Their ideas are a real paradigm shift. People are used to the idea of boards that give advice to company management. This book will help owners understand the role of true directors, who balance the needs of the owners with the needs of the business.

—JIM BURNS, *President, Burns Engineering*

This book should be a terrific guide for all business owners.

—DIANNE WILSON CARLSON, *Owner, Wilson Tool International Inc.*

THE BALANCE POINT provides a fresh and thought-provoking perspective on the role of boards in private businesses. The enterprising angle from which the authors approach the subject creates exciting alternatives for business owners who have sometimes discounted the importance of process and governance. The book provides keen insights into the unique challenges business owners face; more importantly, it presents numerous examples of pragmatic solutions.

—ANN KINKADE, *Director, Family Business Center, University of Wisconsin–Madison*

This book should be a must read for owners and managers of any closely held company who want to minimize the significant risks associated with transitions among owners, managers, and family. A long-time client of mine has implemented many of the concepts presented by Cary and Larry. It is not an exaggeration to state that their approach has been life changing for the owners and nonfamily management of this highly successful manufacturing firm over the last five years. Among other things, the founder/owner/president/CEO/board chair evolved from [relying on] a strong board of advisors to an even stronger board of directors, hired a nonowner president, and is genuinely and comfortably pulling away from the business and recognizing the board as a true balance point between the business and the owners.

—ORIE BEUCLER, *Business Consultant*

The alternative board structures provide owners with practical information to help them put together and train a board that works for their unique situation rather than rely on a "one size fits all approach."

—GLENN AYRES, *former President of the Family Firm Institute and business consultant with Doud Hausner & Associates*

THE BALANCE POINT offers practical guidance on a much deeper level than other books intended to help businesses in transition. This book explains what owners, managers, and directors need to learn to navigate transitional issues successfully.

— ABIGAIL BARRETT, *national business consultant & owner of Leadership Transitions Inc.*

The clarity in describing the problems and solutions is a welcome relief and will be a great help to readers. THE BALANCE POINT doesn't shy away from the difficult issues, but offers pragmatic ways to solve them.

— MARILYN MASON, PHD, *national business consultant and noted author*

I learned that when I separate the roles of owners, board members, and management, I open up the possibility for my children . . . to continue to own this company.

— TOM SCHLOUGH, *Owner and CEO, Park Industries, Inc.*

Brilliant! Using the owner, board, management model with my business clients has met with resounding success. The authors have created a unique and in-depth relationship of accountability that points the way to smoother and more sustainable transition planning. Using this model, the family business can navigate the transition waters with a clear and exciting long-term plan.

— IRIS CORNELIUS, PHD, *Consulting Psychologist, Cornelius & Associates, LLC*

THE
BALANCE
POINT

NEW WAYS BUSINESS OWNERS
CAN USE BOARDS

THE
BALANCE
POINT

CARY J. TUTELMAN
LARRY D. HAUSE

FAMILLE PRESS
www.famillepress.com

Published by Famille Press, Edina, Minnesota
www.famillepress.com

ISBN-13: 978-0-9799551-0-5
ISBN-10: 0-9799551-0-6

Library of Congress Control Number: 2008921076

Printed in the United States of America

TABLE OF CONTENTS

PREFACE

This book was born out of real-life challenges for our clients and our insatiable curiosity to understand, explain, and resolve the fundamental issues they face as they and their businesses transition.

One significant issue almost always present involves the integration of ownership interests with the business interests. This issue presents itself in many different forms, but the essence is always the same. Two examples may help explain the issue.

> An owner grew tired of the day-to-day grind of his business and wanted to transition from management. He hired a president to manage the business, and created a board consisting of himself and two outside directors. He never clearly told the board or the president what he wanted as an owner, the board never asked, and the board always sided with him when he objected to plans the president presented. The president got frustrated and quit, and the owner had to reinsert himself into management. What the owner wanted never got integrated into the plans of the business.

> In another case, an owner wanted to give his business to his four children so they could all share equally in its benefits. He gave voting shares to his two sons (who worked in the business) and nonvoting shares to his two daughters (who didn't work in the business). The brothers ignored their sisters, assuming they didn't understand the business. As a result, the sisters felt unfairly excluded and began to distrust their brothers. Then the two brothers developed different concerns. No mechanisms existed to help resolve their differences, and a power struggle ensued, with the eldest brother claiming the right to make the ultimate decisions. Eventually, they sold the business and the sibling relationships were significantly damaged.

In the second example, the owner confused his daughters' legal rights with management authority, telling his sons that their sisters should not be involved in management because they didn't under-stand the business. As part owners of the business, his daughters had a legitimate right to participate, but under the owner's transition plan they had no way to do so. The owner also mistakenly presumed that as managers his sons would always have similar interests. What happened, of course, is that the sons' ownership concerns changed as their individual circumstances changed, and the owner's transition plan did not provide a way for the brothers to resolve their differences.

It is no surprise that people have differing interests. So the challenge is not to understand that the interests of owners and managers are different, or even what those differences are. The challenge is *how* to identify, understand, and resolve those differences with minimal adverse impact to the business, management, and the ownership group. And, more important, how to do this without knowing the specific differences, and regardless of the people or business involved.

We started our analysis by looking at how entrepreneurs of successful businesses function. These individuals are able to identify, understand, and resolve significant differences in their businesses within a short period of time and with minimal disruption. What is it that these individuals do that is so effective? And can these functions be duplicated to help businesses where ownership and management are not vested in one individual?

We identified three basic functions of successful founders/entrepreneurs: a management function, an ownership function, and a balancing function. We then allocated those functions to the three basic groups involved in most businesses: management, ownership, and the board. We think the balancing function is key to integrating ownership interests with the interests of the management. We allocated the balancing function to the board.

Of course, this created another problem for us—talking about boards. In working with owners of private companies, we can discuss many emotional issues: owner conflicts, succession goals, transition challenges, children in the business, "incompetent" management teams, and so forth. Although owners have difficulty working through these issues, we usually find them at least willing to talk about them. However, when boards came up, we got a different response. We found that owners did not want to talk about boards at all. Not at all! We found a number of reasons they didn't want to talk about boards.

» Some had read stories in newspapers and magazines about the scandals, greed, corruption, illegalities, and cover-ups of public companies and their boards. Such stories cast a negative pall on all boards.

» Many had anecdotal information about boards. They told us things like, "I heard about a guy who got kicked out of his own company by his board." This scenario would be enough to scare any business owner away from having a board.

» Others looked into establishing a board and did not feel there was much flexibility if they wanted to set it up "the right way." They learned such things as "You have to have your CEO on the board; you have to have at least two outsiders on your board; you can't have family members on the board," and so on. Hearing these statements, owners of private businesses come away believing that such requirements will not work in their company. What these owners are really saying is that they don't want others telling them what to do in their own company.

From this investigation, we concluded two things. First, with misinformation our clients had, we could understand their not wanting to discuss boards. After all, who wants to get kicked out of their own company; who wants to be told what kind of board is required and how it has to work; who wants to give a board the power to corrupt their corporation?

Second, we realized that almost all the sources about boards were based on principles for publicly held companies. Missing from these sources was the essential ingredient of all closely held and family companies: owners. Typically, owners of private companies are active in their business, commit most of their adult lives to the care and feeding of it, and are intricately involved with most if not all aspects of it. Shareholders in public companies are not active in the same way that owners of private businesses are. Anyone who has worked with business owners will tell you that. An individual may own a thousand shares of a Fortune 500 company, but does not feel or act like a business owner. Boards in public companies do not work the same way as do boards in closely held and family businesses. That is why our clients resist talking about boards or taking any action to have a board. And who can blame them?

If we talked to our clients about boards, they demanded to know *why* a board was needed for their private business and *how* this board would help. Our clients wanted practical, rational, and easily understandable answers to these questions. We think our book does this.

The Balance Point identifies and explains fundamental issues owners face as they and their businesses transition. The book helps owners understand why challenges exist in the first place and provides different alternatives on how to resolve them. Most importantly, this book explains the existence of an essential function in closely held and family businesses—the balance point—and how to transition the balance point to increase the chance of successfully transitioning the business.

We hope that this text will be the beginning of other books, scholarship, and research about the balancing function in private businesses. We are excited about where these ideas may go. And we hope that our book accomplishes our main objective: to give business owners a practical and reasoned approach to successfully address the challenges involved in transitioning their businesses.

ACKNOWLEDGEMENTS

This book represents years of learning by us, mostly through real-life experiences and working with real-life clients and professional colleagues, but our personal trials also added helpful perspectives. This type of learning requires the active involvement of many people to be effective. We are blessed to have this support, and use this acknowledgement to give thanks.

Our clients were central in helping. They demanded our best thinking and efforts. They gave us the opportunity to help, learn, and become better consultants and people in the process. Thanking specific clients and owners, managers, employees, and family members of clients would breach confidentiality, but we hope to thank you privately.

The support, encouragement, insights, and learning we received from our professional colleagues were staggering. We especially are thankful for those professionals who are in the Family Business Alliance or have been in it over the years: Abigail Barrett, Orie Beucler, Steve Coleman, Iris Cornelius, Michael Holsten, Glenn Ayres, and Jim Redpath. We are grateful for the support and continued encouragement and ideas from Ann Kinkaid, the director of the Family Business Center at the University of Wisconsin–Madison. She gave us her time in editing our manuscript and her trust in working with her families. We appreciate the tips Marilyn Mason gave us before the editing stage. Her input made for a better manuscript. We thank the professionals who served with us for several years on the board overseeing the professional part of the Family Business Program at St. Thomas, Sandra Shearer and Rick Francis, and we thank Bill Monson, Pat Tollefson, and Roxie Johnson who are or were associated with the University of St. Thomas' Center for Family Business.

We also thank the people who were intimately involved in the preparation of this book. Pat Judd opened our eyes to the world of publishing. We were also fortunate to work with two experienced professionals in publishing. Our editor, Terri Hudoba, tightened the manuscript considerably. She was committed to doing a first-class job and offered creative insights in how to solve some organizational and presentational challenges. Peter Gloege and Kendal Marsh, our graphic artists from Lookout Design, Inc., provided value-added creativity and great patience. We appreciate their touch in the graphics, cover design, and page layout. Rachel Hause, who agreed to be our project manager, tirelessly navigated through all the details of publishing.

I (Cary), besides the above mentioned people, thank Norm Stoehr, who strongly supported my interest in writing a book, edited the very first draft, and provided key insights that shaped our book; my fellow business owners in my Inner Circle International group for their timely feedback; Mike Tikkanen and Linc Shea, members of "The Junto" whose motto "Do well by doing good" served us well; and Ron Raymond, who continually reminded me that the patterns of the past are important in consulting. I thank my children, David and Emily, who grew up to be fine ethical people and who, until they grew up, never let on that they were actually listening to my words of wisdom; and my wife, Kathy, who has always encouraged my entrepreneurial dreams and as the operations manager of CJT Company is the other half of our little family business.

I (Larry) thank Glenn Ayres, who involved me in my first consulting project; Abigail Barrett, who encouraged me to pursue business dynamics from the beginning and challenged me all along the way; Jim Redpath, who worked with me on a number of engagements and always supported me and provided his insights; Iris Cornelius, who brought a patience and maturity to the chaos that was helpful; Denny Maas, who offered me valuable insights as a nonowner president/employee in a number of companies; and Bob Rubenstein, who offered me wise perspectives and unending encouragement. I'm grateful for the support and assistance I received from my law firm, Fredrikson & Byron, and particularly the lawyers who work in the family business group, estate planning group, and business and tax group, and, of course, my secretary, Paula Bernard. I relied on the valuable insights from my fellow attorneys in the Attorneys for Family Held Enterprises (AFHE) and my colleagues in the Family Firm Institute (FFI) (notably Mark Voeller). While I didn't realize it at the time, my parents, siblings, and experience gained while working in our very small, but dynamic family business and small Midwestern town provided an early immersion in transition planning and personal dynamics that made a profound impact on my professional life. Finally, I thank my wife, Rachel, and my sons, Nathan and Jonathan, who provided effective observations, caring support, and humbling humor when needed most, whether I knew it or not—a benefit of an involved and caring family.

AUTHORS' NOTE

All stories and examples in this book are composites of our personal experience and events that others shared with us. Companies and individuals named in any story or example in this book are fictional. Any similarity between any story, example, company, or individual in this book and companies or individuals in real life is only a coincidence.

1

A NOTE TO
BUSINESS OWNERS

This book is for owners of closely held and family businesses. We've worked with you for years. We know how important your business is to you. We understand the sacrifices and the enormous effort you have made to keep your business successful.

This book is especially for owners in transition. We understand the challenges you face as your business grows and expands to include senior managers and other owners. Whether you are transitioning your role in management, your relationship with other owners, your level of involvement in the business, or just altering the way you think about your future, these challenges are significant and real. Here are some of the challenges you may be facing:

» You may want your senior managers to take on more responsibilities. What do you do? What is your role if your senior managers do take on more responsibilities? How do you guide your business, retaining the role you want yet giving others the responsibilities you want them to have?

» You may want to transition your business to your children. How do you do this? You know it isn't as simple as just "letting go" by establishing a board that includes outsiders and giving the next generation their chance.

» You may want to sell your business in the next few years. What can you do now to increase its value? How can you show potential buyers that the company is not just you? And how can you do this and still keep your power until the business is sold?

» You may want to sell your stock to other shareholders. How do you ensure that you receive all your payments without staying involved in the company's operations? What can you do?

» You may be a next-generation owner who works in the business. You (or your spouse) may wonder what your role is and when your time will come. You may be told to bide your time, that you cannot do anything until the senior generation "lets go." You may see this as the best (or perhaps only) solution, but at some level you wonder what happens to you and your family as you wait. Is there another way?

» You may be a next-generation owner who doesn't work in the business. You (or your spouse) may have questions such as, Am I supposed to do anything? Can I speak up about my concerns or ideas? How do I find out what is going on? Are my siblings who are employees supposed to take care of my shares when Dad and Mom are gone, and, if so, what can I do if I have different ideas? You may be told that your ownership is a gift, so be happy with it. Or you may be told that the managers will run the business and that as an owner you don't need to do anything. You may be given nonvoting shares with the understanding that you have ownership but no say in the business.

These are just some of the challenges you may face when you and your company begin to transition. We believe you will be in a better position to handle these challenges if you understand the fundamental principles of business transition and if you have a practical framework to help you implement solutions. *The Balance Point* provides this information.

We know you will take what is useful from this book and discard the rest. That's OK. If you find ideas in this book that you like, begin implementing them at your own pace, in your own way, and keep moving forward.

OWNERSHIP

Our book focuses on ownership. In most businesses we work with, owners don't have clear responsibilities (if they have any at all). And while owners generally get along with each other, they usually don't have a lot of experience working together. Often they have different (sometimes conflicting) interests and ways to pursue them. If owners can't reach common ground or don't know how to "speak with one voice," each will pursue their individual interests. When this happens, conflict often results.

Most conflicts can be traced to differing values, needs, and goals among owners, or between owners and managers, and how these differences are resolved (or not resolved). This book explains how business owners and managers can get their values, needs, and goals addressed in a way that helps closely held businesses grow and strengthens family businesses.

THE BALANCE POINT

This book also focuses on an idea we call the "balance point." All closely held and family businesses have a balance point. The balance point is a place where owners' values, needs, and goals are integrated with managers' values, needs, and goals. "Balancing" is the act of integrating ownership and management interests.

We believe all business owners should know where the balance point is in their company and how it works. Also, they should understand when to transition the balance point and their transition plan should describe how they are going to transition the balance point.

UNDERSTANDING THE BALANCE POINT IS KEY TO RUNNING A SUCCESSFUL BUSINESS, AND TRANSITIONING THE BALANCE POINT IS KEY TO TRANSITIONING THE BUSINESS SUCCESSFULLY.

Understanding the balance point is key to running a successful business, and transitioning the balance point is key to transitioning the business successfully. This book provides a comprehensive yet practical approach to balancing owners' and managers' interests and explains when and how to transition the balance point.

OUR BASIC BELIEFS

We want to explain, up front, the basic beliefs that underlie our ideas in this book. We hope you agree with them, and won't feel we are persuading you to do something you don't want to do.

» Owners have an important role and significant responsibilities *as owners*. Individuals who ignore their ownership role and responsibilities substantially increase the risks of long-term conflict and affect the company's well-being, especially when there are multiple owners or when owners are different than managers.

» Owners, managers, and directors have separate and distinct responsibilities and different roles yet are interdependent, so they must work together.

» Owners and managers are the primary problem solvers. Owners solve ownership problems; managers solve management problems. The board is the balance point between the owners and managers, helping each solve their respective problems.

» Conflict may result when

- owners don't know what they are supposed to do.
- owners don't have specific responsibilities or don't perform them.
- owners don't work at the company but try to manage it anyway.
- managers don't perform their specific responsibilities, especially when the manager is also an owner.
- managers don't know, and have to guess, what the owners want or ignore the owners' values, needs, and goals.

    - boards manage the company or decide what the own-
    ers will get from the company.

» Decisions balancing the interests among the owners and between
the owners and managers are made in every closely held and family
business. Family business owners should understand how these
balancing decisions are made and who is making them.

» To be successful, every board must serve a purpose. If you can't
see the value of changing your current board arrangement, then
keep the arrangement you have.

» No single type of board arrangement works for all closely held
or family businesses. The arrangement you choose must reflect
what you want to accomplish and are willing to accept.

» Sometimes the existing board arrangement in a closely held or
family business will work just fine. Not every business needs every
arrangement discussed in this book.

» It is possible to have a board of one. A board is defined by what
it does, not by its size.

» Boards don't have to include nonowners and nonmanagers—individuals commonly referred to as "outsiders." Likewise, boards
don't have to include owners or managers—individuals commonly
referred to as "insiders." A board is defined by what it does, not
by who is on it.

» Board arrangements must satisfy several legal standards. Directors
have the duty to ensure that the company is properly managed,
along with duties of care and loyalty to the business. The principles
in this book are entirely consistent with the law and actually help
directors fulfill their legal responsibilities.

AN OVERVIEW

Chapter 2 explains our idea of the balance point and the act of
balancing. We discuss who generally acts as the balance point. You'll

see that balancing occurs all the time in your company. Chapter 3 identifies four circumstances when you may want to consider changing who acts as the balance point. If you already changed your board arrangement, but aren't happy with the results, this chapter will help you understand why the board is not meeting your expectations.

Because balancing integrates owners' and managers' interests, Chapter 4 explains what owners do, and Chapter 5 explains managers' responsibilities in the act of balancing. Chapters 6 and 7 explain how the balancing is done—that being the balance point is the responsibility of the board of directors and the act of balancing is its major activity. Many entrepreneurs and managers have a great deal of resistance to boards and, often, for good reasons. Throughout this book, we make it clear that those

> A BOARD IS DEFINED BY WHAT IT DOES, NOT BY ITS SIZE OR WHO IS ON IT.

serving as the balance point have a critical role in the company's success and the owners' well-being. Board members may include only the dominant business owner (making it a board of one); all owners, family, managers, or outsiders; or any combination of owners, family, managers, and outsiders.

Chapter 8 identifies seven ways to structure the balance point. We explain the essential characteristics of each structure so you can choose the one that works best for you and your business. There is no one "best" arrangement for every business.

Chapters 9 and 10 describe the nuts and bolts of putting together a board that can act as the balance point in your company. Chapter 11 shares some thoughts for the professionals who work with businesses in transition. Chapter 12 contains our conclusions.

WORDS WE USE

We want to give you some insights as to the words we use in this book. An *entrepreneur* is that one person who is the driving force and significant decision maker within the company (but not necessarily the creative innovator of new products, services, or businesses). *Owners* or *business owners* are those who own stock or other equity in a closely held or family business. They may be managers, employees, investors, or members of the same family or two or more different families, or any combination of these relationships.

Managers include those officers or senior executives responsible for the company's business planning process and the business results. That may include only the entrepreneur, or also the company's senior executives or a management team.

We tried to avoid using the word "governance" because often it is a foreign word to business owners. We prefer to use the word "balancing." *Balancing* is the process of working with owners and managers to help them fulfill their respective responsibilities and work through their competing or unclear values, needs, and goals. In other words, balancing (or governance) is the act of integrating the interests of the owners on the one hand and the interests of the managers and the business on the other hand.

The *board* is the board of directors, the group doing the balancing—it has a purpose that the owners and managers understand and has a clearly defined decision-making process. A balancing board is the *balance point*. We are not referring to boards having no function other than to comply with the law, nor are we referring to a board of advisors. We call a board of advisors an *advisory group*. Unless otherwise noted, when we use the word "board" in this text, we are referring to the balancing board.

We use the term *balance point* in two ways. It's another name for a board of directors who do the balancing functions we describe in this book. You will encounter phrases like "the balance point makes sure that" (the board makes sure that) or "the entrepreneur's role as the balance point" (the entrepreneur's role as the board).

Balance point also refers to who is doing the balancing. In this case, we mean the individuals doing the balancing. You will read phrases like "the entrepreneur is the balance point" (the entrepreneur wants to do the balancing himself or herself) or "who will be the balance point?" (who will make the balancing decisions?). So, while the balance point is the place where the balancing gets done, it's also who is doing the balancing.

When we talk about owners, managers, boards, the business, and the company, our context is usually a corporation. As a result, owners are shareholders, board members are directors, managers are, well, managers and/or officers, and the business or the company is the corporation. Some readers may assume that officers are those who sit on the board. That is incorrect. Officers are those individuals elected by the board to hold specific positions within the corporation. Common titles include chief executive officer (CEO), president, chief financial officer (CFO), treasurer, chief operating officer (COO), vice president, and secretary.

We use *company* and *business* synonymously. Generally, these terms are universally applicable to all business entities. When referring to legal arrangements, however, the terms are not universally applicable. For example, when we refer to the legal duties existing between the board and the company, we mean duties the law imposes on directors of a corporation. If your entity is not a corporation, but is, for example, a limited liability company or partnership, the precise terms may differ from what we use in this book. Differences may also occur based on state laws. Address particular legal questions to a lawyer experienced in business law, family businesses, and/or succession law.

A glossary at the end of the book includes the more important terms we used in the text. Appendix 1.1 includes some perspectives that will help you apply the principles in this book to entities other than corporations.

We thank you for reading this book. We believe it will help you make your business even more successful and enjoyable for yourself, your other owners, your managers, your employees, and your family.

2

THE BALANCE POINT

Before we launch into our explanation of the balance point, some key points from Chapter 1 deserve repeating. First, our book is about business owners in transition. This includes owners who are contemplating transition, those who know they should transition and would like to understand how to do it in a way that works for them and their company, and those who are in the transition process. Second, there are no absolutes when discussing boards. The owners determine whether a board is needed, what it does, and who should be on it. In other words, the owners decide what happens. In this chapter we explain the balance point.

THE BASICS

Business owners (individuals who own stock) and managers (individuals who run the company) often have competing interests. This is most apparent in companies having more than one owner, or where some owners don't work in the company, or in companies where the CEO or president is not an owner.

The basic objectives of balancing these competing interests are to keep the company viable and healthy and to make sure that the owners' values, needs, and goals are met. This is a large responsibility. If the owners' values, needs, and goals are met at the expense of the company, it is only a matter of time before the company's well-being is jeopardized. If the values, needs, and goals of the company are met at the expense of the owners, it is only a matter of time before the owners demand change.

The person or people who balance these competing interests act as the balance point. The balance point role is usually held by one of the following:

» the entrepreneur

» the majority owner

» a husband-wife team

» a next-generation individual who has been given the role by someone in the previous generation who had the same role

These people typically make balancing decisions intuitively. They usually don't separate the owners' needs and goals from those of the managers and then balance them. They just do what they do. They make decisions they know are right. They use their instincts, their business sense, their technical skills, and their common sense. And, for the most part, this process works well; owners get their needs and goals satisfied and the company grows and is successful.

A typical balancing process is similar to what Frank did in his business.

Frank's Story

Frank started CIGNA Metals ten years ago and watched his company steadily grow. He recognizes that to remain competitive, CIGNA must expand into a new and growing market in the next two years. The expansion will require significant capital for new machines and additions to the sales force. Frank estimates the costs of expansion and concludes that to expand without increasing the company's debt, he needs to reduce by half the distributions he receives from the company for two years. Frank advises his wife, Susan, that their household budget needs to be adjusted and they will draw on savings so the company has the cash to expand.

We could say that Frank analyzed all the facts and then carefully balanced what CIGNA Metals needed along with what his family needed. But when asked about his decision, Frank just said he made a good business decision. In reality, Frank, acting as the balance point, went through a decision-making process that balanced his interests as the owner (the need for distributions and reasonable debt limits) and the interest of the business (expansion). Frank just did the balancing intuitively. (See Figure 2.1.)

The act of balancing in a closely held or family business is critical because most of the conflicts in business, at their root, involve differences over values, needs, or goals either among the owners or between the owners and managers, and how the person acting as the balance point balances those competing interests. If the balancing is not done effectively, differences become open conflicts and the balance point becomes the boiling point.

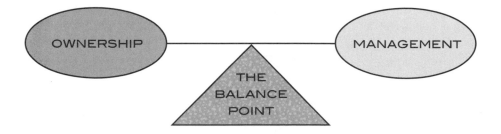

Figure 2.1 The entrepreneur as the balance point

Many business conflicts are about power. This includes such questions as, Who makes key owner decisions? Who makes key management decisions? Who makes the decisions about the roles and responsibilities of owners who work in the company? What should our profitability be? What should our growth rate be? How should we differentiate ourselves in the marketplace?

Many business conflicts are about money. This includes such questions as, Who makes decisions about paying dividends to owners? Who determines how much is reinvested in the company? Who determines the owners' risk and debt tolerance? Who determines how much owners or family members are paid? What about philanthropy?

Many business conflicts involve love or inclusion. This includes such questions as, Who gets the stock? Who participates in owner meetings? Who makes the decisions about succession? Who decides whether children are to be treated fairly (all things considered) and/or equally (all things the same)? Who decides whether and how employee/owners are evaluated? What kind of culture do we want in our company?

Conflicts about power, money, and love can cause great tension and leave long-lasting scars. Two examples illustrate this point.

> In a closely held business with a majority owner, the minority owners may feel that they are not valued and that their needs are not considered. And when crucial balancing decisions are made that directly affect their life (distributions, increased debt, etc.), they are not consulted at all. Failure to clarify and agree on the balance point increases the risk of shareholder disputes, minority shareholder lawsuits, and the untimely and financially burdensome buying of stock.

> In a family business, passing ownership to the next generation often occurs without any plan of how the balancing should be done. For example, if the entrepreneur acted as the balance point, it is likely that a child will think it is his or her right or responsibil-

ity to step in and make balancing decisions for the good of all the owners and employees of the company. This may work well if the other owners accept the arrangement. But if more than one child feels entitled to act as the balance point or if the sibling group doesn't accept the child's appointment to the position, trouble ensues. Without a plan to transition the balance point, the next generation is left to resolve critical balance-point issues at a time in their lives when they often have little experience working together. Sometimes they can work it out, but often the next generation is left to fight it out. In any case, not clarifying who will act as the balance point increases the risk that the ownership group will fall apart, which in turn increases the risk to the business.

The possibility of conflict increases with additional generations and family branches in a family business. Each generation or family branch may have different expectations about when the balance point should be transitioned and how it should be structured. Developing a plan that clarifies where the balance point is located and how it works, and getting that plan accepted by the different generations and family branches, lessens the chances of a power struggle among the owners (allowing them to concentrate on solving owner problems) and managers (allowing them to concentrate on solving management problems).

To summarize, those who do the balancing ensure that decisions about such critical matters as dividends, debt and risk tolerance, growth rate, business culture, profit levels, diversification, acquisition and replication, philanthropy, and differentiation are made after considering the values, needs, and goals of the owners and the business.

We believe the act of balancing is the essential role of a board of directors. However, we are *not* referring to the type of board found in public companies or in most closely held or family businesses. And we are *not* referring to the type of board that you are probably thinking about. We mean a board of directors with the primary task of balancing.

We know that business owners often have a great deal of resistance to boards—and for good reasons. For now, we just ask that you focus on understanding the balance point and the act of balancing. As we go forward, we will explore why the board, as we envision it, is an ideal place to locate the responsibility of balancing.

3

CLARIFYING AND FORMALIZING THE BALANCE POINT

In Chapter 2, we introduced the idea of the balance point and the act of balancing. We hope it is apparent to you that the interests of the owners and managers are balanced in every company. Ask yourself, Who is doing the balancing in our company? Where is our balance point? When companies are in transition, it is critical to clarify and formalize the balance point and to have a plan to transition it. This chapter discusses four specific transition circumstances.

THE BASICS

Typically the entrepreneur, the heir apparent, the majority shareholder, or a husband and wife team perform the act of balancing. In many businesses these individuals do a fine job balancing the owners' and the company's interests. They make good decisions. The owners are satisfied, and the business prospers.

However, when the transition of a closely held or family business involves passing ownership and management accountability to others, clarifying who does the balancing is critical to the viability of the company, the success of the transition, and the cohesiveness of the ownership or family group. It is necessary to clarify and formalize the balance point in the following circumstances:

» when entrepreneurs want to significantly change their role

» when owners and managers are different people

» when there are multiple owners

» when entrepreneurs want to sell the business or their shares

Each of these circumstances involves transitioning the responsibilities and authority allocated to owners, managers, and whoever balances the competing interests of the owners and managers. If these responsibilities and related authority are not clarified and formalized during the four transitional circumstances, it is highly likely there will be confusion over who does what and who has what authority. Confusion over responsibilities and authority often decreases the accountability or increases the defensiveness of those having the perceived authority.

In this chapter we will discuss clarifying and formalizing the balance point in each of these four situations.

WHEN ENTREPRENEURS WANT TO SIGNIFICANTLY CHANGE THEIR ROLE

It is natural for entrepreneurs to consider transitioning their involvement in the company. High-level transition occurs when entrepreneurs appoint new leaders to run the company, expand the ownership group, or change who speaks for the owners and the managers.

These actions require entrepreneurs to review all of their roles and responsibilities and decide which ones to keep and which ones to transition. High-level transitions are complicated because it is often difficult to identify just what the entrepreneur wants to transition and because of some common misconceptions about how to transition. And whatever is hard for the entrepreneur is hard for others. One thing we have learned from working with entrepreneurs is that when they are in transition, the entire ownership and management groups are in transition too.

IDENTIFYING WHAT IS TO BE TRANSITIONED

It's hard for most entrepreneurs to sort out and identify their key roles. For example, most entrepreneurs do not typically ask themselves, What is the difference between what I do as an owner and as a manager? What do I do as a director? When their companies were small, entrepreneurs did most all jobs—sales and customer service, purchasing supplies, pitching in to get product out the door. As one business owner memorably said, "I cleaned the toilets when they were plugged up." There was little separation of their roles and responsibilities.

However, as their businesses grew, roles and responsibilities did begin to separate. Salespeople were hired to grow and maintain the customer base along with bookkeepers or accountants to manage the general ledger; supervisors were promoted to help others provide the services and products customers demanded. Entrepreneurs provided less direct labor, if any at all, realizing that they couldn't possibly continue to do all the jobs. Even entrepreneurs get tired, become overworked, and at times are unable to manage all the details. When this occurs, they begin to change their roles and responsibilities by delegating, even if they are not aware of doing so.

As their businesses continue to grow, entrepreneurs usually establish some form of a management team to help run the company. As the management team develops, entrepreneurs begin to delegate more and more of the senior management functions to them. Long-term employees or family members may begin to take their place as leaders within the company.

Transitioning within management is natural in a growing, healthy company. And most entrepreneurs embrace this type of transition, realizing that they can't be attentive to all of the challenges as their companies become more complex. They also understand that it is good when others begin to take on leadership roles.

But regardless of how much transition has occurred within management, entrepreneurs almost always hold on to the power and control of management and ownership. They retain the title senior executive (or at least perform those functions). They usually retain voting control or may allocate voting control only among trusted individuals according to thoughtfully constructed plans. This is especially true in a family business even when they have transferred ownership interests to or for the benefit of their children.

At some point, though, entrepreneurs begin to consider seriously what they want to do and what will happen to their companies in the long term. For example, some grow their businesses to the point where they say the "fun is gone." These individuals think about why they got into business in the first place, and wonder whether they could get back to doing what they like to do and let someone else "run the business."

Swen's Story

Swen liked to design solutions using aluminum. He liked the feel of the metal—it was more substantial than plastics. He started designing door and window casements for the construction industry and then broadened to home products. His ideas were novel at the time and quickly accepted. As the company, Alumi-Design grew, Swen did less designing and more management. Though he hired others to help, it seemed he just couldn't get to the drawing board enough. The people he hired were doing well and the engineers were continuing to come up with new products, but for

Swen the fun was gone. He asked, "How can I hire a president to run my company so I can go back to the shop and do what I like to do?"

Other entrepreneurs get to the point of wondering how long they want to continue carrying the burden of holding all the power and control of management and ownership.

Roberto's Story

Roberto invented a game and decided to sell it on his own. He bought a plastic extruder, cutters, and labeling equipment, and began manufacturing and marketing under the business name GamePlay Inc. He experienced some success with his own game, but over a number of years he started producing and selling games for other inventors, and that is when his company began growing. While GamePlay's manufacturing, distributing, marketing, and sales systems expanded, the cyclical nature of the industry and increased competition from overseas weighed heavily on Roberto. He knew GamePlay could make and sell products other than games, but he tried to diversify once and the experience was not a good one. Roberto wanted to create new games. He didn't want to sell or liquidate the company because he wanted to keep his employees happy, and he wasn't ready to retire yet. But he also didn't want to lead the company through the transition it had to go through to remain successful. He wondered, "How can I get someone else to lead my company?"

Some entrepreneurs also wonder about what will happen to their business, employees, and customers if something unexpected happens to them.

Joey's Story

Joey was driving home after attending Peety's funeral. Peety had been Joey's right-hand man from the day Joey started McGilvery's

Advertising. Peety did all the stuff Joey didn't like doing, and the employees and customers loved him. Joey remembered the day less than six months ago when Peety came to tell him that he was diagnosed with a rare form of cancer. The news was hard for everyone to hear, but Peety was proud when employees stepped up to take over his duties. Joey knew McGilvery's was going to be all right after Peety was gone, but Joey started thinking what would happen to his company if it was he who had cancer rather than Peety. He thought that his wife and children could continue to own the company while the people Peety put in place could run it. But his son and daughter expressed some interest in being more involved. "How do people like me plan for this sort of thing?" Joey asked himself.

At some point, entrepreneurs do begin to consider seriously what will happen to their companies long term. They get to the point of wondering how long they want to continue carrying the burden of holding all the power and control of management and ownership. They start thinking about what would happen if their management team assumed total responsibility for operating the business or what the company would be like if their children were the sole owners. With these types of thoughts come significant, high-level (and sometimes high-risk) challenges, and the transition focus is no longer limited to changes within management. The transition involves changing management and ownership power, which can be difficult for everybody.

BELIEFS ABOUT TRANSITIONING

The second reason that high-level transitions are hard to do is that entrepreneurs of closely held and family businesses often believe they either have to control their business or sell it. They may believe that the only way to maintain control is to do it themselves because, in the end, they can't really trust anyone else to do it right; in other words, no one can run their business as well as they can and no one else will ever have the feel or touch that is so critical to its success. It is hard for these individuals to see a role for themselves that does not involve functional control of the entire business, and it is hard for them to see anyone else in this role.

Sometimes they hear, "Just sell your shares and retire." Some may say they are clinging to old ideas, not open to change, losing their edge, or keeping others from gaining necessary experience. It is hard for entrepreneurs to accept this feedback, not to mention accept the recommendation to retire.

In family businesses, entrepreneurs are often told that to transition they need to let go and leave the business. Such entrepreneurs don't want to transition from the person who runs it all and loves every minute of it to the owner who watches from the sidelines. It is very hard for them to hear that they have to let go for the good of the family and the business.

> IF ENTREPRENEURS SERIOUSLY WANT TO TRANSITION THEIR ROLE, THE TRANSITION PLAN MUST CONSIDER THE NEEDS OF THEMSELVES, THEIR BUSINESS, AND THE OTHER INDIVIDUALS WHO WILL ASSUME THEIR RESPONSIBILITIES.

If entrepreneurs really want to maintain all the power and control until they sell their company, then they should do so and never worry about who does the balancing. But if they want to transition their role, they should have a transition plan that meets their needs and the needs of the company and those who are key to the company's future. This point cannot be overstated. If entrepreneurs seriously want to transition their role, the transition plan must consider the needs of themselves, their business, and the other individuals who will assume their responsibilities. Transition cannot happen without change.

All entrepreneurs want a way to control their own destiny and that of their company. They want to ensure that as they transition their company it will survive and ownership harmony will be preserved. They want the transition plan to be their plan, not a plan dictated by others. And they want to determine the pace of the transition. Transition simply does not occur any faster than the entrepreneur allows, no matter what the transition plan says.

All of these wishes are understandable if you consider the entrepreneurs' perspective. They have worked their whole life nurturing their company—in many ways their company is their life. They are deeply committed to their employees, their customers, and the values of their business. Their company gives them purpose, identity, status, power, control, wealth, a feeling of great accomplishment, and the opportunity to create a legacy. If someone tells them they have to let go or that it is time for others to take over, they will naturally resist because the change is too big and too abrupt.

But we don't believe that most entrepreneurs should just let go and get out of the way. Asking them to leave is not only disrespectful but usually detrimental to the business because others involved in the company and ownership are usually not ready to assume all of the roles and responsibilities entrepreneurs hold as the senior leader and primary owner. Transitioning the responsibilities of senior management and ownership to others is more complex than the transitions that occurred within management as the company grew.

To make matters more difficult, entrepreneurs often can't see how it is possible to transition their business because they do so much and so many other people are involved. As the entrepreneur, they are in charge. Entrepreneurs struggle to understand who among the other owners and senior managers will hold everything together. Entrepreneurs may believe that these senior managers and owners will do the best they can, working to do what good managers and owners do; but entrepreneurs have held the reins for so long. It's just hard for them to imagine how everything can still work without one person at the center, holding everything together.

Usually the senior managers and owners know they don't have the experience to assume all of the responsibilities of management and ownership. They also know that they can't get the necessary experience so long as the entrepreneur holds the reins. Managers can't help but defer to entrepreneurs who are still actively involved in management, and children who are owners defer to entrepreneurs who are active in ownership. The presence of the entrepreneur is just too expansive to give others the room they need to learn how to responsibly exercise the functions of managers and owners when the entrepreneur is no longer involved.

At some level we believe entrepreneurs understand this reality, and it is just more frustrating for them. Entrepreneurs believe they can't give their successors the opportunity to learn how to assume all of the responsibilities of management and ownership without their exiting, but to exit entirely from the company puts the business at risk because the successors don't have the experience entrepreneurs think is needed to hold it all together. This is why entrepreneurs often refuse to deal with transition.

Alex's Story

Alex knew he was stuck, but didn't want to admit it. Alex built ManPower Equipment into the largest construction tool and equipment distributor in the Pacific Northwest. He successfully expanded the company into retail sales and now entered the catalog business, notching large revenue gains and even greater profitability. Alex thought he had a quality management team, but he always had to keep pushing them or they would rest on their laurels. He constantly revised their goals and thought of new products to offer. Alex got frustrated when his managers didn't take on more responsibilities even after he had made it possible for them to buy 20 percent ownership in the company.

Alex has two daughters and a son, all of whom work in the business. He wants them to run the company, but is disappointed in what he has seen so far. He does not see them as hard drivers—and hard drivers are necessary to keep the business going. None of his children are in upper management, although Alex gave them responsibility for different aspects of the business so they could get experience. He wanted his president to train them, but had second thoughts. Alex also wants his children to meet the distributors and look over the retail stores to make sure people are doing things right because he believes that owners need to keep tabs on the distributors and store managers or they, too, will begin to relax.

On the advice of professional colleagues and his oldest daughter, Alex formed a board of advisors, but doesn't know why it is necessary because he never needed a board before. He tolerates it mostly because the board doesn't slow down the company and isn't where the real work is done anyway. He does not see how anyone could learn how to run the business by meeting only four or five times a year, and believes that anyone who doesn't know how to run the business is of no help. He tells himself that if having the company's attorney and a couple of other business people involved at this level helps his daughter and keeps him legal, then he will put up with meeting a few times a year.

Alex loves what he does and doesn't want to quit, but knows he can't go on forever. Yet no one else seems to do the work the way it needs to be done. "Who is going to hold everything together if I'm not here?" he wonders. Selling the business isn't an option for him because, in his opinion, ManPower Equipment is something special and an outside buyer will ruin it.

Clearly Alex is the center of ManPower Equipment. Everyone answers to him, and everything is organized to serve his needs. His view of transitioning his role is to some day find someone who can do what he does. Right now he thinks one of his children could do this; that is, run the company and hold everything together. This is not an uncommon view among entrepreneurs. But it has certain limitations:

» It keeps Alex in the center of everything until he is ready for or has to let someone else take over. Is this what he wants? Or is he looking for choices lying between keeping it all together and total retirement?

» Management relies on Alex's involvement and doesn't know what to do or whether they can do it without him. Is senior management ready to take over when Alex transitions his management functions? How does anyone know this?

» Alex's children will succeed in their father's eyes only if they display behaviors and characteristics similar to his. What happens if none of them do? If some do and others don't? Or if they all do?

» And just what does Alex do? If someone "replaces" Alex, what is it that this person can do or can't do? Alex does everything now, so can his replacement do everything? If the replacement is one of his children, what do the other children or other managers do? If the replacement is a nonowner, what roles do the children have?

These are just some of the questions that Alex's situation presents. Clarifying and formalizing the balance point will give him more ways to answer these questions than by simply continuing to do the same thing until he is ready for someone to replace him. (You will learn what Alex did at the end of Chapter 4.)

THE BALANCE POINT SOLUTION

Instead of transitioning from the role of owner/CEO to the role of a retiree watching from the sidelines with one person replacing him or her, the balance point solution gives entrepreneurs more options.

» Entrepreneurs can officially establish themselves as the balance point and become the only member of a balancing board of directors. Or they can share the balancing function by adding others to the board. Clarifying that they are the balance point and formalizing how they do the balancing will help entrepreneurs determine just how much management and ownership control they want to retain. It will also help senior managers and other owners understand their roles, responsibilities, authority, and accountability versus those of the entrepreneur.

» If entrepreneurs want to remain involved to mentor successor senior managers, they can so do by limiting the level of management control they transition.

» If entrepreneurs want to remain involved to mentor the future owners, they can do so by limiting the ownership control transitioned.

The balance point solution lets entrepreneurs tailor solutions to meet their own unique set of circumstances. This additional flexibility is created because the focus is not on finding someone who can replace the entrepreneur but rather on transitioning the entrepreneur's functions when the entrepreneur and others are ready.

Addressing the balance point requires entrepreneurs to identify and clarify their roles and responsibilities in three distinct areas: ownership, board, and management. Entrepreneurs then pick and choose which of these functions to delegate. Usually we find entrepreneurs wanting to delegate management and employment functions first. And, we suggest that entrepreneurs transition the balance point function last because this is the function that ties ownership and management functions—and hence the company—together. (See Figure 3.1.)

Clarifying and allocating the entrepreneur's functions in this manner illuminates how these critical functions can be handled by many different people while the entrepreneur keeps everything else together. The entrepreneur can observe and guide the development of others as they assume higher positions, exercise greater authority, and increase their involvement. The successors will then have a clearer idea of what they are supposed to do and how the entrepreneur is involved. They will learn about the separation of and links between ownership and management responsibilities.

Transitioning from a single person who has all the power and control in a company to a group of managers and other owners is less risky if entrepreneurs are involved in the balancing function. This allows them to retain their power and contribute to the management and ownership groups in clear and meaningful ways. As the balance

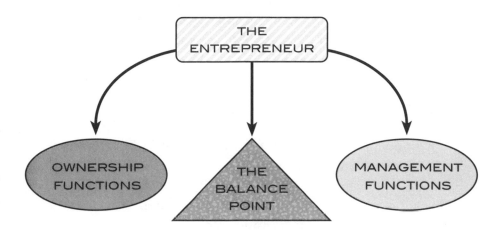

Figure 3.1 Transitioning alternatives for entrepreneurs

point or part of a balance point, entrepreneurs direct management and ownership, preparing them to do what is needed when the entrepreneur is no longer involved. Acting as the balance point role gives entrepreneurs a legitimate and purposeful platform from which to ask senior managers and owners relevant questions and to ensure that the answers from each group meet the company's and owners' needs. When entrepreneurs are ready to share balancing responsibilities or retire from balancing, successor managers and owners will be trained to work with the balance point. Then the entrepreneur has only to transition the act of balancing to a new board.

Transitioning in this way breaks down entrepreneurs' complex and intertwining functions so they can choose what to transition, when to do so, how to do it, and who to involve—a more manageable process than transitioning all at once. It also resembles how entrepreneurs transitioned their involvement in management as the company grew, making it easier to envision how this high-level transition is possible.

For example, when an entrepreneur transitions from being an account manager for the biggest customer, the entrepreneur will want to approve the new account manager's development strategy. Similarly, when the entrepreneur transitions from annual planning, the entrepreneur will want the board (of which the entrepreneur is a member) to approve the plan. In both cases, the entrepreneur transitions roles yet maintains involvement in the processes.

TRANSITION WITHOUT CHANGE

We have worked with many entrepreneurs who believe they are transitioning when they really are not. In these cases, the entrepreneurs do spend less time at the office (often in their second home for part of the year) and they are not involved as much as they once were. They call this transition. However, their role has not changed. They still decide on operational matters; talk to key managers, employees, and customers; and require detailed information about what happens at the office. They have not transitioned any control or power, and the company still relies on them for important decisions. What has changed is the amount of time the entrepreneurs work and how they work.

Transition without change is not transition. It is only change. True transition requires a commitment to changing the control and power structures in the company and/or ownership group.

Transition without change should not be the goal. If an entrepreneur is not ready to transition, the entrepreneur should make that clear to the other owners, directors, and managers. And if the entrepreneur has the power to plan the transition, the transition process will be on hold until the entrepreneur is ready to begin. Waiting for the entrepreneur to actually begin transitioning is far better than going through the motions of transition without change, because sooner or later, the entrepreneur will dig in, stopping the process and maybe even undoing some of the progress made by other managers or owners or by the next generation.

TRANSITION WITHOUT CHANGE IS NOT TRANSITION.

SUMMARY

» Clarifying and formalizing the balance point (that is, identifying who will do the balancing and making the act of balancing deliberate and visible to others) lets entrepreneurs control the pace of their transition. Letting entrepreneurs control the pace greatly increases the odds of them transitioning to a role in which they are comfortable.

» Clarifying and formalizing the balance point helps the other managers and owners understand their roles and responsibilities during this period. It also allows them opportunities to learn how to carry out these functions and, most importantly, develop their skills.

» Clarifying and formalizing the balance point gives entrepreneurs a legitimate platform from which to guide other owners and managers. It helps entrepreneurs control how they want to participate and helps the new president and other owners and managers understand how to relate to the entrepreneurs.

» Clarifying and formalizing the balance point makes it easier for the family business entrepreneurs to transfer ownership to their children. Entrepreneurs can transfer ownership to children, giving them the opportunity to learn how to work together and become responsible owners. Entrepreneurs can retain the legitimate authority to direct the new owners if their values, needs, and goals become inconsistent with the capabilities of the business or the managers' values, needs, and goals.

When all the key people of a company are in transition, a clear balance point plan clarifies who does what. As a result, entrepreneurs can retain whatever management, director, and ownership responsibilities they want, while at the same time the other owners, managers, and directors understand how to work in the system. The questions of power and control, responsibilities, and expectations of transitioning entrepreneurs and transition timelines are all made easier if entrepreneurs transition to some balance point role and not to a seat on the sidelines.

○

THE BOARD OF ONE

We work with many entrepreneurs who tell us they want to transition, but who are reluctant to change. They do not want to give up their power. They like the role they have. Getting them to participate in their own transition plan is often a challenge.

Once the idea of the balance point is fully explained, entrepreneurs tend to be more open to transition if they can do the balancing themselves. Usually they aren't willing to share this role with others. Nor are the businesses usually ready for the entrepreneurs to transition from the sole balancing role. When entrepreneurs express these desires, we tell them that it is clear to us that they want to do the balancing, and, since all businesses need a balance point, they should act as the balance point. They should be the board: the board of one.

This may seem like an unusual idea, but the board of one can play an important role in business transitions. Being the board of one (acting as the balance point) does not diminish the entrepreneurs' power in any way. On the contrary, it keeps them involved in the planning process, the satisfaction of owners' needs and goals, and the resolution of critical issues. Most important, it shows the entrepreneurs' willingness to transition from their unconscious and informal role as the balance point to a formal role. This change often helps start the transition process.

Formalizing the entrepreneurs' role as the balance point clarifies the decision-making process and others' roles and responsibilities. For example, everyone will know that the entrepreneur, as the sole board member, is going to balance the interests of owners and managers. Managers learn to develop and implement plans they believe the company needs to prosper, knowing that the entrepreneur will ensure that their plans are consistent with the owners' values, needs, and goals. In family businesses, entrepreneurs may decide to transfer shares to the next generation in order to involve them as owners while ensuring that their values, needs, and goals will be consistent with the company's capabilities. The board of one gives everyone a chance to test the transition plan and make changes if needed.

Once established, the board of one becomes the foundation for the future development of the balancing board consisting of additional directors. It also helps build a disciplined and integrated process for future owners, managers, and board members. Making this happen while entrepreneurs are active is often the key to a smooth business transition and successful completion of a family business succession plan.

Sometimes entrepreneurs tell us that they want to control the balancing but they want some input on the critical balancing decisions. We suggest that they form an advisory group to provide input, but that they remain the balance point—a board of one—and thereby retain control of the important balancing function.

WHEN OWNERS AND MANAGERS ARE DIFFERENT PEOPLE

In some businesses, the owners and managers are not the same individuals. A closely held business may have nonactive partners or investors. In a family business the founder may want all of his children to enjoy the benefits of ownership, but only some of them will work in the company. Or the entrepreneur may die and his shares pass to or are placed in trust for his family, who will own but not work at the company. When owners and managers become different people, it is essential to clarify and formalize the balance point.

Without a clear sense of where the balance point is, either the owners or the managers will tend to take on the task of balancing. When owners take over, they usually try to directly influence management, often involving themselves in individual management matters by making decisions for and, in some cases, managing the managers. Owners may feel that the managers are not doing the job, and they need to fix things because it is their company. This can cause great turmoil.

If owners manage, then managers may feel frustrated or defensive because they think the owners are involving themselves in areas where they don't belong. Or, the managers may feel confused or conflicted when different owners give them different orders. Whatever the case, managers don't know what to do, which can lead them to becoming less accountable and cause good managers to leave while poor managers stay on.

When management takes over the balancing, they believe owners will have to accept their decisions. Managers' decisions may be based on what they think is in the best interest of the owners or the business, or based on their own interests. Owners must either accept management's decisions or they must act. But taking action is difficult if managers do the balancing. If owners want to balance the managers' interests with their own interests, they may need to take over or replace management, both of which may have considerable consequences and may greatly impair continuity of the business.

31

Figure 3.2 shows the "push me-pull you" that can occur between owners and managers when competing for the balance point.
Without a board acting as the balance point, owners tend to get involved in management, and managers tend to have more trust issues
with owners.

Power struggles are likely as long as the balancing function is
located in either the ownership group or management. When owners hold the balancing authority, they are responsible for overseeing
management—only one small step away from managing. When management holds the balancing authority, they must maintain the owners' confidence or risk the owners taking action, which can be drastic
for management, the company, and the owners.

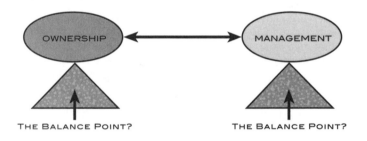

Figure 3.2 Owners and managers without a balancing board

With a clearly established balance point located between ownership and management, owners can develop their plan (stating their
values, needs, and goals), which is communicated to the balance
point, and given to managers. Knowing the interests of the owners,
managers can then develop their plans and communicate them to the
balance point. The balance point then ensures that managers' plans
are consistent with the owners' plan. The owners can concentrate on
ownership issues, while the managers make management decisions
and run the company. Figure 3.3 describes how a balancing board
helps both owners and management.

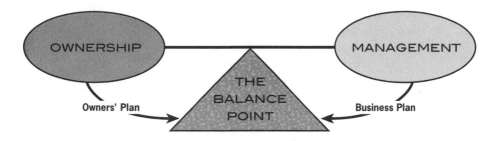

Figure 3.3 Owners and managers with a balancing board

With a board acting as the balance point, owners can plan for what they want, managers can develop plans for the company, and the board can ensure that plans from both groups fit together.

Roberto's Story—Continued

Earlier in this chapter, we introduced you to Roberto, the founder of GamePlay. He wants to hire someone to run his company so that he can go back to creating games. He does not want to lead the transition of his company. Roberto decides to hire Dick, a hard-working, personable individual, as president of the company. Dick has twenty years' experience in plastic manufacturing along with experience in diversifying companies. It is critical for Roberto and Dick that Roberto clarify and formalize the balance point in GamePlay.

If Roberto continues to informally balance his interests as an owner with the interests of the company as he has in the past (that is, if he doesn't clarify or formalize the balance point), Dick will be unclear about his responsibilities and authority, and may become frustrated or defensive. Roberto will adjust Dick's plans without either of them knowing what he is doing or why, which can lead Dick to believe that Roberto doesn't approve of the job he is doing. If this scenario continues, trust is eroded and the relationship will be irreparably damaged. However, if Roberto abdicates the balancing function, Dick will begin to make decisions that may or may not be consistent with what Roberto wants.

Roberto will either have to accept Dick's decisions or reinsert himself into management. (The conclusion of Roberto's story is found in Chapter 7.)

WHEN THERE ARE MULTIPLE OWNERS

Closely held businesses commonly have more than one owner. In some instances, key managers may receive ownership interests to give them a stake in the action. In other cases, investors receive stock for their capital contributions. In family businesses, the senior generation commonly begins transferring shares to their children and grandchildren, either outright or in trust. They see this as furthering their goal of continuing the business and reducing estate taxes. As the ownership group expands, it is essential to clarify and formalize the balance point.

In many businesses, entrepreneurs continue to act as the balance point even when there are multiple owners, and this arrangement works well. However, a time may come when the other owners are uncomfortable with having a single person doing the balancing. This usually happens when

» entrepreneurs die or retire

» power struggles occur in the ownership group

» the company is stagnant and/or unprofitable

» the owners don't believe their needs and goals are or will be met

» the person acting as the balance point is running the company and is (or is perceived to be) not acting in the owners' best interests or is in over their head

When any of these situations happen, the owners want to be part of the balance point, or want the person acting as the balance point to share the role with others or to give it up if they can't do a better job. Leaving the location of the balance point unresolved or in conflict often leads to long-term ownership conflict and a possible lifetime of dissension. The balance point becomes the boiling point. Figure 3.4 shows that conflict is likely when multiple owners have not worked out an acceptable arrangement for who has the balancing authority.

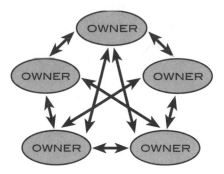

Figure 3.4 Multiple owners without a balancing board

Three examples illustrate the potential conflicts that can result in an ownership group having multiple owners and how a balance point located between ownership and management can help.

» Conflicts about fairness and performance comparisons among owners can be destructive. Compensation can be an issue in companies where owners who are vice presidents report to an owner who is the CEO/president. A balance point located between the owners and managers can help determine compensation for those owners. The balance point can set the compensation of the senior managers by relying on the owners' values, needs, and goals.

» Disagreements about how much money owners should receive and how much should be left in the company for growth can result in destructive conflicts in companies where some of the owners are not employees. The balance point, relying on a set of approved owners' values, needs, and goals, and on management's approved plans, can help the owners and managers balance the competing needs of the company and owners, resulting in a dividend distribution that has widespread support.

» Career paths of the next generation are often in conflict in companies owned by multiple families. This conflict can be so intense that one or more of the families may feel they are being forced out, triggering buy-sell provisions or an all-out war for dominance. The balance point, relying on the owners' values, needs, and goals, can help identify leadership criteria and opportunities to ensure the well-being of the company and help preserve or create family harmony.

A company operates most effectively when the owners' and managers' roles and responsibilities are separated, defined, understood, and agreed to by all. It also works most effectively when the owners define, understand, and agree on the roles and responsibilities of the balance point. With a balancing board, owners have to come up with one plan for the company. Figure 3.5 shows how a balancing board can help the owners work out their individual differences to come up with a single plan.

Tom and Cynthia's Story

Using recipes from Cynthia's mother and grandmother, Tom and Cynthia opened two high-end restaurants in Kansas City. Between Cynthia's culinary talents and Tom's administrative expertise, they beat the difficult odds in the restaurant business—their two locations grew to fifteen, located in four other large Midwestern cities. To obtain the capital needed to open the additional locations they sold 45 percent of their business to thirty different investors. Tom and Cynthia worked hard to make sure the money was used wisely. They carefully planned to protect the owners' investment while also building their dream business.

After the additional locations opened and showed a profit, differences began to surface. The plans Tom prepared for the next three years had the business slowly expanding and diversifying through earnings, minimizing debt, and seeking no additional capital. Several of the other owners objected to Tom's plan as well as other decisions Tom and Cynthia made. Some disliked how Tom handled the business generally and, to Tom, seemed to criticize most everything he did. So Tom just kept doing what he thought was the right thing to do for the business, which agitated the other owners, leading some of them to threaten a lawsuit for mismanagement if they didn't get their way. Everyone thought their respective positions were in the best interests of the company.

The investors initially supported Tom and Cynthia's acting as the balance point when they began expanding their business. It worked well. The additional restaurants were built and became profitable. Tom and Cynthia thought they could continue to operate in the same manner, making what they thought were good decisions for the business and all the owners. But some owners

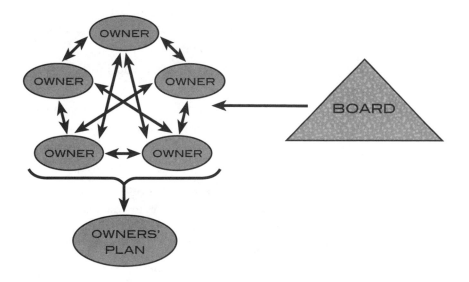

Figure 3.5 Multiple owners with a balancing board

became uncomfortable with Tom and Cynthia doing the balancing. Believing their needs were not being met, these owners began inserting themselves into the balancing role. Tom reacted by firming up his authority to make balancing decisions, thus upsetting even more owners.

In Chapter 7, we give you the conclusion of Tom and Cynthia's story, and there you can examine the board's role.

WHEN ENTREPRENEURS WANT TO SELL THE BUSINESS OR THEIR SHARES

When entrepreneurs want to do the balancing, run the company, harvest their investment, and then retire, they do not need to clarify and formalize the balance point or the balancing process. They will run the company the way they see fit. However, if entrepreneurs want to increase the value of their business before selling it, clarifying and formalizing the balance point can help.

If entrepreneurs want to increase the value of their company before selling it, implementing the balancing concept will assure buyers that the company has professional managers who know how to successfully work with boards and who understand how to integrate the owners' values, needs, and goals into their plans. When managers actually manage the company for the owners' benefit, their expectations and usually their salary and benefits are consistent with the general market, making it more likely they will stay on when the company is sold. Buyers are often willing to pay more for a management team with this level of development. (The principle exception is when a buyer's ethics or values differ significantly from those of the entrepreneur—in which case the buyer may not see the benefit of a management team that is responsive to the owners.)

Jane's Story

After leaving a Fortune 500 company, Jane started Test Match, an electronic testing business. Jane put her best efforts into the business, realizing it was the source of her retirement income. Test Match had a solid reputation for quality products and service. Jane planned to sell the company within the next five years, and she thought she could get the highest price by selling to an investment group or to a large company wanting to expand the products and services. Most of her managers were young except for two who had been with her from the start and would probably retire when she did.

Jane believed that she could get more for her business if she had a well-trained management team that she could sell with the business. Her process worked like this. First, Jane described her values about running the business, and she gave the managers a written list of her needs and goals for the business. She then asked the managers to develop and implement plans for the company that would provide what she was looking for. She formalized the board arrangement, and instituted a monthly presentation where managers explained their plans and how those plans met the objectives Jane identified. Managers also presented solutions to problems that arose. If Jane disagreed with management's plans, she explained how she was balancing her interests as an owner with the interests managers identified and directed management accordingly. Jane also modified the compensation arrangement so managers received bonuses for plans that achieved what she, the owner, wanted.

Jane's managers learned that they serve the owner. They came to understand what is important to an owner and how to develop plans to deliver what she wanted. They also became accountable. When Jane marketed the company, she received a higher bid from an investment firm wanting a management team who could meet specified goals for growth and profitability and who were willing to position the company for resale within five years. Jane demonstrated that her management team had in fact done this and sold the idea that her management team deserved rewards for their efforts if they succeeded. The investment firm agreed to reward managers if they met their goals, and the management team agreed to stay on, knowing they could meet the objectives and be well rewarded.

When entrepreneurs want to sell their shares to the other owners, having an effective balance point ensures the continued viability of the business, and thus the likelihood that they will be paid. The board, acting as the balance point, will make sure payments to the departing owner are included in the owners' plan and in management's budget. The role of the balance point is to ensure that the remaining owners, managers, or the new board can make decisions as needed to keep the company healthy and the financial interests of the remaining owners in proper perspective (all of which increase the probability that the departing owner will be paid). A board acting as the balance point is a safeguard for the departing entrepreneur.

Jane's Story—An Adaptation

Suppose Jane wanted to retire by selling Test Match to her management team rather an investment group—but the company could not finance the full amount of the purchase price she wanted. Having earlier formalized and clarified the structure and process of the balance point, she will have greater confidence in her managers' ability to pay her and in their receiving direction from a board of outside directors. Her managers will also benefit from the balance point arrangement. It will help the new owners clarify and formalize their interests as owners; their varying roles, responsibilities, and authority as different types of managers; and how they will be accountable individually as managers and collectively as owners. Having a process acceptable to everyone for addressing potential conflicts among multiple owners can greatly minimize the risk that turmoil within the ownership group will jeopardize Jane's payments.

If entrepreneurs want to bring in outside investors, a balancing board can help to define the relationship between the managers, directors, and investors. A typical example of this is bringing in venture capital.

If entrepreneurs go to outside investors such as venture capital firms for cash to grow their business before selling it, they may have to give up ownership and possibly one or more seats on the board. Venture capitalists usually ask to join the board so they can protect their investment by shaping decisions to satisfy their interests (i.e., financial returns and exit goals).

The balancing point process requires all entrepreneurs and outside investors to speak with one voice. Doing this before obtaining capital clarifies the investors' expectations and may help find an investor who will truly have the same interests as the entrepreneur. For example, asking an investment firm to articulate its values, needs, and goals will allow Jane to assess whether and how the interests of the investment firm coincide with her values, needs, and goals. The investor can also compare its interests with Jane's objectives. The balance point process requires the board of directors and the investor to align the interests of all the owners (not just those of the investor) with the interests of the business and to ensure that management's plans are designed to satisfy all owners' interests. Directors can focus on directing rather than advancing their individual ownership interests because the entrepreneur and the venture company already agreed on an owners' plan that works for both of them.

The balancing point process has limited downsides for the investor and tremendous upsides for the business. Entrepreneurs seeking investment may still pursue their interests but have to be open about them within the ownership group. Outside investors are still able to look out for their interests, but integrating them with the interests of other owners means actually looking out for the interests of all owners. The other owners know what their "new partner" is looking for, and management knows what the company must produce to be successful in the owners' eyes. With potential competing interests resolved, outside investors are free to provide skills and experience to help management develop the best plans and obtain the best results.

LOCATING THE BALANCE POINT

When entrepreneurs make significant decisions about their companies, we suggested that those decisions involve balancing the interests of the owners and the business. We acknowledge that entrepreneurs don't usually make these balancing decisions consciously; they just do what is needed to get the job done. But, in essence, they are balancing ownership and business interests (and probably doing it well too).

Balancing the interests of the owners and those of the business is what we believe effective boards do in closely held and family businesses. The "balance point" is another name to describe an effective board of directors. Figure 3.6 can help you visualize the board as located between ownership and management. When placed in this position, the board can more effectively understand its role of helping the owners and managers align their respective interests.

The current balance point works just fine in many businesses so it is sometimes hard to understand the need to clarify and formulate the balancing function. Understanding the role of the balance

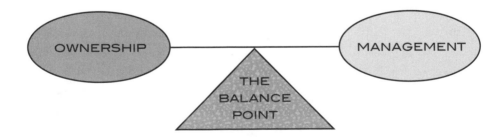

Figure 3.6 The Board as the "balance point"

point and the importance of the balancing function becomes easier when entrepreneurs want to significantly transition their role, when owners and managers are different people, when there are multiple owners, and when entrepreneurs prepare to sell the business or their shares. Clarifying and formalizing the balance point and locating the balance point in a balancing board during these transitional phases will greatly help identify and accomplish what the owners want and the business needs.

Three statements form a solid foundation for a discussion about making the board the balance point:

» Every business has three groups: owners, managers, and the board.

» Owners, managers, and the board each have separate and distinct roles and responsibilities.

» While separate groups, owners, managers, and the board are also interdependent and must work together.

THREE GROUPS

We acknowledge that in businesses led by entrepreneurs, ownership, management, and the board are usually not thought of as separate groups having separate and distinct responsibilities. Entrepreneurs most often perform the functions of all three groups just by doing what they normally do. Entrepreneurs function as an owner when signing a personal guarantee, as a manager when implementing a business plan, and as the board when deciding how much to take out of the company and what to leave in for operations. But the separate functions of ownership, management, and the board exist whether they are recognized or not.

SEPARATION OF ROLES AND RESPONSIBILITIES

If the entrepreneur and the company are in transition, it is essential to think of these three groups as separate and distinct from each other. If ownership, management, and the board are not separated with distinct roles and responsibilities, the balance point remains

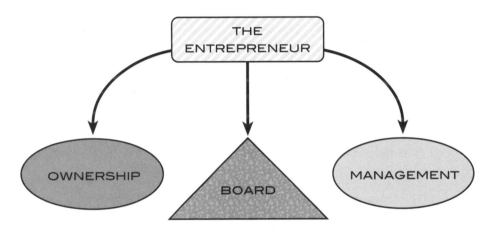

Figure 3.7 Separating into three groups

unclear and a power struggle may ensue to fill that role. Remember, the person or group doing the balancing is making key decisions affecting owners and managers. The cohesiveness of the owners and the well-being of the company depend on good balance point decisions. This separation involves identifying the key functions of the entrepreneur and allocating those functions among the three groups that exist in any business as illustrated in Figure 3.7.

What does separating ownership, management, and the board mean? In its most basic terms, it means that owners do what owners do and managers do what managers do, and the board becomes the "balance point" between the two, helping the owners and managers accomplish their separate and distinct responsibilities. While we cover this extensively in Chapters 4, 5, and 6, here are some characteristics of this separation.

Separating ownership and management means that

» owners, as owners, have no role or responsibilities inside the company (i.e., in management). Owners have ownership roles and responsibilities, and should focus on being effective owners.

» managers, as managers, have no role or responsibilities inside the ownership group. Managers have management roles and responsibilities, and should focus on being effective managers.

Separating ownership and the board means that

» owners have no role or responsibilities in directing management. Owners communicate their values, needs, and goals to the board; the board directs management around these parameters.

» the board has no role or responsibilities in deciding why the owners want a board and what the board is supposed to do. Directors focus on providing the services requested by the owners. Sometimes, directors disagree with the owners. We address the potential standoff that can exist between owners and the board in Chapter 6.

Separating management from the board means that

» managers have no role or responsibilities in determining owners' wants and needs. Managers need to understand the owners' values, needs, and goals; focus on developing plans for the company that are consistent with them; and run the company effectively.

» the board has no role or responsibilities in actually running the company. Their responsibility is to evaluate and approve management's plans for the company, and track and oversee management's efforts throughout the fiscal year.

Table 3.1 summarizes where we suggest key functions are best located.

Table 3.1 Separation of Owners, Managers, and Board

Who has a role . . .	Owners	Managers	Board
• inside the company	No	Yes	No
• inside owner meetings	Yes	No	No
• in directing managers	No	No	Yes
• in deciding what a board will do	Yes	No	No
• in determining what owners need	Yes	No	No
• in running the company	No	Yes	No

INTERDEPENDENCE

Although owners, managers, and the board have separate and distinct roles and responsibilities, the groups are interdependent, requiring them to work closely together. Often, owners are also managers and directors, so an individual may hold several positions at the same time. This complicates their working relationship.

In essence, each of these three groups must be separate and interdependent at the same time. To accomplish this effectively, boundaries must be clearly established. One way to do this is to think of each group's roles and responsibilities as separate, but the process in which they work as interdependent. In Chapters 6 and 7 we explain how the three groups work together. For now, remember that the owners communicate their values, needs, and goals to the board through an owners' plan. The board evaluates this plan and if and when they accept it, managers receive a management version of it. Management then develops the company's strategic and annual plans to accomplish the owners' plan within the company's capabilities. Management then presents those plans to the board, and the board evaluates and eventually approves these plans. Figure 3.8 shows this process.

An unclear balance point process puts the company at risk. A board that functions as the balance point makes the separation and interdependence of ownership and management much easier to accomplish. When serving as the balance point, the board

» clarifies the owners' and managers' roles and responsibilities

» ensures that the roles are understood, the boundaries maintained, and the responsibilities discharged

» acts as a third party to help discuss and resolve contentious issues

» reduces conflict between the owners and managers

The board as a balance point strives for the cohesiveness of the ownership group and the well-being of the company. This is its role.

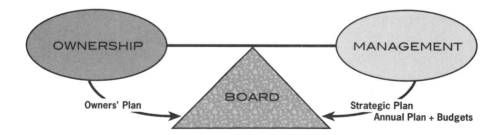

Figure 3.8 How the groups are connected

A COMMENT ABOUT STRUCTURE

We work with many entrepreneurs who tell us they don't like structure and bristle at words like "system" and "process." We try to remind these individuals that they already have a system, structure, and process—the way they make business decisions and obtain results are their system, structure, and process. When entrepreneurs deny this, they are either saying that their system, structure, and process will work just fine in the transition (which may be absolutely true) or that they want to transition but don't want to change. When entrepreneurs understand the concept of the balance point, it often becomes easier for them to understand they can retain authority while making changes that others may need to be prepared to do their job.

The steps involved in considering necessary changes are relatively straightforward.

1. UNDERSTAND YOUR SUCCESSION GOALS. It is also essential to understand where you want to go before you can assess whether the arrangements you have in place now are adequate or whether changes are needed.

2. UNDERSTAND YOUR CURRENT SYSTEM, STRUCTURE, AND PROCESS. It is essential to understand how business decisions and results are really obtained before you can decide whether the current arrangements will work for you. Do a reality check!

3. ASSESS YOUR CURRENT SYSTEM, STRUCTURE, AND PROCESS. Be honest in identifying the strengths, weaknesses, challenges, experiences, skills, and so forth of your business and the people involved. Only then can you adequately determine what changes (if any) are needed to accomplish your goals.

4. DECIDE HOW YOU WILL MAKE ANY NECESSARY CHANGES. Altering your current system, structure, and process will produce fundamental changes. Before beginning these changes, come up with a plan supported by the key people involved. This is part of your transition plan.

5. MAKE THE CHANGES. Implementing these type of changes is often hard but also rewarding. This is where people can practice and learn what they have to do during the transition.

6. TEST THE CHANGES. Evaluating the plan and changes are important to any well-developed plan.

7. MAKE MODIFICATIONS AS NEEDED. Make sure that the system, structure, and process work for you, thus ensuring that your succession goals will be met.

4

WHAT OWNERS DO

Before you continue reading this book, take a moment and ask yourself whether any of the circumstances that call for clarifying and formalizing the balance point (Chapter 3) exist in your situation. If you can identify with one or more of the circumstances, you may begin to realize a new way to create an action plan that works for you. In this chapter, we will focus on the role and responsibilities of ownership. We describe the basic role and responsibilities of an effective ownership group and suggest ways for owners to fulfill their responsibilities.

THE BASICS

A board cannot act as the balance point unless the owners carry out their role and responsibilities. Balancing cannot occur unless the owners identify their values, needs, and goals and let the board know about them. Neither directors nor managers can read the owners' minds, nor should they be expected to. It is the owners' responsibility to do this work. And owners find it difficult to determine their values, needs, and goals as a group without having some structure and process to help them.

Shareholders, partners, and members of a limited liability company are the owners of businesses—that is their basic role. Though their responsibilities as owners will differ from one business to the next, some basic responsibilities for owners of all closely held and family businesses include

» developing an owners' manual

» developing an owners' plan

» electing directors

» evaluating the board

» staying informed

» understanding the difference between power and control

DEVELOPING AN OWNERS' MANUAL

When you buy a car, you get an owners' manual describing how to operate the car. Similarly, it is essential to have a guidebook describing how to own your business. We call this resource or guidebook an *owners' manual*, but you can call it whatever you want.

WHY IS AN OWNERS' MANUAL NECESSARY?

An owners' manual is the primary source for explaining the separate roles and responsibilities of the owners, board, and management and how they work together; the owners' policies, procedures, and structures; and the board's structure. (See Figure 4.1.) Developing this resource when the company is in transition provides direction for owners, managers, directors, and professional advisors who need to know how these groups function separately and how they work together.

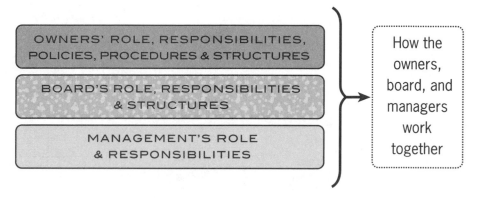

Figure 4.1 The owners' manual

WHAT DOES AN OWNERS' MANUAL INCLUDE?

The owners' manual answers the fundamental questions that owners need to address to successfully own their company. Questions include Who can be an owner? How are we going to work together to make decisions? What happens if we don't agree on important issues? When and how do we review and update the transition plan? What board arrangement do we want? Under what conditions would we choose to sell the company rather than carry on as a business? Failure to address any of these questions may result in conflicts that can undermine the well-being of the ownership group, the company, and the family.

Worksheet 4.1 contains an extensive list of questions to guide owners in developing their owners' manual. Appendix 4.1 suggests topics to include in an owners' manual. Another good idea is for the owners to simply brainstorm about what they believe needs to be addressed and identify the results they want to include in their owners' manual. We discuss the basic topics that belong in every owners' manual below.

Owners Working Together

The owners' manual should include ground rules for working together. All ownership groups and families have domineering members, sensitive issues, old conflicts, discussion traps, and so forth. Ground rules define appropriate behavior before, during, and after owners' meetings. For example, "Speak for yourself and not others" or "Everyone is responsible for staying on task." In this way, group members can more effectively conduct discussions.

Each ownership group must identify how they will make decisions as a group. Owners can usually just talk through minor differences and come to a decision that works for everyone. But what happens when significant differences come up? When do owners vote to make decisions?

SUCCESSION PLAN OR TRANSITION PLAN?

What is the difference between a succession plan and a transition plan? Often these terms are used synonymously, but we think it is important to distinguish between the two.

A succession plan describes the goals the owners have for the succession of their company, such as selling or giving the business to one or more owners, family members, managers, employees, or third-party investors. Succession goals may include going public or liquidating the company.

A transition plan outlines what has to happen and how these things will be accomplished in order to make the succession goals a reality. For example, if the succession plan is to sell or give shares to family members, none of whom will work at the company, the transition plan identifies what needs to happen to make this situation work and how those events will occur.

What happens if conflicts within the ownership group can't be resolved by voting?

When the question relates directly to developing the owners' manual (or the owners' plan as discussed below), we suggest owners commit to talking through differences rather than moving too quickly on a vote to decide. Calling for a vote too soon tends to stifle minority viewpoints, which can adversely affect the minority's commitment to continuing as an owner, or may motivate the minority to express their views in less constructive ways. How soon is too soon depends on each group of owners and the significance of the decisions; no one procedure works for all situations. Some groups allow a minority group of owners to ask for an outside facilitator to help the group work through issues involving significant differences or those having a substantial impact on the ownership group or the business.

Franklin Printing's Story

Stephan, Brian, and Roxanne are the senior managers of Franklin Printing and plan to buy equal shares of the business from Herb, its founder and sole owner. Roxanne will be president and Stephan will head up sales. Brian, the founder's son, will lead operations. The three of them have worked together for about five years and are friends. Their families socialize together. They don't want ownership to get in the way of their personal relationships. Stephan, Brian, and Roxanne agree that ownership will be the one place where the three of them are equal. They came up with a list of what they expect from each other as owners and how they want to be treated as an owner by the others. They also want to ensure that all three of them are satisfied as owners. They agree to work toward decisions that each of them can live with. If any of them disagrees with a position taken by one of the others, they will adjourn the meeting and reconvene within two days to reconsider the issue. If all three still do not support the decision, any of them can ask one of their professional advisors to help find a solution that will work for all three. And if they still cannot agree, then they will use a majority vote to decide.

Distinct roles and responsibilities

The owners, board, and managers have separate and distinct roles, and, as a result, separate and distinct responsibilities. The owners' manual should identify the roles of each group and their different responsibilities. We described the owners' basic role and responsibilities at the beginning of this chapter. Chapter 6 describes the board's basic role and responsibilities; Chapter 5 describes management's basic role and responsibilities. The owners, of course, can tailor these basic duties to fit their particular company. In any case, we suggest putting these responsibilities in writing and including them in the owners' manual.

While the roles and responsibilities of the owners, board, and managers are separate and distinct, they must also be integrated because the people are all part of the same system. The owners' decisions affect how the board directs management and, therefore, how management runs the day-to-day activities of the company. For example, owners of closely held and family businesses often discuss their values (as described in the owners' plan). They spend a lot of time identifying values, writing them down, and communicating them to management. In many businesses, however, the owners' values aren't visible inside the company because management hasn't promoted them to the employees, and the board hasn't required management to do so. In this case, either management or the board has "decided" that it is not their responsibility to ensure that the owners' values are visible inside the company. When this happens, the integration of ownership, board, and management falls apart (if it ever existed to begin with). Each group acts separately, with its own agenda. On the other hand, when ownership, board, and management are fully integrated, management understands that they need to instill the owners' values inside the company, and that the board holds management accountable for this and asks for tangible evidence that it is done.

The board's decisions directly affect the extent to which the owners' values, needs, and goals are followed and how management runs the day-to-day business activities. A board that understands the owners' values, needs, and goals as described in the owners' plan will approve management's plans only if those plans are consistent with the owners' plan. If the board doesn't understand the owners' values, needs, and goals, it won't be able to evaluate management's plan effectively.

If the board approves a management plan that is inconsistent with the owners' plan, then the board, owners, and management will not be integrated. A board that is integrated with the owners and managers evaluates management's plan and, if it finds inconsistencies, determines whether to rework management's plan or the owners' plan (or both plans) to remove the inconsistency.

Management decisions directly determine how the owners' values, needs, and goals are treated inside the company. Management and the board are not integrated when management adopts policies without knowing whether they contradict the values in the owners' plan, or when management knowingly adopts policies that are inconsistent with the owners' values and, in addition, don't seek board approval. Management that is fully integrated with the board and owners knows the owners' values and understands that board must approve policies that are inconsistent with the owners' plan.

When the responsibilities of the three groups are not integrated, the system breaks down and individual interests become more important than the common good, resulting in significant conflicts at all levels. The owners' manual should describe how to integrate the owners, board, and management.

Franklin Printing's Story—Continued

Stephan, Brian, and Roxanne have now worked together for quite a while, so they have an idea of what each of them does within the company. The only new position is Roxanne's elevation to president, which required that all three prepare a job description for Roxanne. They also reviewed Herb's responsibilities and allocated them to Roxanne. The three are less sure of their responsibilities as owners (because they haven't ever been owners) and don't know what the board will do (because Herb's board wasn't active). To protect their personal relationships, they want to be sure they are all on the same page regarding what they want from the business and what their expectations are for the board and management.

Stephan, Brian, and Roxanne are already beginning to distinguish between owners, management, and the board, and are learning how to determine what these groups should do and how they should work together.

The balance point or board

The owners' manual should identify the location of the balance point. It is important for the owners to discuss the situations reviewed in Chapter 3 that prompt changing the balance point from where it is currently located to a board. Those situations are

» when entrepreneurs want to transition out of day-to-day business activities but still want to make a contribution

» when the owners and managers are (or will be) different people

» when there are (or will be) multiple owners

» when entrepreneurs want to sell the company or their stock

IS A BALANCING BOARD REALLY NECESSARY?

This book provides a step-by-step approach to help owners decide whether they need a balancing board and how to establish one. These steps involve answering the following basic questions:

» When do we need a board? (Chapter 3)

» What do we want this board to do? (Chapter 6)

» How will the board work with the owners and managers? (Chapters 4, 5, and 7)

» What board structure best serves our needs? (Chapter 8)

» What board structure will those in power accept and endorse? (Chapter 8)

» What do we expect from our board and directors? (Chapter 9)

» What characterizations, skills, and attributes do we want our directors to have? (Chapter 9)

» What process are we going to follow to select potential candidates and elect directors? (Chapter 9)

The answers to these basic questions will describe the role, responsibilities, structure, and process of the balancing board. These answers should be documented in the owners' manual so everyone knows what they are.

If the owners decide that one or more of these situations apply, and they want to be prepared when it occurs, then it is time to discuss establishing a balancing board.

Franklin Printing—the next questions

Herb was the balance point for Franklin Printing when he was involved in the business. As the founder, he decided what owners would get from the company based on what he thought the company needed. After Herb sells his shares to Stephan, Brian, and Roxanne and retires from the business, where will the balance point be located? This is a question the new owners need to answer. If they locate the balance point within management, Roxanne as president will probably decide that she has the authority to balance the interests of the owners and the business. If the balance point is located within ownership, Stephan, Brian, and Roxanne will be the only people who make balancing decisions so they will need to figure out how they will share this power. However, if the board is the balance point, the owners will have the additional advantage of appointing people to help them make balancing decisions—when and if they want assistance.

WHO IS INVOLVED IN PUTTING THE OWNERS' MANUAL TOGETHER?

All of the owners should be involved in developing the owners' manual. Including everyone in this process increases their understanding of how things fit together; provides an opportunity to practice listening, understanding, and making decisions; and allows owners to assess each other's level of commitment for common ownership.

Nonvoting owners

Some ownership groups and families want to involve only those owners or family members having voting shares and exclude those with nonvoting shares. But consider the consequences of excluding someone merely because they don't have a vote. Excluding them sends the message that they are not welcome—and that does not build commitment or trust. Usually a business is better off when all owners commit to keeping their capital in the business, and this type of commitment requires that the owners be a part of what they own. If an ownership group or family wants to distinguish between voting and nonvoting shares, they can ask all owners to help develop the owners' manual, but leave final approval of the contents to those members owning voting shares.

Some ownership groups and families want to involve only those owners or family members who work in the business and exclude those owners who do not. Again, consider the consequences of excluding someone merely because they don't work at the company. If an ownership group or family wants to make a distinction regarding employment, a more effective way would be to limit ownership to those individuals whom the business employs. This eliminates the possibility of an ownership class that is excluded from participating in discussions of ownership involvement.

Managers or directors with shares

Some ownership groups and families give shares to managers or directors, but they don't want to include those people in the process of developing the owners' manual. Perhaps they gave these managers or directors shares as a form of compensation or a "piece of the action" in case the company is sold, and alternatives to giving them shares would not provide the type of tax benefits sought. Whatever the reason, the ownership groups and families must clarify and agree to the role and responsibilities of these managers or directors—or misunderstandings and conflict may result. When managers or directors who own stock are excluded from the ownership planning process, they may not be thought of as "real owners."

One way of resolving this issue is to ask managers or directors to participate in those parts of the ownership discussions that pertain to them. For example, they may participate in discussions about the balance point, but not discussions about the criteria for estate planning and keeping shares within the ownership group or family. Giving managers and directors different classes of stock (nonvoting shares rather than voting shares, for example) may help to highlight that their participation is different and their share ownership is intended for a particular purpose.

When managers and directors do own shares, we encourage the other owners to find a way to include them in developing and maintaining the owners' manual. Doing so will give those managers and directors a much better idea of what it means to be an owner. From this, managers and/or directors who own shares will either become better informed owners and thus better understand their role and responsibilities, or it will become clear that it is best that they not own shares. In either case, resolving this issue will most likely avoid significant conflict with a group that is central to the company's success.

Trusts

Some ownership arrangements involve trusts. For example, an owner may transfer her shares of a business to a trustee to hold in trust for the benefit of her children or other relatives. Or an entrepreneur may die, leaving a will directing that his shares be held in trust for the benefit of his wife and, following her death, for the benefit of his children and grandchildren. When the ownership interests are held in trust, the trustee is the legal owner, and the beneficiaries of the trust are sometimes considered the beneficial owners.

Another common trust arrangement is the employee stock owner-ship trust (ESOT), which is sometimes referred to as an employee stock ownership plan (ESOP). ESOTs are created to buy ownership interests. The ESOT trustee holds the ownership interests as the legal owner for the benefit of the company's employees who are the beneficiaries of the trust. An ESOT is popular because it offers a tax-favorable way for owners to sell all their ownership interests and for all of the employees to own a portion of the business in which they are involved.

When trusts own shares, some ownership groups or families want to involve only the legal owners, but there are benefits to including the beneficiaries in developing an owners' manual. For example, upon ter-mination of a trust (other than an ESOT), the beneficiaries will own the shares. Including the beneficiaries in developing the owners' manu-al will increase the likelihood that they will support the policies in the manual when they legally own their shares. Involving the beneficiaries of a trust (including an ESOT) provides a great opportunity to educate them about the roles and responsibilities of the company's owners, board, and managers and how these three groups work together. This can be particularly helpful if shares are owned in an ESOT because the employees are actively involved in the company and can significantly affect how these groups perform. Involving beneficiaries in the owner-ship planning process doesn't mean that the beneficiaries are physi-cally present in owner meetings. Sometimes, the trustee obtains input from the beneficiaries separately (through small groups or as one large group) and then takes this information to the owner meetings with the interests of the beneficiaries in mind.

Different ownership situations require involvement of different people (or groups of people) in the ownership planning work. We en-courage owners to consider the impact of excluding any owners versus the benefits of including everyone who has an ownership interest in the business. If including a class of owners raises concerns, consider alternatives that address those concerns or consider buying out their ownership interests entirely.

CHAPTER 4

Family members who are not owners

Some family businesses involve family members who are not owners in ownership meetings. Typically these nonowner family members are spouses, but sometimes they are next-generation individuals who are invited to owner meetings to learn about the business. Some family businesses even form family councils as an initial step in their transition work and invite spouses and children who may not own shares into the decision-making process. (See the Sidebar at the end of this section for an explanation of family councils.)

Huntington Telephone's Story

Phil and his four sons, Jack, Dana, Steve, and Jon own equal shares of Huntington Telephone, but only Jack and Dana work in the business. Phil, Jack, and Dana worked with us to transition Phil from management and to hire a nonowner president to lead the company until either Jack or Dana are ready to step into that role. They also formed a family council consisting of all five owners and their spouses.

The first family council meeting we attended included discussions about life insurance for the owners who worked at the company and reimbursement policies for employees' business travel expenses. Because these topics were on the agenda, everyone, including spouses, had something to contribute to the discussion. After the meeting we asked the group about the purpose of the family council.

"It's to keep everyone informed about what is happening at the company," said one respondent.

"Does keeping everyone informed include asking family members to decide business policies?" we inquired.

"What do you mean?" they replied.

The members of the family council were not aware they were making policy. We explained that the agenda included seeking approval from the council and asked, "Who is the appropriate person (or people) to approve reimbursement policies and the amount of insurance the company needs to carry on key owners?" No one responded.

Another owner stated, "We were told it was a good idea to have a family council so we formed one."

We then asked the spouses (only one of whom worked in the business) what they thought would be helpful to talk about as a family. Their responses varied, but they were all interested in understanding the business, what it meant to be owners, and how the business affected their personal lives. Essentially, the spouses wanted information, but not the type that was discussed at the meeting.

"Do you mind if your spouses are not invited to meetings where business policies are discussed?" we asked the owners.

No one wanted their nonworking spouses excluded if the spouse who was working at the company was involved in discussions about policies. These owners had not distinguished between the roles of a spouse who works at the business and spouses who don't. To move things forward, the owners agreed to meet as owners where they would discuss the role and responsibilities of owners, managers, and the board, and when and how to involve spouses in the decision making.

How to include nonowner family members is a critical decision that often is not well thought out or planned. Many families involve nonowner family members or form family councils without understanding the purpose of a family council or how the family or family council relates to the owners. They do it because they are told that this is what families owning businesses do.

Owners must discuss the roles and responsibilities of owners and family members who are not owners and how the roles and responsibilities of these two groups might be the same or different. Owners decide whether nonowner family members are involved in owner meetings. If they are to be included, the owners also need to decide how the nonowner family members are involved and on what issues they may participate or vote. If the decision is not to involve them in owner meetings, the family owners must then decide how the nonowner family members will obtain the information they need to support the family owners. For example, owners can differentiate between owner issues and family issues. On family issues, every family member might be involved in the meeting and vote; one person = one vote. On owner issues, meetings may be limited to family owners, or if the meeting includes all family members, only those with shares may vote on ownership issues.

Family councils

When they begin transition planning, most of the family business owners we have worked with want to limit participation in owner meetings to only those family members having an ownership interest in the business. These individuals want to have the opportunity to decide for themselves how they are going to work together as owners. Eventually, however, the owners begin addressing issues that impact the broader family. When this occurs, it is helpful to distinguish between owner issues and family issues. Then owner matters can be addressed in owner meetings by those family members holding ownership interests, and family matters can be addressed by the broader family. A family council can be a useful mechanism to help organize broader family involvement in addressing and resolving these family matters.

We strongly support the formation and use of family councils to help family members address family issues and to provide owners with input from the broader family. We do not support using a family council or otherwise including nonowner family members in general business decision making without first having the owners distinguish the roles and responsibilities of owner and nonowner family members and deciding how each group should carry out their roles and responsibilities. Involving nonowner family members in ownership decisions when the owners have not discussed the implications of their decisions increases the risks of creating expectations among nonowner family members that may not be sustainable, blurs the boundaries between owners and nonowners, and creates the possibility that owners may have to take back some of their decision-making responsibilities, which can lead to disappointment and dissension. Ideally, family councils should not address ownership issues unless the owners invite nonowner family members to participate in decision making, and then only after the owners consider the role of the broader family and the implication of involving nonowner family members.

The family council is distinct from the ownership group. The ownership group is limited to family members who own stock. The family council can include owners and nonowners. While this distinction is quite obvious, it is important because many of the family council's decisions need ownership group approval before they become part of the owners' plan and owners' manual.

The family council should give the annual plans of the broader family to the owners. If they agree to do so, the family owners can then incorporate into their annual owners' plan those parts of the broader family's plan relating to the business.

The owners' manual should spell out the family council's involvement in the business, their decision-making authority, and how they interact with the owner group. How to decide these issues is up to the owner and family groups. Each family creates a relationship between the broader family and the family owners that fosters the well-being of the family

A FAMILY COUNCIL CAN BE A USEFUL MECHANISM TO HELP ORGANIZE BROADER FAMILY INVOLVEMENT IN ADDRESSING AND RESOLVING THESE FAMILY MATTERS.

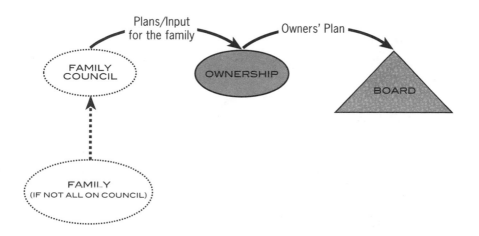

Figure 4.2 Relationship between family, family council, and owners

and the business. This model is shown in Figure 4.2. Sharing decision-making power is a necessary ingredient for a harmonious family.

Some of the structures and processes in this book can be adapted to fit a family and a family council as long as the owners agree. For example, if the family council consists of a subgroup of the entire family, the family council can be authorized as the balance point between the family and the owners (much like a balancing board is the balance point for a family business) for those issues that the ownership group has delegated to it. As the balance point, the family council balances the differing interests of family members and the owners, helping all family members align their interests so the family is cohesive and acts as a group. The key to making this work is an ownership group that is clear about what decisions the owners make and what responsibilities they delegate to the family council.

The bottom line is that the business owners decide who is going to be involved in developing the owners' manual. Typically, conflicts arising among owner groups are based on a lack of clarity as to who is involved with what decisions.

THE FAMILY COUNCIL

A typical family council includes the entire family (as defined by the owners or the family) or is a smaller group of family members chosen to make decisions on behalf of the larger family. It often includes family members who are not owners. The family council's main role is to address the "business" of the family and family involvement issues.

A family council is different than the ownership group. But each family council develops its own unique reasons for its existence and operation. Also, each has its own unique areas to address. Five general areas family councils usually address include

» developing healthy and strong family relationships

» preparing responsible next-generation owners

» providing education and development opportunities for family members

» interacting with the ownership group

» coordinating family stewardship

Out of these five areas come specific topics for family discussion and resolution. Discussion items may include

» developing and updating a family charter (a shared dream)

» discussing and understanding the authority of and the boundaries between family members, owners, and the business—such as who makes what decisions, who makes recommendations, and what is out of bounds for family members who are not owners

» discussing who can own shares, owner entry and exit arrangements, and tax issues

» developing policies or requirements regarding employment for future family members

» exploring gender and age issues

» developing codes of conduct and family values that suggest how family members relate to each other in and out of the company

» developing confidentiality policies regarding the family business and family discussions

» discussing the involvement or noninvolvement of family members as individuals

» discussing expectations family members have of each other

» developing an annual priority list for discussion and decision making

» discussing and resolving issues of fairness

» imparting a sense of family and company history to the next generations

» deciding what stewardship means for the family and how the family will be involved as a group

» developing an annual statement of values, needs, and goals for the family

THE PROCESS OF PUTTING THE OWNERS' MANUAL TOGETHER

There is no one way to put together an owners' manual. But the process most owners use usually includes

» following initial ground rules and other guidelines for working together

» identifying how the owners want to be involved in developing the manual

» assigning one person to take notes at the meetings and write the drafts

» deciding on the manual's contents and those parts needing the most attention

» commenting on and recommending changes to the drafts

» allowing time for individual owners to discuss the manual with their attorneys or other advisors

» getting final approval from each owner

» presenting the manual or relevant parts of the manual to the board

» scheduling meetings to do all of the above

» monitoring owners' and directors' reactions to the owners' manual

» monitoring how well the owners' manual is working

It's helpful if the owners understand the process for putting the manual together so their discussions can focus on the content.

General guidelines

1. The owners' manual should be in writing—making the information easily available to the different owners, the board, managers, and professional advisors who will need to refer to it. Writing down the guidelines also makes the information more reliable (it is not based on recollections) and makes changes deliberate.

2. Owners should work on those items that matter most to them as owners. This may include obtaining information about the company in order to understand concerns about owners' employment issues (compensation, qualifications, evaluations, accountability); the long-term stability of the business; owners' risks; philanthropy; the entrepreneur's level of involvement in the business; estate tax liability and the ability to pay estate taxes; and relationship difficulties within the ownership group affecting trust, commitment, communication, and decision making.

Addressing the issues having the highest level of interest means the owners deal with the hardest issues first. Usually, this is a good thing—it means the owners will be engaged and more likely committed to do the work. It often brings integrity and meaning to the work of the owners. Sometimes, though, an owners' group must become more cohesive to tackle the hardest issues. In this case, resolving easier issues first helps build cohesion—it shows the group that they can make decisions together and permits individuals to open up to the group at their own pace.

When addressing these matters, some ownership groups are able to go deep; that is, identify and address what is at the core of their concern (which sometimes is not immediately evident by the question). For example, an ownership group wants to talk about dividends. In a closely held company, the lifestyle that one or more individual owners want to maintain is at the core. In a family business, the next generation's fear that they may be negatively judged by their parents if they talk about money is at the core. Other ownership groups work better if they address questions at a level reflecting their current ability to work together. As long as the owners are satisfied with the result, there is no need to go deeper. Going too deep too soon can damage the confidence or desire to address the real issues later. If the entire ownership group is satisfied with the answer, address deeper issues at a later time when either the questions come up again or when the core issues surface in another context.

The Peterson Family's Story

Dad and Mom Peterson told their five children they would receive all of their parents' ownership interests in Dexter Chemicals, a second-generation family business. Dad purchased the business from his father and grew it into one of the largest privately owned chemical companies in the nation. He continues to be the company's CEO but delegated the responsibility for the day-to-day operations to a management team. None of the children work at the company, but all five understand the benefits of ownership (they would be wealthy) and the responsibilities that come with ownership (taking care of the employees and helping the small community where the business is located). Each child wants to be an owner, and they are all honored to be involved in Dexter Chemicals becoming a third-generation family business. They also deeply appreciate their parents' generosity.

Dad and Mom started transferring ownership interests to their children and modified company documents to make sure that ownership would go equally to lineal descendants of the five branches of the family. Dad talked often about how he wanted to treat his children equally. So he authorized them to meet and learn how to be responsible owners. Mom spoke freely about her concerns that money would destroy her children's values. As the Peterson family met and the children considered how they would own the business together, they increasingly began to criticize each other. One daughter, concerned about whether management could function without him, asked Dad when he was going to retire. Her siblings responded by telling her she was getting too personal with Dad. A son wanted to know how much he might receive from the company in dividends. His siblings told him not to ask out of fear that Mom and Dad would be offended.

Finally the children decided to meet on their own to discover the underlying reasons for their criticisms of each other. Eventually, they discussed their fear that, if offended by a question or comment, Dad or Mom would retaliate against all of them by withholding annual cash gifts or freezing dividend distributions, which all five siblings depended on in varying degrees. So whenever a sibling's question might increase the risk of offending a parent, the others would step in and stop the exchange. They did not want to be their "brother's keeper"—but their fear resulted in exactly that. Not confronting or criticizing Dad or Mom became a family rule.

Discovering the root cause of their conflicts was extremely painful for the children. A son remembered a hurtful time when Mom decided to not talk to his spouse because of a disagreement over the son's religious beliefs; his siblings joined in the cold shoulder. A daughter who had worked for the company recalled the time when Dad insisted on firing rather than demoting her to another position that she could handle; none of her siblings lent her their support even though they thought Dad's decision unjustified. Basically, they all recalled times when they weren't there for each other, and each said they never wanted to do that again.

While no one understandably wanted to revisit this family "no confronting no criticizing" rule because of the painful memories, its existence shouldn't be ignored. The dynamics caused by this rule will continue to exist until the siblings address it at a level deep enough to learn what they must do to keep it from adversely affecting how they get along. And left unresolved, this family rule will limit their transition work in two ways. The siblings will continue to judge each other's behavior (which is frustrating to those siblings whose behavior is being moderated, and results in power struggles among them), and they will not tell their parents what they need, as siblings, when they own the business together. Their fear of reprisal is so great that some believe Dad and Mom will disinherit them if they try to negotiate for what they need. What is truly sad is that Dad and Mom don't see that their children are hurting because the children aren't telling them. Here is an example where the family has to go deep to move forward, but they are unwilling to do so, believing that ignoring the issue is the preferable alternative.

Problems can arise when some owners are willing to go deeper than other owners. To even talk about this issue, the owners need to address their differing comfort levels. Those owners wanting to address core issues may need to be more patient or to explore what issues the other owners can resolve before participating at a deeper level. Owners who are reluctant to participate at a deeper level can help their fellow owners if they can identify their reluctance and prepare themselves to participate at a level where the other owners want to go. What is most important is that the group continues to discuss how to resolve the issue (rather than pretending that it doesn't exist), with each person striving to help the others.

An ownership group may benefit greatly from using outside facilitators if the facilitators have experience in working with business owners. Worksheet 4.2 contains guidelines that owners can use to select a business facilitator. Facilitators are outside of the ownership dynamics so they can point out what impedes the owners and suggest alternatives. Facilitators can help owners having difficulty participating, making the environment safe to address real issues.

WHAT PARTS OF THE MANUAL ARE LEGALLY ENFORCEABLE?

The owners' manual is usually not a legally binding agreement. Rather, it provides evidence of the overall structures and processes that the owners identify for ownership, management, and the balancing board. In a family business, it may document the structures and processes involving family members who are not owners. The idea is to have all of these arrangements written down in one place that can easily serve as a guide and can be easily reviewed and revised as needed.

However, it is essential that legal counsel review the owners' manual. Some provisions are agreements that the owners want to make legally enforceable. Some may be contrary to state or federal law, so the owners will either need an exemption from the law or they will need to modify that particular provision. The balance point solution offers structures and a process that gives owners more opportunities to manage power struggles, conflict, and disagreements without litigation. These structures and process should be consistent with all state and federal laws, and the agreements that are fundamental to the operation of the balance point and managing differences should be made legally enforceable. Appendix 4.1 (the table of contents for an owners' manual) identifies items that often appear in the company's bylaws, shareholder or owner control agreements, or similar owner contracts to make the agreements legally binding. It is difficult to generalize, though, because each ownership group has its own unique agreements.

Don't forget that any legal documents will need to be amended if the mirror provisions in the owners' manual change. Likewise, the manual should reflect any changes made to the legal documents. Including legal documents in the annual review of the owners' manual is a good way to keep all documentation synchronized.

MAKING CHANGES

Changes will certainly occur, and each ownership group must include a mechanism for change. The owners' manual should include a plan to review it on a regular basis in order to keep current with the owners' changing perspectives. Any changes need to be recorded and included in the owners' manual. Additionally, as the owners work together over time, the fundamental questions may change, and the answers to the fundamental questions may change. When they do, owners need to update their manual.

Sometimes a change seems subtle but, in reality, can affect the entire owners' manual.

» Changes in the ownership structure. For example, creating non-voting shares requires that the owners think through and distinguish the duties of owners with voting shares from those with nonvoting shares.

» Changes in the succession plan or concerns about the transition plan. For example, an entrepreneur may decide not to transfer some of his ownership interests to his children, electing instead to sell some shares to a third party or to give working control to only one child. Or a child scheduled to be the next president may decide to do something else.

» The ground rules may not be working or are not being followed For example, none of the owners identify what they want from the business as a group or a couple of the owners decide for the entire group. Or guidelines about how owners talk to each other are not being followed.

» The relationship between the owners' group and the family council may need changes or adjustments. For example, the owners consider changing the transfer of ownership interests and realize that spouses should be involved in the discussions. Or the owners discover they need to involve next-generation members to a greater extent to prepare them for leadership.

In each of these cases, the owners' manual may need substantial changes.

Sometimes an earlier generation of owners who are no longer involved in the business developed the owners' manual. Too often current owners take their predecessors' answers to the fundamental questions as gospel out of respect for the departed owners or out of the desire to "let sleeping dogs lie." When this happens, owners become unhappy with the arrangements and conflict results. For example, on the issue of buying out a senior partner, an owners' manual includes a structure and a process that has long ceased to make economic sense. Reviewing and changing this structure and process is essential in this case. Each generation of owners should review their fundamental questions and revise their manual as needed. Doing so on a regular basis avoids risking the well-being of the ownership group and the company.

DEVELOPING AN OWNERS' PLAN

Owners need to develop a unified statement identifying their collective values, needs, and goals as they relate to their business. We call this statement an owners' plan.

WHY IS AN OWNERS' PLAN NECESSARY?

Having an owners' plan ensures that all of the board's activities and all of management's plans and day-to-day operations reflect the wishes of the owners. The owners' plan is a single statement supported by all of the owners that provides only one set of "marching orders" for directors and managers. Having clear direction from the owners eliminates the problem of directors and managers "serving two masters" or having to "guess what they [the owners] want." When the owners develop a unified statement, the owners, directors, and managers can better function as an integrated unit.

Figure 4.3 The owners' plan

WHAT DOES AN OWNERS' PLAN INCLUDE?

The owners' plan states the values, needs, and goals of the own ers as a group. (See Figure 4.3.) Just what these are depend on the particular ownership group and the type of business.

Values

Owners' values are the basic principles that drive all planning, decision making, and behaviors relating to the company. Owners' values define what is most important to the owners as a group. Other words used to describe this portion of the owners' plan include owners' principles, commitments, guidelines, and ethics. This section of the owners' plan typically includes statements about

» *Ethics*—the basic moral compass that directors and managers will use in all their decision making and behaviors. Ethics define "doing the right thing."

» *Culture*—how owners, directors, and employees are valued and treated. These are usually written as standards of behavior or codes of conduct. Culture defines "acting the right way."

» *Work environment*—the company's culture. Work environment defines "what it feels like to work here."

» *Performance*—the owners' expectations for results. Performance defines "how well I must do."

» *Accountability*—how employees are answerable for their performance. Accountability defines "being on the hook."

» *Confidentiality*—how closely owners, directors, and managers guard information (financial, research, development, owner, family, and general business). Confidentiality defines "what I can and cannot say."

» *Commitment*—what the owners' group pledges to do and how they are going to keep their pledge. Commitment defines how the owners "walk the talk."

Certainly, there are other owners' values. Each owner group has the responsibility of identifying their collective values, recording them in their owners' plan, and communicating them to the board. The board then communicates them to management.

From these values, the owners make specific decisions affecting the board and management. Examples from clients include the following statements:

» We will include at least one woman on the board.

» We will advance a family member based on merit and the availability of a position.

» Our company will be an asset to the community by financially supporting local charitable activities and encouraging community involvement by our employees.

» Our company recognizes the importance of family life and supports employees balancing their home life and work life.

» We will develop excellent relationships with all our customers and vendors.

» We will ensure strong financial performance realizing that profit and growth create the most good for the most people.

Needs

Owners' needs are what they ought to have right now but are lacking, or what they have and can't do without. Need statements address items like the following:

» *Information about company performance and plans*—including financials, market share, growth strategy, actual results compared to budget, and so forth. Performance information defines "how we are doing."

» *Information that educates the owners about their business*—who buys the company's products or services, how the company gains new customers, how it delivers products or services, and so forth. Educational information defines "what I need to know to be a responsible owner."

» *Debt and risk tolerance*—the level of risk owners are comfortable with and how much debt they or the company have. For example, owners will state their personal guarantees and how they want to share any financial risks among themselves. Some owners will include statements about debt levels compared to assets, accounts receivables, or other benchmarks. Debt and risk tolerance defines "what I am willing to risk."

» *Evidence of their value to the company*—what the owners will do to contribute to the overall process. Evidence of their value defines "how I can help."

» *Evidence of a competent, working board*—what the board's deliverables should be. This evidence defines "how the board is doing."

» *A return on investment (ROI) or equity (ROE)*—how profits will be allocated among the business, the employees, and the owners. Owners define the return they need so management can include these numbers in their strategic and annual planning. ROI/ROE defines "how much money we need."

> » *Clear boundaries among owners, directors, and managers*—the performance expectations for each group. Clear boundaries define "who does what."

From these needs, the owners make specific recommendations affecting the board and management. Here are some examples from clients:

» We need distributions from the company to pay taxes on the income that is taxable to us.

» We need $100,000 per year in addition to any amounts needed to pay income taxes.

» We want an annual stock valuation.

» We will provide quarterly company tours for owners and family members.

» An annual report will cover financials for the previous year as well as one-year, three-year, and five-year plans for the company.

» The company will provide income streams and benefits for retired owners throughout their lifetimes.

The more specific owners can be about their needs, the more guidance they provide to their board and management. By specific, we mean stated in a way that is understandable to anyone reading them.

High Peak Electric's Story

Jack, Dana, Steve, and Jon asked for our help after they purchased High Peak Electric from its founders. The new owners, all in their early to mid 40s, were married and had families, worked in management, and owned the company equally.

When we got to the topic of what the owners needed from the business in terms of money, the conversation became uncomfortable. One said they each should continue getting the salary they got before buying the company because they should pay off the original founders before paying themselves any more. Two suggested deciding on a formula to measure a reasonable return on their investment that takes into account the debt to the founders. One suggested getting a cash dividend equal to 3 percent of net income, but someone else thought 3 percent of the company's value was a better indicator. Another owner didn't think they should talk about money at all right now.

We explained that each owner's financial well-being was directly tied to the business. And we gave them two reasons to be as specific as they can in this area. First, if each owner's financial well-being is tied to the company, each owner ought to be able to describe what that is. In other words, each owner ought to understand what he is looking for from the company to meet his (and his family's) short-term and long-term financial objectives. Second, if each owner's financial well-being is tied to the business, the expectations one owner has about money will affect the other owners' expectations. They need to understand each other's general expectations regarding money.

We suggested that each owner meet with a financial planner to figure out and understand their personal financial situation. We asked them to consider values, needs, and goals for their standard of living; their children's education; their retirement; their health concerns; their charitable goals; and any other special financial considerations. We told them to consider their current financial resources (the assets they own now) and what other financial resources they had available (additional income from their spouse, inheritances, etc.). We wanted them to project and identify the amount of money they *need* from the company to meet their minimum objectives and the amount they *would like to receive* to meet their goals. We encouraged them do this work with input from their spouses.

All four owners balked at our suggestion, raising a number of reasons for not doing the work in this manner.

Steve: We can't pay anything out to ourselves—other than our salaries—until we pay off the founders, so why not wait?

CT & LH[1]: The goal here isn't to determine what has to be paid out this year or even the next five years—when you have to pay for the stock. The goal is to determine what you need from the business over the long term so you can plan for how you all will get that done. Why not get a sense of that now so you have a better sense of what you have to do?

Jack: This is too personal. What I need is my business and no one else's.

CT & LH: True, it is personal. But you can decide how much you are willing to share with your partners. Your partners may ask for more information, but you don't have to share it with them if you don't want to. You have control over that.

Dana: Why don't we just decide on a formula? Then we don't have to share anything with each other.

CT & LH: A formula doesn't tell you whether it will provide more or less than what you need. Ultimately, you have to know what you need from this venture to know if it works for you.

Steve: But our numbers are all going to change, so let's just wait and do it later.

CT & LH: Of course your numbers will change. And the numbers for the business may change. That is why you need to look at this regularly. But doing this now will give you an idea of where you are at currently and what has to be done to get all of you where you need to be.

---

[1] The authors, Cary Tutelman and Larry Hause.

Jon: You mean we have to do this more than once? I'll do it this one time, but only once.

CT & LH: Do it once, see how it works, and then as a group decide if and when you need to do it again.

Jack, Dana, Steve, and Jon each worked with a financial planner to assess their individual financial values, needs, and goals. Each was surprised by the result and a bit concerned about how much they would need to meet their modest objectives. Each determined what he was comfortable telling his fellow owners. They all identified a minimum lump sum they needed to meet their financial objectives, and they all described a specific amount they hoped to get. They agreed that their compensation could be salary, bonuses, or payments for stock. They also pointed out when they hoped to see the payments increase and when the payments had to increase.

While their specific numbers and time frames will undoubtedly change, they all thought the exercise yielded a lot of useful information. They took the highest minimum and maximum number for their target amounts. They learned that they couldn't meet the targets right away—the company needed to grow first.

This process helped the four owners see that planning is not only useful but necessary to their well-being. They learned more about working together to help meet all their objectives. Helping each other is a key part of what owners do. They were able to negotiate boundaries for discussing personal issues in a way that respected everyone's concerns about confidentiality but still yielded useful information. As Dana put it, "Now we know how to plan for our financial future. This is important."

Owners tend to balk at the extra work of clearly and specifically stating their needs. And they often react negatively to the term "needs"—it may make them feel selfish, guilty, demanding, greedy, or ungrateful. While some owners choose to use a different term, we usually encourage them to explore why "needs" carries negative connotations. Understanding the basis of this reaction often leads to a more fulfilling participation in the ownership work and a higher quality owners' plan. All owners have needs regarding their business—not talking about them doesn't make them go away. Once owners understand and accept this, they can learn to identify and express their needs in a clear, mature manner, rather than feeling guilty or shameful.

In family businesses, the negativity associated with needs often revolves around the next generation's attitudes toward finances—they feel guilt about receiving a financial return without having to work for it or they want a bigger financial return because of their commitment and dedication to the business. Meanwhile, the older generation worries about increasing a sense of entitlement or decreasing the incentive to be financially self-supporting.

> **ALL OWNERS HAVE NEEDS REGARDING THEIR BUSINESS—NOT TALKING ABOUT THEM DOESN'T MAKE THEM GO AWAY.**

To manage these concerns, the owners have to discuss what kinds of information, commitment, participation, or support they as owners require from each other and the company in order to do what owners do. After addressing these topics, they can begin to form a more helpful association to "needs" and they can talk about the financial return the owners need.

Needs and money. When it comes to discovering the needs (and goals) of owners regarding money, some find it helpful to adopt the following ideas or concepts

- » *Everyone* has needs and goals involving money.

- » Talking about the need (and goal) for money is usually more helpful than ignoring the issue. (Not talking about something rarely solves the problem.)

» Some owners who receive their shares as gifts experience guilt or shame about receiving dividends. One client remarked that with each dividend check came the unspoken question from her father, "What did you do to deserve this?" Owners should remember the tremendous amount of work required of them to develop, implement, and maintain a balancing board, and to be responsible owners in general. Transition work is hard, and is a way to convert what some might consider "unearned" income into "earned" income.

» Some owners who receive their shares as gifts develop a sense of entitlement. Remember, though, that the opportunities made available through stock ownership came at a cost to someone and carries with it responsibilities to follow and further develop the ownership group's values—values that should be greater in importance than any position, opinion, or need of an individual owner. This approach allows for the owners' group as a whole to help each individual owner maintain an appropriate perspective and level of humility.

» Owners who bought the company from other owners or their parents may have a sense of guilt, shame, or entitlement about money—feelings that are not exclusive to those who received shares as gifts.

» Including the owners' monetary needs (and goals) in an owners' plan does *not* mean the owners will get what they ask for—it's only the first step in the process. The balancing process requires the board to evaluate the owners' positions. After the board accepts the financial requests in the owners' plan, management has to assess the impact of the requests on the business. Management then prepares plans for the company that management believes satisfy the owners' plan but not at the expense of the business. If management believes that the owners' financial needs and goals are not achievable or will not sustain the company, management must reflect this in their plans. The board then needs to assess whether the owners have to revisit their financial requests.

Goals

Owners' goals are what owners want long term, and typically include statements about

> » *Long-term involvement*—how long owners want to be involved as owners. Long-term involvement defines "when I expect to sell or gift my shares."

> » *Long-term roles*—how owners see their specific roles as owners or directors or employees changing, how they want their roles to change, and over what period of time. Long-term roles defines the "specific role I want to have."

> » *Stewardship*—what owners want to pass on to the next generation or to charity. Stewardship defines the "future I'm building for my children."

> » *Image in the marketplace or community*—how the owners want others to view the company; for example, as the national expert in its marketplace. Image defines "what people say about us."

> » *Long-term return on investment (ROI) or equity (ROE)*—the ultimate financial rewards the owners desire. Long-term ROI or ROE defines "how much we want overall."

> » *Growth parameters*—the appropriate areas of growth, rate of growth, and method of growth. Growth parameters define "how management will grow our company."

From these goals, the owners make specific recommendations affecting the board and management. Examples from clients include

> » We will not build plants outside our home state.

> » Acquisitions are acceptable as long as they occur within our industry.

» We will actively contribute to our local community with money and time.

» Dividend amounts paid to the owners should always be low enough to make each owner work for a living.

» The company needs to be ready for the second generation to retire in ten years.

WHO PUTS THE PLAN TOGETHER AND HOW?

Earlier we stated that all owners involved in putting together the owners' manual should also be involved in putting together the owners' plan. The purpose of the owners' plan is to have a unified statement supported by all of the owners.

Just as with the owners' manual, there is no one way to put together an owners' plan. But here are some principles that we found helpful.

Assess the need for facilitation

Owners tend to struggle more in putting together an owners' plan than an owners' manual, probably because the plan requires more intimate conversations than does the manual. For example, the owners' manual talks about such things as how they will treat each other and make decisions. While personal, these topics are often much less intimate than how much money each will need to continue as an owner. As the topics become more personal, unspoken relationship issues begin to surface. If any owner expresses concern about whether the group can handle the level of conversation needed to complete an owners' plan, hire a facilitator. The cost of involving an outside business consultant pales in comparison to igniting (or reigniting) hurts that fractionalize the ownership group.

Consensus

Getting all the owners to agree on a single owners' plan is often a tall task. However, the incentive to do so is great. When the owners speak with one voice, the board speaks with one voice, and management manages the company under one set of marching orders.

Because the owners' plan is the plan for the entire group of owners, it is important that the owners work to reach a consensus on the plan.

Consensus does not mean that every owner agrees with every point in the plan. As we use the term, consensus means that all owners can live with the overall plan, knowing that they have the opportunity each year to revisit the plan.

Owners need to ask themselves, Can I live with the plan? If the answer is "yes," they must publicly support the plan, and contribute to its success. If the answer is "no," owners must decide how long they can live with the plan—for a year? Then they must publicly support and contribute to the plan's success during that time. If they cannot live with the plan at all, they need to explain the changes they'd like to see.

If discussions progress to this point without resolution, it is usually time to bring in an outside business consultant to help the owners work through the issues. If this step fails to bridge the gap, the individuals who cannot support a proposed plan with otherwise widespread support need to reassess whether they want to continue as owners. If they choose not to continue as owners, the exit described in the owners' manual (and accompanying legal document) may be necessary.

Appendix 4.2 can be used to explain the consensus process. The process described there addresses the touchy subject of money, though not all policies need to be this detailed. The text provides a number of ideas that can be adapted to work in a broad context.

Identifying where the owners are

As with their manual, the owners should discuss those values, needs, and goals that most of them wish to discuss. An owner may seek to resolve some issues that have immediate consequences to all owners; for example, a need for information or to take care of a current or potential monetary crisis. The group should address such needs before discussing their investment values and goals.

It doesn't matter what the ownership group starts talking about first. The important thing is that the owners start working together to come up with a statement that all of the owners can live with describing their values, needs, and goals regarding the business.

Some owners may work well by asking themselves the basic question, What are our values, needs, and goals? They write down their answers individually, share them with the group, and then consolidate the responses on a master list in such a way that all of the owners can support the single statement. Use Worksheet 4.3 for this purpose.

Some owners begin by listing everything they can think of to be addressed. This "brain dump" identifies what is on their mind. They ask what they value, what they need, and what their goals are. They ask what challenges must be resolved for them to own the business together, what management may need from them, what concerns they have about owning the company together. These questions often will produce a long list of topics that can be prioritized (so the group knows what to work on first) and then allocated between the owners' manual and the owners' plan (so the group knows where the answers belong). Worksheet 4.4 has a list of questions for this exercise.

Some owners start in right away with a topic, like distributions, employee well-being, culture, growth, or family employment. They discuss their individual values, needs, and goals for the topic, consolidate individual responses into a group position, assess whether the consolidated statement has the support of the group, record the conclusion, and determine whether it belongs in the owners' manual or plan. Appendix 4.3 offers a number of topics our clients have identified.

As the owners resolve the concerns that most bother them, the resolutions should be written in either in the owners' plan (or in the owners' manual if appropriate). As owners answer each of the questions or challenges they identify and as these are written down, the owners' plan (or manual) becomes more complete. Appendix 4.4 includes sample values, needs, and goals found in owners' plans.

EVALUATION AND CHANGE

Owners should review their plan annually. Just as management needs an annual plan to address last year's performance and make course corrections for the future, owners need to address last year's owners' plan and make adjustments for the future. Changes in the owners' plan need to be communicated to the board, and the board needs to communicate to management those portions of the owners' plan they need to effectively operate the business. In this way, the current owners' plan remains the fundamental document for all planning. An owners' group that effectively addresses current issues and calmly discusses future issues is more likely to stay together and, in a family business, preserve family integrity.

COMMUNICATING THE OWNERS' PLAN

Owners should submit their plan annually to the board for acceptance as part of the planning process. And, at least once a year, the owners should review their plan, make changes as needed, and submit the revised plan to the board. When we say submit, we suggest that the directors receive copies of the plan before the meeting with the owners where the actual review takes place.

Olson Manufacturing's Story

Oscar, Susan, and Jim jointly own Olson Manufacturing. Susan and Jim don't work in the business but try hard to be responsible owners. Oscar is happy that Susan and Jim want to be responsible owners. The three of them worked on an owners' plan that Susan and Jim agreed to present to the board. Oscar chairs the board; just five months earlier the three of them elected three independent directors to the board.

Oscar set aside time on the agenda for the presentation of the owners' plan and Jim and Susan put a presentation together. The directors received advance copies of the plan along with the other board materials. Oscar thought the directors would read through the plan before the meeting, and because two of them know Jim and Susan personally, he suggested simply asking whether anyone had any questions. No one did, so within five minutes the directors were talking about other matters.

Needless to say, Jim and Susan were disappointed and didn't think the directors understood their plan. They presented the plan again at the next board meeting, taking time to review each provision along with the owners' expectation that the directors will ensure that managements' plans will meet every need and goal expressed in the owners' plan. Jim and Susan's review got the directors' attention this time. They asked a lot of questions to clarify what the owners were saying, and they directed the owners to consider modifying some provisions of the plan. The directors decided to hold off accepting the plan until the owners had a chance to consider these proposals. The owners met and changed their plan before the next board meeting; after approving it, the board gave the plan to management.

ELECTING DIRECTORS

Owners elect directors. Many owner groups do not take this responsibility seriously. They see a board as a waste of energy or something that they don't need.

A clearly identified balance point is essential for the well-being of the company and its owners and managers. Legally, the balancing board has the responsibility to sufficiently manage the business,

> A CLEARLY IDENTIFIED BALANCE POINT IS ESSENTIAL FOR THE WELL-BEING OF THE COMPANY AND ITS OWNERS AND MANAGERS.

and directors have specific duties of care and loyalty. Ethically, a balancing board is responsible for the overall well-being and success of the business. Practically, a balancing board ensures that the owners and managers fulfill their obligations. These are large responsibilities that the owners should not take for granted.

Electing directors is the process of choosing individuals who will best accept and fulfill their responsibilities. Before electing directors, the owners as a group ought to answer the following questions:

1. When do we need a board? In other words, how will a balancing board help our succession and transition plans? What is the purpose of the board?

2. What do we want our directors to do?

3. How will the board work with the owners and managers?

4. What board structure will those in power accept and endorse?

After answering these questions, owners should consider the makeup of the board:

5. What characteristics, skills, and attributes do we want our directors to have?

6. How are we going to select potential candidates and elect directors?

Chapters 2 and 3 will help you answer questions 1 and 2. Chapters 4 through 7 will help with question 3; Chapter 8 addresses question 4; and Chapter 9 provides information for questions 5 and 6. Only after owners have answered these questions should they elect directors to their board.

Once owners began to grasp the idea of a board, they immediately begin to think about appointing directors. Who do we get to sit on our board? and How much do we pay them? are two frequently asked questions. We encourage owners to defer answering these questions until they answer the questions noted above.

EVALUATING THE BOARD

Owners must ensure that the board fulfills its responsibilities. Too many owner groups elect a board and then don't interact with it, and don't hold it accountable for its performance, evaluate it, or train board members. When this happens, the board begins to act on its own or loses motivation—a dangerous situation because a board makes decisions affecting whether and how to address and implement the owners' values, needs, and goals inside the company.

When boards act on their own, they either become an agent of the owners and force management to accept goals that may not be practical, or an agent of the managers and impose management's goals on the owners. In either case, the board ceases to be part of the interdependent system of ownership, management, and governance that defines a successful business. If the board loses motivation, they cease to ensure that owners' plans are implemented in the company and that critical issues are addressed and resolved.

When evaluating the board, owners should consider the following:

Interaction with the board

» How often do we want to meet with the board?

» What do we want to talk about with the board?

» Do we have elected owners who will act as the owner representatives to the board?

» What do we do if we are not happy with the board?

» How available do we want to be to the directors and about what issues?

Accountability of the board

» What is good performance?

» What are the expectations for a director's behavior and communication?

» How do we get rid of directors who do not comply with our expectations?

» How do we react to board decisions that do not comply with our plan?

Evaluation methods

» Do we have a written evaluation for board members?

» What do we want to evaluate?

» How often do we want to evaluate?

» How will we provide feedback to the directors?

Owners attending board meetings

» Do we understand what is to take place at the meeting?

» How do the directors do their work?

» Is the board acting as the balance point?

» Are the directors considering the owners' plan when responding to management?

» Are the directors considering management's plans in relation to the owners' plan?

We address board evaluation more specifically in Chapter 10.

STAYING INFORMED

Owners must stay knowledgeable about the company, the industry, and the functions of the owners, board, and managers.

» Owners of a business should have access to whatever information they need about the company; provided, of course, that they have a legitimate reason for wanting the information and respect any confidentiality policies that are in place. This does not mean the owners should use the information to make management decisions. Owners don't manage. But intentionally keeping owners in the dark leads to suspicion and mistrust and usually results in incomplete owners' manuals and plans.

» Owners stay knowledgeable by reviewing their functions and those of the board and managers on an annual basis. Reviewing their own values, needs, and goals at least annually also keeps owners informed.

» Owners ask their advisors to find other individuals with the skills and knowledge to help them stay informed about the company and the industry.

» Owners may want to attend company functions or trade shows. Attending seminars or participating in educational opportunities can also be beneficial.

Owners can certainly delegate some of these tasks. Not every owner needs to be an expert in every area that owners need to understand. Every owner should have some basic working knowledge, but the task of staying informed can be shared.

Staying informed also involves having a plan to educate new owners. It isn't reasonable to conclude that individuals know what they need to know simply because they are owners.

THE DIFFERENCE BETWEEN POWER AND CONTROL

To many people, power and control are synonymous. But in closely held and family businesses, the differences between power and control are critical to understanding how the influences of ownership or being a family member can significantly affect the company, the board, the management, and the general dynamics of meetings—and even the business.

» *Power* is the ability to influence decisions and behavior regardless of who is in control. Power is almost always earned or received vicariously through someone with proven power. Another phrase that defines power is "functional or practical control."

» *Control* is the authority vested in an individual to accomplish certain objectives or tasks. Control is always given, delegated, mandated, or assigned. Another phrase that defines control is "legal control."

Four examples will help illustrate the distinction between power and control.

Potter Seeds' Story

Dave is the sole owner of Potter Seeds. His wife, Harriet, wondered what would happen if she asked one of the assembly line workers to get her a sandwich. We said, "They would drop what they were doing and get you the sandwich." She was astounded by this response because she had no authority in the company. But she tried it. And guess what? Harriet got her sandwich. Harriet didn't have any authority (control) to make the worker get her a sandwich, but she had power—the ability to influence behavior.

Augusto's Story

As a courtesy, Augusto, a retired founder of a large scrap metal company, was invited to the company's annual planning meeting. The subject of using an overseas vendor came up. Augusto remarked that overseas vendors are unreliable and stated that the company shouldn't ever use them. The planning team immediately dropped the subject because they didn't want to disagree or offend the company's founder. When asked later why the subject was dropped, even though it was the team's decision, an executive said, "All decisions are the founder's as long as he is alive." Augusto had no control or authority, but he certainly had power!

Rachel's Story

Rachel, the sole owner and CEO of Dolling's Distribution, spent the last few years delegating her sales activities to various people. She told her customers that she wanted them to work with her salespeople and develop relationships with them directly. Sean, a long-term customer, called and complained to Rachel about a quote given by Helen, a senior saleswoman. Rachel told Sean she was no longer in charge of quoting, that she had 100 percent confidence in Helen to quote effectively, and Sean should contact Helen or her manager and work it out. Sean said he understood that Rachel wasn't in charge of sales anymore, but thought she still could get the quote changed. Rachel agreed to make the change. Even though she delegated quoting decisions to Helen, Rachel retained the power to change the quote.

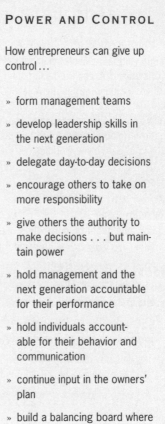

POWER AND CONTROL

How entrepreneurs can give up control…

» form management teams

» develop leadership skills in the next generation

» delegate day-to-day decisions

» encourage others to take on more responsibility

» give others the authority to make decisions . . . but maintain power

» hold management and the next generation accountable for their performance

» hold individuals accountable for their behavior and communication

» continue input in the owners' plan

» build a balancing board where they can use their power while transitioning from management

» build ownership and management groups that are separate and distinct but also integrated

Kathy's Story

Pat is a 50 percent owner-executive of Mid-Atlantic Exports (MAE) along with Kelli, the president, who owns the other half of the business. Pat told his wife, Kathy, that MAE might have to shrink by half because their current bonding company was going to drop them, and they might not be able to get coverage elsewhere. After discovering that Kelli did all the negotiating with the bonding company but hadn't gotten results, Kathy suggested that Pat get involved and ask the bonding company to reconsider its decision. Pat didn't want to interfere but respected Kathy's opinion, and later negotiated a deal with the bonding company. Kathy didn't have the authority in this matter, but she had the power to make things happen.

The use of power to contribute to the well-being of a company or family is essential to maintaining the success of the company and the integrity of the family. Conversely, the use of power for selfish reasons can lead to long-term conflicts in companies, ownership groups, and families.

The distinction between power and control is especially critical in transition planning. Entrepreneurs in transition often hesitate to form a board fearing they will lose control, and believing control is more important than power. But they ought to be thinking about ways to give up control—but retain power.

In other words, entrepreneurs should use their power (not control) to achieve their desired ends. By delegating their control and authority to accomplish specific tasks, others learn to do those functions. Using their *power* to guide the results enables entrepreneurs to act as a balancing board. Retaining *control* simply keeps them chained to the grindstone and inhibits the development of future managers and owners.

Often in closely held and family businesses, entrepreneurs think they have transitioned the control but really haven't. When their management team or someone from the next generation makes a decision they don't like, they will "pull rank" and reverse the decision.

Sometimes entrepreneurs have only given others the authority to do what the entrepreneurs would have done—leaving the management team or the next generation to play "guess what's in the entrepreneur's head." If they guess wrong, the entrepreneur reverses the decision.

Richard's Story

Richard is the sole owner of Consta-Comfort Cooling and Heating. His succession goal is to sell his shares to the management group and retire within the next two years. For the past three years he worked on developing his management team and positioning them and the company for the transition. Richard decides to add four independent directors to serve with him on the board to help evaluate management's abilities. He wants to add these directors now so he can train them to continue overseeing management—at least until he receives the entire payment for the company. Richard doesn't want to continue serving on the board after selling his shares because he doesn't want to influence the managers. He's also concerned that he might influence the new directors, whom he wants to learn to operate as true directors. He is so concerned about having too much power that he decides to cast the last vote on every board decision. In one of its first decisions, the board votes to approve management's long-term plan. Richard doesn't like the plan, so he immediately disbands the board.

Richard never gave away control; it only appeared that way. His actions frustrated his management team and did away with the three years of work preparing for his transition. Richard didn't need to exercise control. He could have guided the outcome by using his power. Specifically, he could have guided the board's agenda so that management's long-term plan wasn't one of management's first decisions. He also could have explained how management's plans affect his retirement timeline. Above all, he should have explained to the board why he did not like the plan and why it was not good for the company. In all likelihood, Richard's opinion about the future of the company would have affected the board's decision.

Jon's Story

Jon told his management team to develop a three-year vision for the company and a plan for how to get there. The management team met over six months and developed a vision statement and a thorough plan to achieve the vision. Jon reviewed the work and modified the vision and plan to reflect his thinking, without consulting the management team. The management team wondered why Jon had them do the work they did if he was just going to do it his way anyway. If Jon acted as the balance point, he could have pointed out that the plan was not consistent with the owners' plan and that the management team needed to modify the plan to align with his values, needs, and goals as the owner.

Nate's Story

Nate transferred about 25 percent of his company to his three children, who worked for about two years learning the responsibilities of ownership. Jointly, they developed two owners' plans during that time. They gave the owners' plans to the board and the board passed the plans on to management to consider when preparing their plans.

Nate wants to be sure his children get the balance point idea down before the trust he created terminates and his children's ownership of the company increases to 75 percent. To test them, Nate has the children create a third owners' plan without his involvement. The children make some revisions Nate doesn't like. They plan to discuss the changes with the board and hope that management considers the modifications' impact on the company.

But Nate rewrote the owners' plan to eliminate the provisions he disliked and presented the plan to the board. His children thought they had the authority to develop a plan as long as they followed the process. Nate isn't really willing to give up that control. His children are frustrated, and Nate lost an opportunity to see how everyone responds to something that might happen when he is no longer involved. Nate could have let the process work and guided the outcome from his seat on the board. He would have successfully delegated control to develop an owners' plan, but could still use his power as the balance point to guide the outcome.

These examples illustrate that delegating control greatly influences how companies are run, the commitment and trust of managers and owners, and how boards function. Delegating control is necessary to any transition plan, and the person transitioning control should understand how much control they want to retain and how much they want to delegate. They must also understand how to use their power (not control) to guide the outcome.

Now that you have a better idea of what owners do and how important it is that they do what they are supposed to do, let us revisit Alex. We described Alex's dilemma in Chapter 3. It is our hope that his story will be an inspiration to you.

Alex's Story—Conclusion

Alex wants to transition but doesn't know how. His children and his managers are unable to lead the company and he isn't confident that he will find his replacement. The balance point solution helps Alex get unstuck by giving him some new ways to think about his transition. He stops trying to find one person to replace himself. (Instinctively Alex knew this was improbable, and eventually realized his goals were probably better served if he didn't try to find a single replacement.) Instead, he identifies the key functions he performs for his company; allocates those functions among ownership, management, and the board; decides what functions he is ready to transition and what he wants to retain; allocates the functions he wants to transition to others within the appropriate group (ownership and management); and continues to perform those functions he wants to retain. This is how Alex initially allocates his functions:

» Believing his management team is ready to be tested, Alex elevates an existing manager to president, and allocates specific management responsibilities to the president, including responsibility and authority to lead the management team that runs ManPower.

» He establishes a structure and process to "test" his managers—to keep them striving for improvement and hold them accountable. The arrangement basically involves three steps. First, he writes down his values, needs, and goals as an owner and gives them to the president. Alex clearly and specifically describes what he is looking for and what he expects his management team to accomplish. Second, as the sole member of the board of directors, Alex directs the president to lead the management team in developing a long-term plan and annual plan to accomplish what Alex says he wants as an owner. Third, as the sole member of the board, Alex evaluates the management team's initial plans, making sure they meet his objectives as an owner, and eventually approves them. He meets weekly with his president and monthly with the management team to evaluate the progress they are making on their plans.

» Alex begins to realize that his children have no idea of what owners do; in fact, he didn't have much of an idea either. He never thought about what he does as an owner. So, he sets up an arrangement where he identifies what he wants owners to do and explains this to his children. He starts by identifying the values, needs, and goals he has for the business. Alex then explains his values, needs, and goals to his children, saying that owners need to do this so the managers know what they have to do to be successful in the owners' eyes. His children ask many questions and through these discussions learn a lot about what their father expects from his business and from them as owners.

» Alex intends to have his children review his work and develop a set of values, needs, and goals that works for all of them as owners because he wants to see how his children will work together and how they might react to the values, needs, and goals he identifies.

When his children come up with their values, needs, and goals, Alex intends to evaluate their work as the sole member of the balancing board. He will either accept their results or send them back for more work. He wants his children to know that owners don't necessary get everything they ask for; that the board evaluates the values, needs, and goals and directs the owners to revise their work if their values, needs, and goals don't meet the board's evaluation criteria.

» Alex also wants his children to review what he identifies as owners' responsibilities and to tell him whether they agree with these responsibilities and what is needed to fulfill them. Alex wants his children to take the lead with this work so he knows how well they understand it and whether they will learn to work together. As an owner, Alex will guide them and clarify his thinking as needed.

Alex clarifies and formalizes his role and responsibilities as the balance point and as a manager and owner. He decides to guide his president and management team from the board, acting as the balance point. He elects to guide his children in their role as the future owners by participating as an owner and also as the board. By clarifying and formalizing his role and responsibilities, Alex also clarifies the managers' roles and responsibilities and those of his children as well as each group's authority and accountability to the board.

Alex's situation is just one example of how an entrepreneur got unstuck. His transition illustrates several common themes that occur when entrepreneurs significantly change their involvement with their company. One key to Alex's success is his wish to do the transition successfully. He stays open to different ways of solving his challenges. He recognizes that others involved in ManPower have their own unique gifts and talents and may need different arrangements. Alex also has the courage to involve others in a meaningful way. Not all entrepreneurs are so willing.

WHAT MANAGERS DO

The previous chapter describes what owners do. It illustrates the importance of the owners' manual and the owners' plan. Take a few minutes to consider what you might want to include in your owners' manual and owners' plan. At first the list may seem daunting, but the task can seem less overwhelming if the owners identify those topics for their manual and those topics for their plan having the highest priority for the entire ownership group. Prioritizing these items naturally results in a step-by-step guide owners can use to work through their lists. In addition, resolving the tasks having the most interest to the group usually taps the energy and commitment of the owners. Remember, a lot of progress can be made by working consistently on those items that are the most important to the group; take your time and work through the process.

This chapter explains what managers do in relation to the balance point. This chapter is less detailed than the previous one. But that doesn't mean managers do less than owners. Much of what managers do relates to the running of the company, not to the balance point. This chapter discusses only the role of management as it applies to the balance point.

Remember, each company has a different management structure. Answering the questions, Who is a manager? and Who is on the management (or executive) team? are vital to understanding the role of management in the company and who interacts with the balance point.

THE BASICS

Managers' responsibilities regarding the balance point differ from one business to the next. The basic role and responsibilities that all managers of closely held and family businesses have to the balance point include

> » developing a strategic (long-term) plan for the company

> » developing an annual plan for the company

> » managing the company in a manner that is consistent with these plans

STRATEGIC PLANS

Managers develop and implement long-term plans for the company's overall well-being that are consistent with the owners' values, needs, and goals. (In other words, managers work within the owners' plan.) We call these long-term plans "strategic plans."

In some closely held and family businesses, the owners' plan is nonexistent, vague, or too general. In these cases, management either tries to figure out what the owners want or just goes ahead and does what they think best. However, the owners' values, needs, and goals are less likely to be met.

When the owners' plan is comprehensive and communicated to management, management's ability to develop and implement a strategic plan that satisfies the owners and enhances the company's well-being greatly increases.

A good strategic plan includes analyses of customers, competitors, and the company itself. It also includes a basic business strategy; a product or service development strategy; and an analysis of such things as current and future technology, pricing, expansion, marketing, organizational structure, human resources, finance, revenue and profit goals, succession planning, leadership development, ethics basic policies, and codes of conduct. A strategic plan is long-term, usually three to five years for most businesses. Development and implementation of a strategic plan is outside the scope of this book; however, Worksheet 5.1 contains a simple outline of a strategic plan describing its nature and scope.

ANNUAL PLANS

Managers develop and implement annual plans, sometimes called tactical plans, for the company's overall well-being that are consistent with the current strategic plan. In other words, managers work within their own strategic plan for the company. Each year, management brings their strategic plan (or its update), annual plan, and budget to the board for discussion and approval. (See Figure 5.1.)

The board evaluates management's plans and approves them if the board finds the plans satisfy the planning criteria. Chapter 6 discusses how the board evaluates management's strategic plan and annual plans.

In some companies, management's annual plans are not tied to the company's strategic plan. This happens when management looks at each annual plan as a stand-alone plan rather than as a stepping-stone to complete the strategic plan.

For example, if a strategic plan calls for the company to double its revenue in five years, the basic ideas and strategies for each of the five annual plans should be laid out in year one. The five annual plans should build on each other, culminating in completion of the strategic plan. If and when the strategic plan changes significantly, annual plan projections must change too.

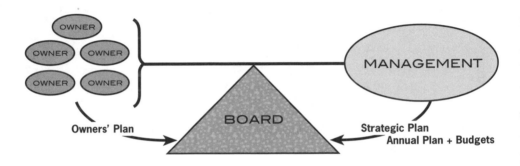

Figure 5.1 Management's plans

When annual plans are not connected to the strategic plan, the owners' plans and the strategic plan are less likely to be met. When annual plans are tied to the strategic plan (and to the owners' plans), management's ability to develop and implement a plan that satisfies the owners and enhances the company's well-being greatly increases.

In some companies, management's annual plans do not contain budgets. This often happens because management has developed a "best case" annual plan or hasn't checked to see whether the plan is realistic. The board should insist that an annual plan have a budget so that the board is confident that the plan can be accomplished.

A good annual plan includes goals and objectives for the fiscal year and an explanation of how they will help accomplish the strategic plan. The annual plan should be one leg of the strategic plan. Development and implementation of the annual plan is outside the scope of this book; however, Worksheet 5.2 contains an outline describing the nature and content of a typical annual plan.

MANAGING WITHIN THE PLANS

When management receives the owners' plan, they integrate it into the strategic and annual plans. Managers then run the company in a manner that is consistent with the owners' values, needs, and goals and consistent with the company's current strategic and annual plans.

In some companies, management's day-to-day decisions may not be consistent with either the owners' plan or its own strategic and annual plans. This happens for one of several reasons.

» Management doesn't do a good job of communicating the strategic and annual plans to the employees or building goals and objectives around these plans.

» Management doesn't think they have to perform according to the plans.

In these two cases, management is not performing up to the owners' expectations. The board, acting as the balance point, needs to address this issue.

» Management identifies opportunities they believe will help the company even though the scenarios aren't in their plans.

» Management believes the approved plans won't be met, so makes decisions contrary to the plans.

When either of these two scenarios happen, management must communicate their analyses and conclusions to the board in a timely manner. The board, acting as the balance point, must ask management to update the strategic and annual plans according to the process described in the owners' manual. If management fails to perform either of these tasks, they aren't meeting the owners' expectations and the board needs to address the issue.

Strategic and annual plans are strong guidelines—not rules. However, they are also part of a larger system of owners' values, needs, and goals. Changes to either the owners' plan or management's plans must be communicated throughout the entire system (owners, board, management, employees). The entire system should be completely integrated at all times.

Forlene Advertising's story shows what happens when management doesn't sufficiently communicate relevant parts of the owners' plan, strategic plan, and annual plan to the employees or doesn't do a good job of building goals, objectives, and tasks around these plans.

Forlene Advertising's Story

Richard and Chris, Forlene's founders, retired from active management and transferred all of their operational responsibilities to Paula and others within the company. Richard and Chris always gave their advertising representatives a long leash because they believe creative people need the freedom to take chances in order to produce the cutting-edge advertising their customers demand. Richard and Chris emphasize this value in the owners' plan they gave to Paula. But she didn't pass this information to the other managers.

Paula's controlling management style soon began to rub off on some of the other managers; the culture shifted toward a top-down environment. Clashes soon erupted with the advertising people, and several key representatives complained to Richard and Chris. As directors, the two of them asked Paula to demonstrate whether their value of a creative environment was being maintained. In learning how to provide this verification, Paula became aware of how her management style clashed with the culture, and she took corrective measures that helped retain key employees.

If Paula had informed the employees of this owners' value, her managers could have helped sustain the culture, not get wrapped into Paula's style or perhaps even have challenged Paula. Luckily for the company, Paula wisely took corrective actions when confronted with her contribution to the problem. That is not always the case, as the next example demonstrates.

Here's what can happen when management's day-to-day decisions are not consistent with either the owners' plan or management's own strategic and annual plans because managers don't think they have to perform according to the plans.

Phillip's Story

Phillip worked for Quic Concrete for twenty years and was instrumental in the company's significant growth. His father wants him to continue operating the business, and so recently promoted Phillip to the position of president. At the same time, his father also announced to the family that he is transferring all of his shares to Phillip and Phillip's two sisters in equal proportion. Phillip's father establishes a board consisting of himself and two other businesspeople.

Phillip was miffed because he expected to own the entire business and certainly didn't want to be held accountable by his sisters or even a board. He wanted the same freedom that his father had when he owned the entire company.

Phillip doesn't participate in writing an owners' plan and when he receives his copy, he tosses it in his lower desk drawer. When the board asks Phillip for the company's plan, Phillip comes prepared to talk about his vision for the company and how he is going to get the company to where it needs to be. Phillip ignores the owners' plan and refuses to follow the guidelines the owners put in place. He thinks he should act as the owner, management, and balance point (like his father did). He planned to take care of his sisters in a manner consistent with the company's ability to do so.

In the above two examples, management didn't perform to the owners' expectations; the board, acting as the balance point, addressed the issue. The outside directors talked to Phillip and, with his consent, hired a facilitator to help Phillip and his sisters understand their father's succession goals and as well as their respective roles, responsibilities, and authority and those of the board. While Phillip was disappointed in having to share ownership of the company, he did come to realize what his father was trying to do and how he (Phillip) could achieve his goals under the system his father put in place.

Here's an example of management identifying opportunities they believe will help the company, even though the scenarios are not included in their plan.

AirRack's Story

Fred, the sales manager for AirRack, received a call Friday evening from his counterpart at StackRite (their largest competitor) wondering whether AirRack might be interested in buying Stack-Rite. The caller explained that StackRite's owner is in significant financial difficulty and needs to sell. Fred called Julie, AirRack's president, who then called the entire management team into the office over the weekend to begin assessing the feasibility of an acquisition. Julie knows that acquiring StackRite would allow her company to expand its core product lines; pick up experienced personnel, especially in the sales and engineering area; and move into two new markets. But she also knows that AirRack is in the middle of a facility expansion and is planning a software conversion. An acquisition of this size is not in any of the company's plans.

Julie also called the chair of AirRack's board and explained the opportunity, the challenges, and what the management team was preparing. She scheduled a meeting with the chair for

Monday afternoon, and asked to hold a special board meeting in the middle of the week. She also asked the chair to contact Sue, the owners' plan coordinator, to join their meeting on Monday.

Julie then reviewed the owners' plan and the company's current strategic and annual plans, mapped out a timetable as well as the advantages and disadvantages to the acquisition, her thoughts on how the acquisition meets the owners' plan, what changes she thought the owners would need to make to their plan to support the acquisition, and some guidelines to follow in any acquisition. She also prepared an agenda for the next morning's management meeting and a preliminary outline of the board presentation and e-mailed both to the management team asking for their thoughts (in writing) on these matters so they could discuss them the next morning.

Julie knows that businesses rarely have an opportunity like this presenting itself, but every company will have something that pops up outside of its plans. The best that anyone can do is to be prepared to respond. Julie was prepared. The owners' plan tells Julie where her owners are at and what they want, and it gives her a good idea of what the owners will and will not support. The owners also understand the business and industry and know how to evaluate and modify their plan if necessary so this opportunity would not frighten them. Julie also knows how the directors will evaluate her acquisition plans. They will ensure that whatever management comes up with is consistent with the owners' plan and is also well thought out, consistent, thorough, and covers any contingencies. And Julie knows that her management team has experience in planning and implementing plans. In fact, her managers fully support this type of planning because they can work out a lot of the problems in advance and have more time to deal with the little things that always came up when plans are implemented.

AirRack actually did not acquire StackRite, but not because they weren't ready or couldn't respond. All of the groups—ownership, management, and the board—acted quickly and efficiently because they had planning experience. Each knew what needed to be done and how each group relied on each other's work. AirRack didn't complete the acquisition because StackRite's economics were not what management thought they were or needed to be. As it turned out, AirRack's management obtained, through competition, about two-thirds of the benefits they thought they might get from an acquisition—and at a much lower cost.

Here is what can happen when management believes their approved plans will not be met and so makes decisions that are contrary to the plan.

New Homes 4 U's Story

With housing starts slowing considerably after a rise in interest rates and import restrictions causing increases in lumber prices, Seymour believes New Homes 4 U will fall far short of the profitability goal needed to make the distributions to owners set out in the plans. He could either delay the company's entry into the commercial building area or reduce the company's workforce. Seymour thinks the business has to diversify, and the best time to do this is now. Reducing the workforce would result in considerable savings, and he could hire contractors to help out if needed on the commercial side. Seymour cut the workforce even though the owners' plan states that the company's employees should be treated on par with the owners' interest. He also let out bids on the commercial projects even though this diversification isn't part of the plans or approved by the board.

Clearly, Seymour did what he thought was right. However, he acted alone—denying the owners and the board an opportunity to consider how they could help. For example, the owners could have reduced the amount of their distributions rather than lay off some of the employees. And the board didn't have the opportunity to balance the company's entry into a new venture with the owners' plan or otherwise review management's reasoning for this action.

When any of the above situations occur, management must communicate their analyses and conclusions to the board. The board, acting as the balance point, must ask management to update the strategic and annual plans according to the process described in the owners' manual. If management communicates its analyses and conclusions to the board in a timely manner and updates its plans, management is doing its job. If management does not communicate its analyses and conclusions to the board in a timely manner, and if it does not update its plans, management is not meeting the expectations of the owners, and it is up to the board to address this issue. (And, as stated in the previous chapter, the board, acting as the balance point, may also ask the owners to review their plan or consider changes based on changing circumstances.)

Strategic and annual plans are strong guidelines, not rules. But they are also part of a larger system designed to meet owners' values, needs, and goals. Changes to either the owners' plan or management's plans will undoubtedly be necessary—and they must be communicated throughout the entire system (owners, board, management, and employees). The entire system should be completely integrated at all times.

6

WHAT BALANCING BOARDS DO

Management's role has probably always been clear to you. By adding the dimension of how management relates to the board, you can begin to understand that management does not operate in a vacuum. They are part of a system—separate, but integrated—with the board and the owners. This chapter focuses on what balancing boards do. Here you will begin to see how the entire system is connected and how the process works.

Chapters 2 and 3 stress that the function of balancing ownership and management's values, needs, and goals exists in every closely held and family business and is essential to the success of every business. We are not overstating the case. Some person or some group of individuals has to balance the needs and goals of the owners and the managers, or the company will not survive long term.

THE BASICS

If you are the entrepreneur of your company, consider for a moment what you do. You answer all the tough questions. You decide where the company will go, how it will get there, what sacrifices you and your family will make to help it grow, and how much it will pay you so you can take care of your family. You are, in essence, balancing the interests of the company and the owners. You are the board and you exercise governance without even thinking about it. You may seek advice from others, but the ultimate decisions are yours. Even if your company has a board of directors, it usually doesn't play a balancing role. It doesn't need to, because you do—you balance the interests of the company and the interests of the owners. If you didn't make these decisions and make them well, the well-being of both your company and your family would suf-fer. Intuitively, you know this to be true.

> **WHAT THE BOARD DOES DETERMINES WHETHER IT IS A BALANCING BOARD.**

In many companies, the entrepreneur usually does a great job of balancing. And if the entrepreneur is not in transition, there is no compelling reason to have a different board arrangement.

Some entrepreneurs confess to having boards. But having a board does not mean it is balancing effectively or balancing at all. In a closely held business, the board is often made up of the entrepreneur and the management team. In a family business the board is often made up of family members—usually the parents and maybe the children who work in the company. This board may include nonfamily executives. The groups may meet as a board, but the board may not be doing the balancing. The way to know is to ask, Does the board ensure that tough questions are answered and that the owners' and managers' values, needs, and goals are balanced? In our experience, boards consisting of management or family generally focus on operational issues, personnel issues, and customer issues, while entrepreneurs do the balancing in their heads and let others know what to do as needed. What is called a "board of directors" actually functions as a board of advisors. As we have said before, what the board does determines whether it is a balancing board.

Furthermore, electing outside directors to your board does not convert it to a balancing board. For example, entrepreneurs often ask their professional advisors or buddies to serve on their board and think this is a real board. But is it balancing ownership and management interests, or is it just a group that gives advice to the entrepreneur? Who does the balancing?

THE BOARD'S ROLE

The defining characteristic of a balancing board is what the board does, not who serves on the board. And the defining function of a balancing board is to balance—to balance the owners' values, needs, and goals of the owners with those of the managers and the company.

Boards balance by directing—directing owners and directing managers. Balancing boards direct owners to do what owners are suppose to do, and direct managers to do what managers are required to do. If the owners' and managers' interests differ, balancing boards balance the competing interests, not by choosing sides, but by directing the owners and managers to reconsider and rework their respective plans until their interests align.

THE BOARD'S AUTHORITY TO DIRECT

The balancing board's most important function is directing management and ownership. The authority to direct managers is clearly found in the board's legal duty to oversee management. The board, however, has no legal authority to direct owners—owners grant authority to the board to direct them. When owners set up a balancing board, they are asking the board to hold them accountable for fulfilling their duties and asking the board to be the balance point. Figure 6.1 illustrates the board's authority to direct.

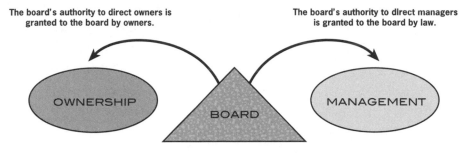

The board's authority to direct owners is granted to the board by owners.

The board's authority to direct managers is granted to the board by law.

OWNERSHIP

BOARD

MANAGEMENT

Figure 6.1 The board's authority to direct

Giving a board the authority to direct owners is a big step for them. Owners will do this in the following circumstances (see Chapter 3 for a full discussion):

» *When entrepreneurs are in transition.* A balancing board can help guide the implementation of the transition plan; help prepare management for their increasing leadership role; and ensure that the owners' plan reflects the transition plan and the values, needs, and goals of all the owners.

» *When there are multiple owners.* A balancing board can help ensure that the owners speak with one voice in their owners' plan. This is especially critical when significant differences occur among the owners. A balancing board can help direct the owners to iron out those differences openly in owners' meetings rather than letting each individual freely influence other directors or managers as they see fit.

» *When the owners and the managers are different people.* A balancing board can help ensure that owners focus on owners' issues and managers focus on management issues. With a balancing board, owners know that directors oversee managers and they (the owners) should direct their concerns to the board. A balancing board can keep the owners from directly and individually influencing management.

» *When entrepreneurs want to sell the business or their stock.* A balancing board can help teach management how to understand and achieve the owners' goals and how to accept direction from a board. This helps management adapt to the type of environment that supports a sale, resulting in managers experiencing less trauma from a sale and being more willing to stay. Buyers are often willing to pay more, or pay on better terms, if they see the potential of working with the existing management team that will accept direction from a new owner. When selling to existing owners or management, a balancing board can also help ensure that payment schedules are met and annual plans and budgets incorporate regular payments to the entrepreneur.

Only when owners give the board the authority to direct them can the board truly function as a balancing board. It is only when the owners give the board the authority to direct them, that the accountability between the board and the owners becomes a realistic possibility.

THE BOARD'S RESPONSIBILITIES

As we stated before, the role of a balancing board is to direct managers *and* owners. Stated another way, the board is primarily the balance point between ownership and management, directing managers to fulfill their functions as managers and directing owners to fulfill their functions as owners. Figure 6.2 illustrates what balancing boards do.

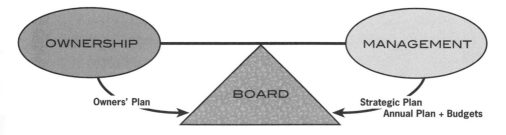

Figure 6.2 The board's basic balancing function

The specific responsibilities of any board are unique to the ownership group and the company. But the general responsibilities of every balancing board require the directors to do at least the following:

» ask for, evaluate, and accept an annual owners' plan from the owners

» ask for, evaluate, and approve management's strategic plan along with any updates to it, and annual plans along with budget updates

» help resolve differences between the owners' plan and management's plans

» make sure owners and managers adhere to the planning schedule

» hire, evaluate, determine compensation for, and fire senior management as defined by the owners

» decide whether to pay dividends

» decide special matters such as approving acquisitions, mergers, sale of assets, actions outside the ordinary course of business, and other decisions as required by applicable law or the owners

Balancing boards *do not*

» manage the company or get involved in its day-to-day operations

» develop the owners' plan

HOW THE BOARD WORKS WITH OWNERS

A balancing board directs owners by holding them accountable for completing their unique responsibilities. The owners' primary responsibilities are discussed in Chapter 4. Each one of these responsibilities is critical to the well-being of a business. Here is what can happen when owners don't fulfill their responsibilities.

» If owners don't develop an owners' manual, the board will not understand its purpose or responsibilities.

» If owners don't develop an owners' plan, the directors have no clear idea about how to direct management or assess management's plans.

» If owners don't update their owners' manual or plan, the shifting values, needs, and goals of individual owners may not be addressed and the board may not know about changing circumstances within the ownership group.

» If owners don't elect new directors, the current directors remain in place and often become ineffective, stale, or "agents" of a particular owner or manager.

» If owners don't make sure the board fulfills its responsibilities, the balancing function may shift to the owners or the managers.

» If owners don't stay knowledgeable about the company and the functions of the owners, board, and managers, they are more likely to act on their own (taking over the role of director or manager), become unreasonably risk adverse, or develop an owners' plan that does not adequately describe the values, needs, and goals of the ownership group.

» If owners don't understand the difference between power and control, they may not understand their boundaries and may use their power inappropriately.

The following steps describe the basic interactions between owners and their balancing board. We will focus first on board acceptance of the owners' plan because we want all business owners to understand that management's strategic and annual planning should begin with the owners' plan.

ACCEPTING THE OWNERS' PLAN

Normally, the board gives the owners a deadline to complete their plan according to the board's annual calendar. The owners (or an owner representative) present and explain their plan to the board. The board evaluates the owners' plan by asking five questions. Directors can ask these questions in any order or any combination. Figure 6.3 presents one common sequence of the questions.

Question 1: Does the owners' plan reflect the values, needs, and goals of the owners as a group?

Question 2: Is the owners' plan comprehensive? Does it address the concerns the board or the managers raised?

Question 3: Is the owners' plan internally consistent? Do some parts of the plan conflict with other parts of the plan? (For example, the owners may want all employees to be treated equally, yet develop a list of perks for owner-employees.)

Question 4: Is the owners' plan clear and detailed, and does it include the risk-reward ramifications to the company and the owners? The plan must be clear so the directors understand what the owners are saying. The plan should have enough depth so the directors believe the owners have thought their plan through well and management has the information they need to develop their plans. The owners' plan must include the risk-reward ramifications so the directors know that the owners understand its positives and negatives.

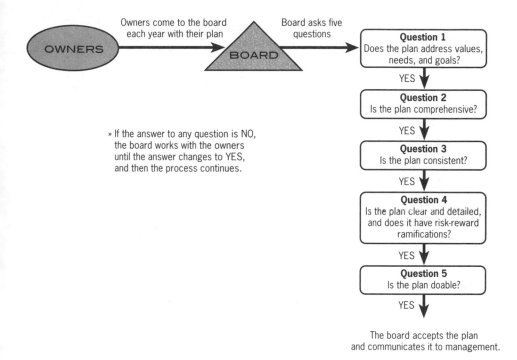

Figure 6.3 Reviewing the owners' plan

Question 5: Is the owners' plan doable? The plan must not only hang together but the board has to believe that it can be accomplished. (For example, owners may want to distribute 90 percent of the profits, yet they want to double the company's revenue in five years but not incur any debt. In this case, the board needs to address the practicality of the owners' plan.)

» If the answer to questions 1 through 5 is Yes, the board accepts the owners' plan and communicates the appropriate parts of it to management.

» If the answer to any question is No, the board asks the owners to work on the plan and resubmit it. If the owners cannot all agree on one owners' plan, the board works with the owners to resolve their issues.

This process has been laid out in its simplest form. Nonetheless, it focuses the board's attention at the right level of inquiry and makes the board's involvement deliberate. Use Worksheet 6.1 at board meetings to help directors stay on task when reviewing the owners' plan with the owners.

However, boards often have trouble directing owners—often because some owners are interested only in achieving their personal needs and goals and have difficulty balancing their needs and goals with those of the other owners or with the company's capabilities. They feel a need to go around the system by persuading management or directors to work on behalf of their particular needs and goals. Other owners go through the motions of developing an owners' plan, but when things don't go their way, they begin acting independently. And some directors don't bother to ask the owners what they want, because the directors think they know what the owners need. Some directors believe that owners can have anything they want and wonder why directors should ask for their input, let alone direct them.

What these directors don't realize is that owners rely on the board to help them fulfill their owner responsibilities. In other words, the owners have no one other than themselves or the directors to get feedback about how well the owners are acting on their responsibilities. And owners don't learn anything if they always get a free pass. A balancing board ensures that all of these issues, including directing owners, are dealt with and that the ownership group, at some point, begins to speak with one voice. The balancing board can be the impetus for resolving ownership differences. Boards can use Worksheet 6.2 to help them identify the owners' positions on issues they bring to the board.

ELECTING DIRECTORS

To make sure the owners plan for changes in director positions, the board reminds the owners about who is up for reelection and who is leaving the board. They will also suggest to the owners what expertise they believe is missing on the board.

EVALUATING THE BOARD

To make sure the board is fulfilling its responsibilities, it reminds the owners to conduct an evaluation of the board and give it critical feedback at least once a year on suggested improvements.

STAYING KNOWLEDGEABLE

To make sure the owners stay knowledgeable about the company and the functions of the owners, board, and management, the board periodically asks what information the owners want and reminds individual owners when they blur the boundaries between ownership, governance, and management.

UNDERSTANDING POWER AND CONTROL

The board gives feedback, positive and negative, to individual owners or the owners as a group regarding how they are handling this issue. Much of the feedback is of a sensitive or personal nature. For the board process to work, directors need to give feedback honestly and respectfully. Hesitating to give feedback to any particular owner only causes more conflict in the ownership group and in management.

TIPS FOR WORKING WITH OWNERS

Once directors identify significant issues for the owners, directors need to ask themselves how they will handle such issues, should one arise. They need to be mindful of the consequences of their decisions. Decisions of the board affect not only the owners, but their relationships with each other, their families, and their company. Here are some items to keep in mind:

» Owners should not be excluded from developing the owners' plan because of their ownership interest or their past positions or actions. Owners can choose not to participate—but the choice should be theirs.

» The board's process needs to start where the owners are at. If the board is ahead of the owners or behind them, the owners may think the board isn't doing its job. Understanding where the owners are at may require discussions about the rights and responsibilities the owners think they have, whether they understand the roles and responsibilities of the board and management, and how the owners are going to work out their differences.

» The board should understand the owners' level of commitment to the business.

» Although the owners' goal is to reach consensus, consensus is not unanimity. Consensus is working together as a large group to come up with a plan having the broadest amount of support possible. When owners evaluate an owners' plan, they should vote yes if it is something they can live with—and not hold out for their dream plan.

» The owners are asking the directors to evaluate their plan using specific planning criteria. If the owners' plan does not meet the criteria of the planning process, the directors need to let the owners know this and direct them to rework their plan.

» In family businesses, spouses are hugely influential and are involved, regardless of whether they attend owner meetings. Directors can ensure that owners recognize and take into account the interests of their spouses and immediate family.

HOW THE BOARD WORKS WITH MANAGEMENT

A balancing board directs management by holding managers accountable for completing their unique responsibilities. Chapter 5 discusses the primary responsibilities managers have regarding the balancing point. Each one of these responsibilities is critical to the well-being of a business. If management does not develop and implement a strategic plan or an annual plan, or does not manage the company in a way that is consistent with the owners' values, needs, and goals, the board needs to act.

MANAGEMENT PLANS

Usually the board gives management a deadline to complete their plans. Deadlines direct management to work on their plans according to the board's annual calendar. The board evaluates management's plans by asking five questions. Again, these questions can be asked in any order or combination. This is the balancing function in action. Figure 6.4 illustrates a common order of questions.

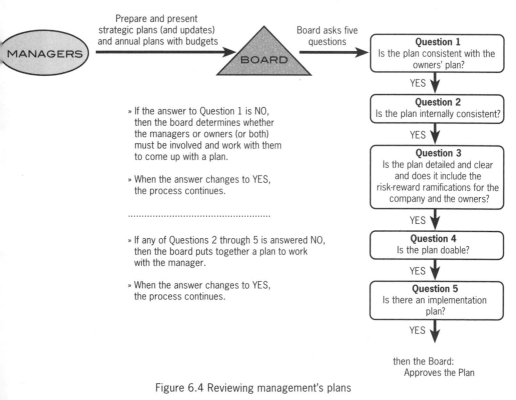

Figure 6.4 Reviewing management's plans

Question 1: Is the strategic plan or its update consistent with the owners' plan? Is the annual plan and budget consistent with the current strategic plan?

Question 2: Is the plan internally consistent? Do parts of the plan contradict each other?

Question 3: Is the plan detailed and clear, and does it include the risk-reward ramifications to the company and to the owners?

Question 4: Is the plan doable? The plan must hang together and the board has to believe that it can be accomplished.

Question 5: Is there an implementation plan, a reasonable timeline, a budget, a built-in evaluation method, an alternative plan and/or a criterion for pulling the plug if complications arise?

» If the answer to questions 1 through 5 is Yes, then the board approves the plan and monitors its implementation.

» If the answer is No, the board asks management to rework and resubmit their plan.

This process has also been laid out in its simplest form. Nonetheless, it focuses the board's attention at the right level of inquiry and makes the board's involvement deliberate. Directors can use Worksheet 6.3 to help them evaluate management's plans.

However, boards can also have trouble directing managers—because some managers are only interested in achieving their personal needs and goals and have difficulty balancing their needs and goals with those of the owners or the realities of the company. Individual managers may feel a need to go around the system to try to persuade the board to work on behalf of their needs and goals. Others may go through the motions of developing management plans, but when things don't go their way, they begin acting independently. A balancing board ensures that these issues are dealt with and that management follows the plans. The balancing board should be the impetus for resolving these issues.

Two points are important here. The board accepts the owners' plan; it does not approve it. (The board has no legal authority to direct the owners.) The board approves management's plan based on its merits, not on the directors' personal opinion of the plan. (Chapter 7 discusses this last point extensively.)

> THE BOARD ACCEPTS THE OWNERS' PLAN; IT DOES NOT APPROVE IT. THE BOARD APPROVES MANAGEMENT'S PLAN BASED ON ITS MERITS, NOT ON THE DIRECTORS' PERSONAL OPINION OF THE PLAN.

TIPS FOR WORKING WITH MANAGERS

Here are some tips directors can keep in mind when reviewing management's plans.

» When managers present their strategic and annual plans, they tend to go into tactics right away—specific details of how the company is going to meet the strategic, annual, and owners' plans. Directors should make sure that the managers understand the owners' plan and understand how their strategic plan will accomplish the owners' plan before getting into tactics. Directors should also ensure that budgets are reasonable and reflect the annual plan.

» As management learns how to develop strategic and annual plans that are responsive to the owners' plan, it can be helpful to designate a director to review management's efforts early in the planning process.

» The company's strategic and annual plans need the entire management group's support. The board should understand who is involved in putting management's plans together to ensure that the plans have the support of those managers responsible for their implementation.

REVIEWING MANAGEMENT'S PROPOSALS

Use this basic process whenever managers come to the board for approval or whenever the board directs management. For example, assume that the board accepts an owners' plan and approves management's strategic and annual plans. Then the CEO seeks board approval to acquire a small competitor in order to gain market share that was not anticipated. The directors can use this process to evaluate the CEO's proposal. The board expects the CEO to present a specific proposal for evaluation. The directors first decide whether the proposal is consistent with the values, needs, and goals as expressed in the owners' plan. If not, the board determines whether they need more information from the owners or from the CEO. If so, the board proceeds to evaluate the CEO's proposal by pursuing the remaining questions. This process helps the board evaluate the proposal at the proper level. It also helps management learn to be prepared because they know what the board will evaluate. Boards can use Worksheet 6.4 to process management's proposals (rather than plans).

SUMMARY OF BOARD'S EVALUATION FUNCTION

Two implications arise out of the specific evaluation process that we suggest the board follow in reviewing the owners' plan and management's plans.

First, the specific process for evaluating management's plans is essentially the same as the process for evaluating any management recommendations falling outside their plan. For example, management has an opportunity to acquire a large competitor in California. The five-year strategic plan addresses the acquisition, but the current annual plan does not on the assumption that the opportunity would not be available for at least two years. Management comes to the board seeking approval for the acquisition. How does the board proceed with evaluating this recommendation?

To begin, the board asks management to present its plan. Management's plan should include, at a minimum, a summary of the opportunity, a description of what management is asking the board to do, and all of the information management thinks that the board will need to approve the plan, that is, the answers to the same questions the board uses to evaluate management's overall plans.

1. Is management's plan to acquire the competitor in California consistent with the owners' plan? Management should present information that answers this question. For example, management can explain that the acquisition is consistent with the owners' current values, needs, and goals. This answer helps directors focus on their responsibility to act as the balance point by assessing whether management's proposal is consistent with the owners' interests. This also helps management understand and integrate the owners' values, needs, and goals into the company's plans and operations.

2. Is management's plan to acquire the California competitor internally consistent? Do parts of the plan contradict each other? Management is expected to provide information the directors can use to assess whether the various areas of management are working together in a consistent fashion. For example, is the financial manager predicting cash flows that are consistent with projections the sales manager uses and expenses projected by operations and human resources? Management ought to ask itself what due diligence it needs to do, assuming that the board will evaluate its plan to determine whether it is consistent.

3. Is the plan to acquire and assimilate the California competitor detailed and clear, and does it include the risk and reward ramifications to the company and to the owners? Management needs to determine what information the directors ought to receive regarding the California acquisition knowing that the directors will want to ensure that management has a complete plan that is clear, detailed, and addresses the potential benefits and disadvantages to the owners and to the business.

4. Is the plan doable? The information management provides to the board should show that the plan is not a "best case scenario" or that everything has to fall into place just right for the plan to work. In addition, the plan should include management's feasibility assessment and the level of support that exists within management for the plan. The board wants to know whether senior management supports the plan and believes that it can be accomplished.

5. Is there an implementation plan, a reasonable timeline, a budget, a way of evaluating the plan, and an alternative plan or criterion for pulling the plug if complications arise? Management should present information describing how they will implement the plan, the various steps that are involved, the projected timelines, the costs, how the benefits and detriments will be evaluated, or the alternatives that might arise to threaten the success of the plan as well as management's responses to these threats.

We've seen management come to boards seeking approval for acquisitions with nothing more than a verbal report about the general opportunity that's available. And we've seen boards engage in significant discussions with management with only cursory information available. When management seeks approval but does not provide information (answers to the five questions) for the directors to review the proposal, the board needs to ask for the answers. Managers will soon learn how to present proposals to the board with the level of content that a proposal needs to include.

The second implication relates to the role of the owners' manual and plan and management's strategic and annual plans. These four documents are center stage for the board's focus. Everything a balancing board does should in some way relate to one or more of these documents. Every board agenda item ought to connect to one of these documents. Every decision the board makes should relate to one or more of these documents. All information the board reviews should relate to one or more of these documents. Connecting every board activity to one or more of these documents will go a long way to ensuring that the board acts as a balance point, takes responsibility for the process and not the result, and acts independently. If the board makes decisions or takes other actions not related to one or more of these central documents, it is likely that the board is either managing the managers or the business, giving advice, or solving owner problems.

THE BOARD'S ACCOUNTABILITY

To whom is the board accountable? This frequently asked question has a very complicated answer.

Owners say the board is accountable to them because they own the company. And most owners say the board is accountable to them because they can elect and remove the directors if the directors don't act according to the owners' wishes. Often, boards in closely held and family businesses tend to yield to the wishes of the owners simply because they are the owners. However, directors are obligated not to act fraudulently, illegally, or in a manner that is unfairly prejudicial toward owners. In addition, the directors owe the company the duties of loyalty and care.

But the question regarding the board's accountability is more complicated. Chapter 7 explains the board's primary legal duties. Briefly, the board has the legal responsibility to manage the company—directly or indirectly, by overseeing management. If the owners so decide, the board is authorized to elect officers and hire all managers.

The legal duties placed on directors and the law providing that owners elect directors create dual accountability for directors—to the owners and the company (see Figure 6.5). Directors are accountable to the company because of their specific duties of care and loyalty and management oversight. Directors are also accountable to the owners because owners elect them and owe them certain duties. This "pinch point" is even more complicated because the owners can sue in the name of the corporation to enforce the duties directors owe to the business.

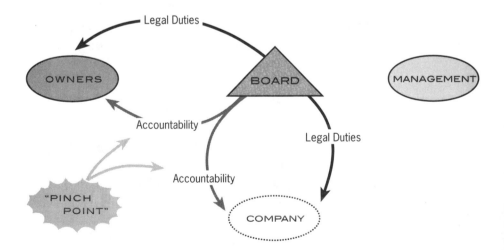

Figure 6.5 A board's dual accountability and the "pinch point"

Usually, this pinch point doesn't compromise the board's ability to balance. However, this pinch point is a very real problem in closely held and family businesses when significant differences occur between the owners and managers and neither group is willing or able to compromise their values, needs, or goals to align the two groups' interests. When faced with an owners' plan and management's plans that are irreconcilable (and just don't appear to be irreconcilable), what is a balancing board to do? This is where the buck stops—and usually, all parties want an answer to this question.

Many business people say that directors should support the owners because the owners elect the directors. This is what business owners hope happens because they want to ensure that they have the ultimate power. But what happens if the owners are wrong?

Others say that the directors must determine the best interests of the company and decide on that basis by choosing between the owners or the managers or by developing their own plan. This is what some lawyers tell their clients, which causes some ownership groups to resist putting a balancing board in place. But what happens if the directors are wrong? If directors side with management, they can be liable if owners sue in the company's name, claiming that the directors did not act in the company's best interests. They can also be liable if the owners claim that the directors' actions were unfairly prejudicial toward owners. Either way the directors are the focus of the animosity and lawsuits, a position most directors want to avoid.

If the owners' plan and management's plans are truly irreconcilable, and the board has tried (without success) to get the owners and the managers to adjust and integrate their plans, then the board only has two choices: If the board believes that management cannot come up with plans that integrate the owners' plan, the board needs to replace management. If management's competency is not the issue, then directors need to come up with a plan to ease their exit, and then resign. Directors should resign rather than choose one plan over another. The board's role is to balance, and balancing cannot occur by taking sides.

The planning and balancing process described in this book reconcile the pinch point the law imposes. The planning process requires the owners to express their view of what is in the best interest of the company through their owners' plan, and management to express its view through their strategic and annual plans. By balancing, directors work to get the owners and managers to adjust their plans so both groups are thinking alike about what is in the best interests of the company. Figure 6.6 illustrates how the planning and balancing process resolve the pinch point.

Ultimately, directors are neither accountable to the owners nor the company; they are accountable to the process—of balancing, of acting independently, of not choosing sides. In other words, the board

Figure 6.6 Resolving the pinch point

owns the process. This is a fundamental principle of balancing boards. If directors follow this principle (especially in irreconcilable situations) they will likely avoid a primary concern about director liability.

Directors will likely avoid liability in irreconcilable situations because they have directed management (the group primarily responsible for the operations of the company) and the owners (the group primarily affected by operations) to agree on just what is and isn't possible and acceptable based on the best knowledge and information available. If these two groups cannot collectively determine the best interest of the company, it is impossible to expect the directors to do so in a way to avoid potential liability. In these irreconcilable (and hopefully rare) circumstances, the directors who are not owners have no realistic alternative but to resign.

If the directors don't resign in these situations, they become part of the problem because they will ultimately be forced to take sides, compromising their accountability to the process. If they side with the owners, they succumb to the owners' power—but if they resign, the owners' power is checked, and this may become a wake-up call that the owners need. By siding with management, directors encourage the owners to exercise their power to replace the board and management—a transition that is usually more disruptive and threatening to the company than a planned transition.

Some may claim that by resigning, directors abandon the owners when they are most needed. However, if the directors have truly tried to work with the owners and managers to align the differing interests of both groups, admitting defeat is *not* abandoning the owners. Rather, it is admitting that the board

> THE BOARD OWNS THE PROCESS—OF BALANCING, OF ACTING INDEPENDENTLY, OF NOT CHOOSING SIDES.

is caught between two groups who are unwilling to work together. The directors determine that they cannot be the balance point. A separate balance point isn't needed, at least at this point. The owners can then assert their authority and take back the role of the balance point.

The owners' ability to take back the balance point (that is, to appoint themselves as directors) can be altered by contract. In certain contexts (such as not wanting a majority vote of the owners to repopulate the board with directors who would do their bidding), it may be highly desirable and advantageous for the owners to be bound to accept a balancing board consisting of an agreed-upon composition that cannot be altered except for the names of the directors. This prevents the owners from taking back the role of the balance point while allowing them to choose other directors. The directors' duty to act as an independent balancing point should prevent any director from siding with an individual owner.

Of course, we hope this difficult situation can be avoided. The principles in this book are designed to help owners, directors, and managers avoid this situation. But we have seen instances where differences between ownership and management cannot be aligned. We have seen what happens when directors take sides, and we have seen what happens when directors resign "planfully." While both situations are difficult, having the directors resign in a planful way is generally less disruptive. It also decreases the directors' risk because the directors remove themselves from the dual accountability scenario.

This section describes the board's accountability, but we also address the accountability of owners and managers. Every group is accountable to someone; every group has a boss. Table 6.1 summarizes the basic ideas of accountability, authority, and responsibilities regarding owners, managers, and boards. This table can serve as a guide to these important concepts.

Table 6.1 Accountability, authority, and responsibilities

Owners	Directors	Managers
Owners are accountable to the board because the owners give the board the authority to direct them	Directors are accountable to the process	Management is accountable to the board
Owners have a fiduciary duty toward each other	Directors have legal duties of loyalty, acting in good faith, and overseeing the management of the company	Management gets its authority from the board
Owners are responsible for coming up with an owners' plan	Directors are responsible for balancing the plans of owners and management	Management is responsible for coming up with a strategic plan that integrates the owners' plan and annual plans

THE RESPONSIBILITIES OF THE BALANCE POINT

B y now it should be clear that owners come up with the owners' plan, managers come up with management plans (within the parameters of the owners' plan), and the board balances the two groups' plans to ensure that both owners and managers are moving in the same direction. As a business owner, you may still be doing this process in your head, or you may be involving others. This balancing process can be incredibly effective if it is done well. Much depends on the owners' ability to speak with one voice and clearly state what they need and want—and whether the board understands its responsibilities, and has the desire and skills to carry them out. This chapter explains how the board acts as the balance point.

THE BASICS

Roles and responsibilities are a mixture of structure and process. For example, we said in Chapter 4 that owners provide in their own-

ers' manual what owners, managers, and the board do, and the procedures and policies they follow; that is, the structure. How each group
works and how the three groups interact is the process. Remember, the
groups, while separate, are interdependent.

The board, acting as the balance point between owners and managers, is in the best position to manage the process, allowing the owners and managers to solve problems. This chapter explores the key to
balancing: owning the process, but not the result.

OWNING THE PROCESS, NOT RESULTS

Owning the process and not the results means that the board
does not create or develop the owners' plan. It means that the board
does not tell the owners what their plan should say. The board expects
the owners to come up with a plan that addresses ownership issues.
Owners own their plan, and the board is there to ensure that the owners' plan is well thought through, internally consistent, and addresses
owner issues. This makes the owners responsible for the results of their
problem solving.

Owning the process and not the result means that the board does
not create or develop management's plans. It means that the board
does not tell management what the strategic or annual plans should
say. The board expects the managers to come up with their plans, and
the board is there to ensure that management's plans are well thought
through, internally consistent, and integrated with the owners' plan.
Managers own their plans; the board ensures that the managers understand their plans and any probable consequences before approving them. This makes the managers responsible for the results of their
problem solving.

Owning the process and not the result also means that the directors ensure that owners and managers own their respective problems.
The board does not solve owners' or managers' problems. Owners

solve owner issues and managers solve management issues. Owners and managers are responsible for the results of their problem solving.

However, a balancing board does make decisions and they do solve problems. They evaluate and accept owners' plans. They evaluate and approve management's plans. They decide whether the plans are integrated. They ensure that business operations are consistent with those plans. They ensure that owners and managers solve their respective problems. But these decisions and problem solving do not constitute owning the results. These decisions are about balancing—or owning—the process. Figure 7.1 summarizes the role the three groups have in the balancing process.

» Owners solve owner problems

» Owners own the results of their problem solving

» A balancing board owns the process of integrating the owners' and managers' plans

» A balancing board makes decisions about how the owners' plan and managers' plans are integrated

» Managers solve management problems

» Managers own the results of their problem solving

Figure 7.1 Who solves what problems

Owning the process and not the result is a subtle, yet perhaps the most critical part, of effective balancing. Many directors take the owners' or managers' problems and attempt to solve them. They do this for many reasons, most of which are well intended. For example, directors usually solve problems in their primary job; it's what they do for a living. In addi-

OWNING THE PROCESS AND NOT THE RESULTS MEANS THAT THE BOARD DOES NOT CREATE OR DEVELOP THE OWNERS' PLAN . . . OR MANAGEMENT'S PLANS . . . [BUT IT DOES] ENSURE THAT OWNERS AND MANAGERS OWN THEIR RESPECTIVE PROBLEMS.

tion, many owners and managers believe that is why they have directors—to solve problems.

However, when directors begin to solve problems, they no longer just own the process. They now own the result as well. In essence, they relieve the owners and managers of responsibility for resolving their respective issues. This is detrimental to the process of developing an owners' plan, because owners need to wrestle with their issues so they can speak with one voice and maintain integrity. If owners accept recommendations from the board, the owners' plan is generally short-lived, one or more of the owners doesn't get their needs and goals addressed, and greater ownership conflict is likely down the road. Similarly, it is detrimental to the process of developing effective management plans because it is management's job to understand the owners' plan and fully commit to the approved strategic and annual plans. If the board tells managers what their plans should be, managers are more likely to stray from the plans and develop an acrimonious relationship with the board or the owners, or both. And the likelihood of fulfilling the owners' needs and goals is diminished.

Let's look at some examples of the board owning the results and not the process, the impact this had on the owners and managers, and what the board could have done to be more helpful.

WHEN THE BOARD SOLVES OWNER PROBLEMS

Rebuilt Motors' Story

Rebuilt Motors is a business with seven owners. Some owners want to expand the business to other states and locations, while the others want to retain one central, local operation. So the owners ask the board what to do. The board decides to expand the business. One group of owners is happy, but the other group is not.

Ackberg Automotive's Story

Ackberg Automotive is a family business wanting to transition to the third generation. Two sibling families who disagree on the succession plan for their business comprise the ownership group. Harry and Hank each think their own oldest son should be the heir apparent. So they ask the board for advice. The board chooses Hank's son rather than Harry's. As a result, one family is happy with the decision, but the other family is not.

In both examples, it appears that the problems are solved. However, ownership and family unity have not been achieved. The owners are not speaking with one voice. The owners' plans do not represent all the owners. In fact, the "losing" ownership group or family may pursue a course of action quite at odds with the owners' plan and the well-being of the business.

In the example of Rebuilt Motors, to own the process rather than the results, the board should have explained to the owners that they (the owners) must agree on expansion. In the Ackberg Automotive example, the board will own the process but not the results if it tells the owners that they (the owners) need to agree on how to choose the successor. If the owners have trouble resolving that issue, they should consider hiring a business consultant. The board can assist the consultant, but it should not try to resolve the issue.

WHEN THE BOARD SOLVES MANAGEMENT PROBLEMS

Taylor Metals' Story

Jim became president of Taylor Metals three years ago to replace Pete Taylor, who has retired and now sits on the board. Jim receives a call from the company's largest customer saying that they are moving their manufacturing overseas and will cut their business with Taylor Metals by 90 percent. This customer represents almost half of Taylor Metals' business, and Jim is greatly concerned. At a special meeting of the board, Jim asks the directors for advice. After some discussion, the board tells Jim what he should do.

Ultra Cleaning Services' Story

Selma, Ultra Cleaning Services' president, and her management team wanted to spend $15 million to buy new equipment and hire additional people to expand and diversify their business. They propose that Ultra Cleaning borrow the funds by taking out a five-year equipment loan and increasing its credit line. The bank debt will increase the company's debt-to-equity ratio to 2.5:1, which exceeds the 1:1 ratio the owners have in their plans. Selma reasons that the owners will actually have less risk under the expansion and diversification plan because the company will be stronger in the long run. The directors agree with Selma that Ultra Cleaning has to diversify and expand if it is to remain viable. They also think management's plan makes sense and is well put together. They accept Selma's explanation about the risk to the owners and decide that the owners will just have to get used to the higher debt. In approving Selma's expansion and diversification plan, the board is acting as management's agent. The board does not require that management wrestle with the issue and thus sets in motion a potential owner-board conflict.

By laying at the feet of the directors a management problem of dealing with a significant sales void created by a departing customer, Jim doesn't learn much. The board should direct management to identify one or more alternatives and come back to the board; they can then ensure that the alternatives align with the owners' interests and otherwise meet the criteria discussed in the previous chapter. If Jim wants advice from the directors, he can call them individually for input before presenting management's proposed solutions to the entire board.

Selma's dilemma is more challenging. In accepting her proposal, the directors solve both a management problem and an ownership problem. Management's problem is finding alternatives to meet their goals without increasing debt. The owners' problem is whether they (the owners) want to change their debt-to-equity ratio. If Selma demonstrates that this solution is the only feasible alternative that she sees, and the board believes her, and the owners refuse to change their debt to equity ratio, the next step may be for the board to direct Selma to project what will happen if the company doesn't expand by increasing debt and then letting the owners decide whether they want to accept those consequences or perhaps sell the business.

When directors begin to solve owners' and managers' problems, they begin to blur the separation between ownership and management by acting like owners or managers. This opens up the possibility of owners getting involved in management issues. It also may affect the success of the transition plan, especially if business owners are successfully transitioning their role. Without the separation of ownership, governance, and management, business owners can, and probably will, reclaim their previous position of power and control.

When the board begins to own the results (rather than the process), the board ceases to be the balance point between ownership and management. The roles and responsibilities of each group become blurred, and governance becomes more informal and not as necessary. When directors solve the problems of ownership and management, the entire system can break down and the conditions that prompted the creation of a board most likely will reappear.

Through effective balancing, the board owns the *process* by which all plans become fully integrated, while the owners and managers own the *results*. In other words, the board ensures that the right group—the owners or managers—or both—work on their problems.

The board's role is to ensure that the owners' plan and management's plans are consistent and that management's plans are well thought through, clear, doable, and fit into the strategic plan. If the owners' plan and management's plans are inconsistent, the board will get the owners and managers involved in the decision-making process by asking either the owners or managers (or both) to reassess their plans. The board does not make decisions for the owners or management.

> THROUGH EFFECTIVE BALANCING, THE BOARD OWNS THE *PROCESS* BY WHICH ALL PLANS BECOME FULLY INTEGRATED, WHILE THE OWNERS AND MANAGERS OWN THE *RESULTS*.

IDENTIFYING WHO HAS THE PROBLEM

Owning the process and not the results requires the board to identify which group—owners, managers, or board—has the problem. Earlier in this chapter we said that boards have to deal with problems relating to the process while the owners or managers (or both) have to deal with problems relating to results.

In practice, identifying which group has to solve what problem is not easy to do. What makes this even more difficult is that, at some level, every problem has elements involving the owners, managers, and board. For example, a job shop has the opportunity to develop a proprietary product—their first endeavor of this kind. Management's role is to provide the board with a well-thought-out analysis complete with due diligence, showing how the proprietary product enhances the strategic plan and how it is consistent with the owners' plan. The owners, having never considered proprietary products in their owners' plan, must decide whether proprietary products are consistent with their vision for the company or whether they are open to changing their vision of the company. Owners must consider whether the proposal affects their debt/risk tolerance and, if it does, they must decide whether they will change their debt/risk tolerance for this new endeavor. And they must determine whether the proposal affects their dividend plan. If it does, they must decide whether the new dividend plan is acceptable.

The board makes certain that the owners think through how a proprietary product will affect these ownership items (debt/risk, dividend plan, vision for the company, etc.) and that the owners' plan reflects their position. In other words, the board ensures that the new owners' plan is consistent with the owners' values, needs, and goals. The board also ensures that the plan for the proprietary product is fully integrated with the owners' plan and the company's strategic and annual plans.

You can see that what might appear as a relatively straightforward issue—whether to develop a proprietary product—affects managers, owners, and the board. Figure 7.2 shows the different levels of this proprietary product issue.

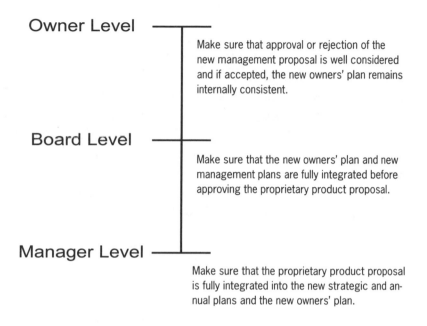

Owner Level

Make sure that approval or rejection of the new management proposal is well considered and if accepted, the new owners' plan remains internally consistent.

Board Level

Make sure that the new owners' plan and new management plans are fully integrated before approving the proprietary product proposal.

Manager Level

Make sure that the proprietary product proposal is fully integrated into the new strategic and annual plans and the new owners' plan.

Figure 7.2 Different levels for a single issue

FIVE STEPS TO IDENTIFY WHO OWNS THE PROBLEM

Here are five steps a balancing board can follow when identifying which group (owners, managers, or board) has what portion of a problem:

1. Define the problem

2. Identify how the owners and managers are involved in this problem

3. Determine the owners' position and management's position

4. Determine what additional information is needed from the owners and the managers

5. Assess whether the final conclusion integrates the owners' and managers' positions

Eventually these steps become automatic. In other words, the directors make sure they understand the issue that is before them; they ask how the owners, managers, and the board should be involved with that issue; they look to the owners' plan to understand the owners' position, and they look to the strategic and annual plans to understand the managers' position; if needed to approve the solution, they ask for information from owners and managers; and they assess whether the solution integrates the owners' and managers' positions. Here are a couple of examples to help you understand this difficult but critical component of effective balancing.

Defining the problem

The following example describes how defining the problem can affect who needs to be involved in problem solving.

CorecTech's Story

CorecTech's accounting department discovers that the company is expensing certain maintenance costs that vendors have not billed. CorecTech's legal counsel tells Martin, the company's president, that CorecTech has no legal responsibility to reveal the error and pay the vendors for their oversight. Martin proposes using the extra money to buy new safety equipment for the employees. The cost of the new equipment roughly equals the amount not charged by the vendors. Because equipment purchases are not in the annual plan approved by the board, Martin asks the board to approve this action. How does the board determine which group—owners, managers, or both—needs to be involved in this decision and how?

Stated Problem #1: Let's say the problem is to determine whether the new equipment will actually increase employee safety enough to justify its purchase. When reviewing CorecTech's owners' plan the board doesn't see anything related to this issue and can't imagine how the owners might want to be involved as the problem is presented. The board evaluates Martin's information to see whether his proposal is well thought through, clear, doable, and fits with the current plans for the company and owners. The board sees the problem as solely belonging to management.

Stated Problem #2: What happens if the problem is a question of what is the best way for the company to use its "newfound" money? The board's review of the owners' plan for CorecTech shows that corporate dollars are to be allocated among the company, employees, and owners. The directors ask Martin whether owner distributions can be made without these funds. The board also considers whether the owners have any interests in how the funds are allocated between the company and employees. Finding none, the board asks Martin whether the company needs the funds to meet its plans, and then evaluates Martin's proposal as indicated above. Again, the board sees this only as a management problem.

Stated Problem #3: But what happens if the board asks whether the money belongs to the company or the vendors? The board reviews the owners' plan and notes that the owners want to treat the vendors the same way we all want to be treated. The directors then consider what treatment the owners would expect if a CorecTech's customer discovered a similar error. The answer is obvious, so the board directs Martin to notify the vendors of the error and pay them the amount they failed to charge. The board now sees the problem as belonging to management but with an ownership context.

Defining the problem should always include identifying how the owners are involved. The directors should review the owners' plan and ask two questions: Is there anything in the owners' plan that relates to this problem in the various ways it can be defined? How might the owners want to be involved considering the various ways the problem can be defined? To help identify management's involvement, directors should evaluate management's position based on the evaluation criteria discussed in Chapter 6.

APPLYING ALL FIVE STEPS

The story of Itasco illustrates how all five questions are addressed in identifying which group should be involved in problem solving.

Itasco's Story

Itasco's new division lost money during the last two years. Next year's losses are projected to be the highest yet, and will prevent the company from paying dividends for the first time. Grant, Itasco's CEO, believes the division will eventually provide substantial benefits to Itasco. Grant goes to the board with a proposal to pay dividends as requested in the current owners' plan, but also to lay off employees to cut expenses. Grant is confident that the layoffs will not jeopardize Itasco's future, but in the short term will lengthen the time needed for the division to recover. How does the board determine which group—the owners, managers, or both—needs to be involved and how?

1. *Define the problem.* Itasco's board defines the problem as how to balance paying dividends, laying off and retaining employees, and timing the new division's profitability.

2. *Identify how the owners and managers are involved in this problem.* The directors know that the owners' plans state a specific dollar amount that the owners say they need, as well as an amount they would like to receive from the company. When reviewing the owners' plan, the directors also learn that the owners want Itasco to commit to the well-being of its employees and expect the employees to be loyal to Itasco. The board correctly determines that the owners need to be involved in this

issue regarding the questions about distributions to owners and employee layoffs.

The board also knows that Grant and his managers need to come up with a plan that addresses changes in the owners' plan and is realistic about what the company can do.

3. *Determine the owners' position and management's position.* Grant's position is clear to the board. He came to the board with a thorough proposal that met the owners' plan as stated. The directors believe he considered all other feasible alternatives and that his proposal presents the best choices available. The only item the directors want Grant to clarify is whether the distribution to the owners will be the amount they stated as their goal or the amount they said they needed. Grant confirms his proposal would pay out the higher amount.

The directors are less certain of the owners' positions on dividends and the treatment of employees. For example, the owners say they need a certain dollar amount from Itasco, but their goal amount is higher than what they say they need. Does that mean the owners would like more but can get by with less? Regarding the treatment of employees, the directors are uncertain about what the owners mean by being committed to the well-being of employees. For example, are the owners willing to reduce the distribution amount they want in order to lay off fewer employees?

4. *Determine what additional information is needed from the owners and the managers.* The board determines that they need to know whether the owners are willing to reduce the amount of their distributions to avoid laying off employees and, if so, by how much and for how long. They ask the owners to consider this request and report their position in two weeks.

If the owners come back and say that they are willing to reduce their dividends by 20 percent for two years, the directors will want Grant to come back with a new proposal addressing the challenges at the new division.

The owners may need additional information from Grant and the board as they respond to the board's directives. Likewise, Grant may need additional information from the owners as he begins to consider their alternatives. Both groups are encouraged to identify the information they need and to ask the board to make the information available.

5. *Assess whether the final conclusion integrates the owners' and managers' positions.* After the owners and managers respond to the board's directives, the board evaluates Grant's final proposal to ensure that it is well thought through, clear, doable, and fits with the modified plans for the company and owners.

If Grant's proposal does not pass this evaluation, it indicates that either the owners or managers may not be focusing on the correct component of the problem or may need assistance in coming up with or clarifying their position; or the board doesn't understand the positions of the groups, or may not know how to integrate them. In that case, the steps need to be repeated.

Some issues are fairly straightforward, and the five steps can be easily completed during a single discussion. Some problems, like the ones facing Itasco, are complicated or significant enough that a written summary of each of the steps is helpful. Figure 7.3 can be used to organize the written responses. (Figure 7.3 is also reproduced as Worksheet 7.1.)

This information is especially helpful when putting the board agenda together. If the chair works through this process for each item that the board needs to approve, the chair will understand the problem; what issues it prompts for the owners and managers; what the board's role will be with respect to the problem; what additional information will be needed at the meeting for the directors to approve the solution; and how to guide the board in making sure that the solution integrates the owners' and managers' positions.

Explanation of the problem: _____

_____

	Owners	Board	Management
What is each group's responsibilities regarding the problem?			
What is each group's known position regarding its part of the problem?			
What information is needed from each group regarding its part of the problem?			

Figure 7.3 Issue identification

ACTING INDEPENDENTLY

For the owners and managers to trust the board with the process, the board must act independently. Acting independently is a "best practice" of a board. It means following three criteria:

1. The board owns the process and not the result

2. Directors are other-centered

3. Directors have no self-interest in the plans or in any particular result

Acting independently means the board owns the process and not the results. As soon as the board becomes responsible for the results, it loses its independence and guiding the process becomes more difficult.

Acting independently also means that directors are other-centered. In other words, their decisions should be based on what is in the best interest of the company and the owners they serve—and not necessarily what the directors themselves would do if it were their company. To balance effectively, directors need to think and act as directors, not entrepreneurs.

For example, a management report to the board explains how to distribute the company's profits for the prior fiscal year among the owners, employees, and the business based on the profit allocation plan found in the owners' plan and the company's strategic plan. It was a good year and the employees are scheduled to receive large profit bonuses. A director expresses concern about how the profit allocation will affect the company's cash flow and equity position in view of the company's plans for expansion. The director's own company had cash flow and equity problems when it tried to expand. Not wanting the same thing to happen here, the director wants to limit the allocation of the profits to the employees and continually comments that the profit allocation must be more weighted toward the business.

Certainly the director's concerns are legitimate. His experience helped him spot a potentially devastating problem in this company. And he may even be correct. What is not helpful, though, is how the director acts on his concern. He pushes to limit the prior year's allocation and to amend the owners' plan. The owners are concerned because they believe that a well-rewarded workforce is the most critical component to their success. The managers don't know whether the director is disappointed in their performance or has a personal agenda, and are concerned about how to effectively work with their board. The director is assuming that what happened in his company will happen here. He is acting out a "self-centered" position and not focusing on the best interests of the company he serves.

Here is how the director might act "other centered." He could explain what he sees as a potential problem; ask for information from the managers and possibly even the owners to assess the legitimacy of his concern for the company; and then assess whether the current profit allocation can meet the values, needs, and goals of the owners and the business. If he doesn't think that will happen, and he is right, the board can use this conclusion to determine who may have to change their values, needs, and goals: the owners or the managers.

Acting this way, the director identifies the problem and seeks information to assess whether the problem he sees is really a problem for this company (that is, can the solution meet the values, needs, and goals of this particular ownership group). If the answer is yes, the board moves on. If the answer is no, the board determines which group—owners, managers, or both—needs to solve the problem by changing their values, needs, and goals. This is acting "other centered."

Acting independently also means that the directors have no self-interest in the plans or in any particular result. Directors should act as third parties, evaluating each plan on its own merits, not on whether they or another director will personally gain from approving or accepting a plan. They should also evaluate each decision on how it is integrated with the owners' plan and management's plans, not how they might gain from the result. When directors evaluate a plan or make a decision based on self-interest, they promote a position that benefits themselves as owners or managers. In other words, they think and act like an owner or manager. The distinction among ownership, governance, and management is blurred, and the board ceases to be the balance point between ownership and management.

For example, a company headquartered in Chicago considers expanding operations to another city—New York City or Los Angeles. The director, also an executive manager, decides that Los Angeles would be the better choice because he has friends there. If the board chooses Los Angeles, he will be able to see his friends more often. This director is ignoring the business reasons for expanding and ignoring the merits of the two cities. This director does not understand that the location decision must represent an integration of the owners' plan and the management plans. He should have looked to these two plans for guidance.

In another case, a company did not meet its yearly projections. So, according to the approved plans, a 50 percent reduction in owner

distributions will take place. A director, who is also one of the owners, asks the board to give the owners 100 percent of their distribution because she has a balloon payment on a mortgage due soon and
is counting on the dividend to meet the payment. The director is not
thinking of the company, the owners' group, or the consequences of
increasing owner distributions. This isn't to say that increasing owner
distribution to 100 percent is wrong. The point is she didn't analyze
how the 100 percent distribution amount would affect the company's
ability to implement and accomplish its strategic or annual plan. She
didn't ask how the increased distribution would change the owners'
plan. She didn't even bring the issue to the owners. She simply acted
out of her own self-interest.

Being independent is hard. It is even harder when a director as-
sumes responsibility for the results rather than the process. This is true
even when the director is acting as a third party out of a true desire to
help (being other-centered). Acting independently is harder for directors who are also owners or managers. Chapter 8 addresses the unique
challenges for owners or managers on the board.

Roberto's Story—The Conclusion

In Chapter 3, we introduced you to Roberto, the founder of
GamePlay. He wants to hire someone to run his company so
he can create more games and not lead the company's transition. Roberto ends up hiring Dick as president of the company.
Dick has twenty years' experience in plastic manufacturing and is
hardworking, personable, and also has experience in diversifying
companies. The board consists of three independent directors,
Roberto, and Roberto's wife LaGretta.

Over the next four years. Dick implements systems throughout
the company that improve the quality of GamePlay's manufacturing and broaden the company's customer base. Dick explains
his vision and has clear and well-thought-out plans for growing
the business. GamePlay's traditional gaming business decreases
from 90 percent to under 20 percent of the total company as

the company makes inroads in the home appliance, construction, and automobile industries. Dick hires new people, expands the facilities, and changes the compensation and benefit systems. Personnel in the sales and market groups completely turn over and engineering grows from two employees to ten. Overall the company is diversifying and doing well.

Roberto, though, grows dissatisfied, starting with little things: Dick does things differently than he; the employees are now going to Dick for answers (and they even like him!); Roberto feels "corrected" when Dick implements different systems, thinking he (Roberto) should have thought of those things himself. Roberto's thoughts continue down this course until he convinces himself that he just isn't relevant to the company anymore—and that really bothers him. Roberto knew this would happen, and deep down is relieved that he doesn't have the burden of diversifying the company. But he wants to invent more games and that isn't happening. Every time he talks to Dick about a new gaming device, Dick either avoids the topic, or tells him it isn't the right time, or seems to listen but never lets the idea make the planning cut.

LaGretta is also becoming agitated, but for different reasons. Dick's plans require a lot of cash, and LaGretta is concerned about how their retirement will be funded. She sees the company grow in value and profits, but she hasn't seen much additional cash coming to Roberto and her. Yes, they have a salary, but she wants to travel, and wants to plan for when she and Roberto can't work anymore, and wants to help her children and grandchildren.

When Dick presents the next long-term plan to the board, Roberto and LaGretta criticize it. They complain about the level of capital expenditures, the number of employees the company has now and will have if the plan is approved, and the lack of focus on the company's core business, gaming. The outside directors don't approve the plan in light of the comments Roberto and LaGretta make at the meeting.

Dick asked Roberto and LaGretta what is troubling them. He wants to know what they need in order to support him. Despite his efforts, Roberto and LaGretta don't tell Dick what they are looking for from the company, and the board doesn't direct Roberto and LaGretta to identify their values, needs, and goals. When Dick places an order for new office furniture to replace the old, Roberto vetoes the order. He believes that Dick and he simply have a different set of values because Roberto thinks the existing furniture is adequate (and in any event, if additional furniture is needed Roberto would have bought used, not new). Roberto asks Dick to resign and they work out a severance arrangement. Roberto goes back to managing the business but is now out of place with all the changes that occurred. Employees soon begin to leave, production quality suffers, customers drop off, and eventually Roberto is forced to sell the company. Dick loses out on an opportunity to reap the financial reward for his efforts that would have funded his retirement.

The position of a nonowner president may be one of the more difficult jobs that exist. One of the biggest challenges is to ensure that the nonowner president understands the values, needs, and goals of the owners and develops plans that meet the owners' interests. Failing to do this means that the president either has to continue correctly guessing what the owners want or will eventually be replaced. Dick and Roberto were in agreement when Dick started diversifying the business. Somewhere along the line, however, Dick's views of what was important to Roberto and LaGretta differed from what Roberto and LaGretta thought they wanted.

What happened at GamePlay is common when boards are not effective in their role. When Dick was hired and began diversifying the company, he acted as the balance point. He set the vision for GamePlay and developed plans to implement that vision. Roberto and LaGretta were initially pleased, so the board didn't evaluate whether Dick's vision was consistent with Roberto and LaGretta's vision. Later, as Roberto and LaGretta grew concerned, they took over the balance point. They criticized Dick's plans and decisions without identifying their own values, needs, and goals. In essence, they began to manage the company by objecting to management's plans based on their belief that management's plans wouldn't provide them with what they wanted.

The outside directors were certainly not acting as the balance point. They supported Dick when Roberto and LaGretta had no objection, and they supported the owners when Roberto and LaGretta didn't approve. If the outside directors acted as the balance point, they would respond in one of two ways when the differences between the owners and the president became apparent. First, the outside directors would instruct Roberto and LaGretta to identify what they wanted from the business and from Dick as president. The outside directors were in a better position than Dick to ask Roberto and LaGretta for this information because the directors could challenge the owners' conclusions without risk of impunity. The directors should also hold Dick accountable for meeting the owners' interests. Instead, they gave Roberto and LaGretta a free pass to object without explaining why they were objecting. The outside directors thought their role was to support Roberto and LaGretta's positions at the board meeting because they owned the company and could ultimately do what they wanted anyway.

Alternatively, the outside directors could ask Dick to explain how his plans for the business satisfied the owners' values, needs, and goals. Then Dick could identify what he thought Roberto and LaGretta were looking for, and the owners could respond and correct any misunderstanding. By using either approach, the outside directors would have facilitated involving the owners and management in the primary issue: what Roberto and LaGretta wanted and whether Dick could provide it.

In the case of GamePlay, the owners and managers are different people; when this happens it is likely that their interests will not align naturally. Furthermore, the likelihood of the differences in the owners' and managers' interests increases over time and as circumstances change. The balance point solution requires the board to regularly ask the owners to identify their values, needs, and goals regarding the company and the managers to complete plans demonstrating how the company will achieve the owners' interests.

DIRECTING, ADVISING, AND MANAGING

In order for directors to be effective at owning the process but not the result, they must also understand the differences between directing, advising, and managing. Most directors do not understand the differences; in fact, they view these activities as interchangeable.

DIRECTING

For the most part, directors should direct. Directing has two components. First, directing is asking the owners and managers to develop plans and solutions to problems. That is, they should direct the owners to deal with owner issues and they should direct managers to deal with management issues. Directing in this manner, of course, requires the directors to identify for each issue before them what information may be needed from the owners and from the managers. It also requires the directors to identify who is responsible for resolving the issue and what role the board should play.

Acting in this manner requires the directors to act as third parties. If they act in their own self-interest, they will not gather the pertinent information and will not make an objective decision. Acting in this manner also requires the directors to be other-centered. If their decisions are based on what they personally would do or how they would do things if it were their company, their decisions will not be based on what is in the best interest of the company and the owners they serve.

The second component to directing is the skill of asking questions to draw out information, rather than simply giving an opinion as soon as an issue is presented. This skill helps the director ascertain whether the owner or manager really understands the issue, has thought it through, and has a potential solution that meets both the owners' and management's plans. While directors are often eager to give their opinion and offer solutions, doing so does not encourage the owners and managers to own their respective issues.

For example, a president may come to the board to discuss problems with the sales manager. The board has two basic options. First, the directors can gather the pertinent data and then give their recommendation. When a board takes this option, it owns the result. It is, after all, the president's responsibility (not the board's) to find a solution to this personnel decision. If the board makes a recommendation and the president doesn't agree with it, the boundary between the board and management becomes blurred and the relationship between the board and management becomes more adversarial.

Second, the board can ask pertinent questions of the president to help clarify the issue and help the president make the decision. When a board takes this option, it continues to own the process, but not the result. The boundary between ownership and management is protected, and the relationship between the board and management is strengthened.

The board's role, in this case, is to help the president do the president's job. The directors determine whether the president has thought the issue through, has looked at the risks and rewards of the president's decision, and has reviewed its consistency with the owners' plan and the strategic and annual plans. The board's role is not to decide for the president or to do the president's job. Directing management prevents directors from "doing management."

ADVISING

Advising is participating as a resource, expert, or guide. Generally speaking, owners elect certain individuals as directors because they have wisdom and experience that are helpful to management. Directors should be free to share their wisdom and experience. The key to effective advising, however, is understanding when and how to advise.

Advising is most appropriate when management puts its strategic and annual plans together. At this time, it is the managers' responsibility to learn as much as they can about how to achieve their plan. They will find it useful to talk with individuals who have been through similar experiences or are experts in their particular fields. Often, the individuals who can best help the managers sit on the board. Asking the directors to advise managers is not asking the directors what to do. It is asking them for a perspective that will help managers develop their plans. Usually, these conversations occur outside of the board meeting.

When directors evaluate management's plan (according to the process outlined in Chapter 6) advising also is appropriate. If the board feels that part of management's plan is not thoroughly researched or demonstrates a lack of perspective, individual directors can help managers understand what they need to do to complete the plan.

For example, assume a president wants to buy a competitor and his acquisition plans don't include a strategy to integrate the two company cultures. Directors who have expertise in this area can explain why the integration of two cultures is important, describe their experience, and suggest ways management can look into the issue further before asking the board to approve the plan.

Overadvising disrupts the balance point. Overadvising usually includes a director telling management what to do and how to think; in other words, what they must do if they want their plans approved. In essence, overadvising becomes managing the managers. When directors overadvise, they act as managers and, as a consequence, they own the result. They lose the ability to be the balance point between ownership and management, and they cease to act independently.

When a board is advising, the board should make it clear that it is advising. There are three ways to do this.

» The board agenda sets a time in the meeting devoted to topics on which management wants the board's advice.

» When directors offer their perspective during the plan evaluation process, they should declare that they are advising.

» When managers seek advice from particular directors outside the regular board meetings, the directors should declare that they are advising and are still acting as the balance point.

Getting advice from directors can be helpful—so can giving advice. But how and when advice is given determines whether the director is doing an effective job.

MANAGING

Directors should never manage. When directors manage, they become agents of either the owners or the managers. In essence, they represent one group—and end up pushing the owners' plan onto the managers or management's plans onto the owners. When this happens, the directors are managing and, when they manage, they own the results. They cease to be the balance point between owners and managers.

For example, assume the owners' plan calls for a 20 percent annual return on investment. Management has been unable to develop a plan that will accommodate this need because of a slow economy, bank covenants in their loan agreement, and other outstanding debt. They present a plan for an 8 percent annual return on investment for two years in order to ensure the company's well-being. Even though management's plan looks reasonable, the board tells management that 20 percent is a firm number and they have to do whatever it takes to make it happen.

In this case, the directors are acting as agents of the owners. They are not trying to find a way to integrate the two plans. They are not facilitating discussions with the owners about the owners' expectations or with the managers about how to overcome limitations on growth. Clearly, the directors are not independent or acting as the balance point between ownership and management. It is very likely that significant conflict will arise in the ownership group, between ownership and management, between the board and management, or among all three groups. This may be a difficult issue to resolve, but if the board is serious about its responsibility to direct the process and act as the balance point, it is likely that a solution will be found.

Tom and Cynthia's Story— The Conclusion

Tom and Cynthia's restaurant needs capital so they bring in investors, most of whom are on the board. This board begins to turn down Tom and Cynthia's proposals and approves only cost-cutting proposals.

In response, Tom increasingly does things without seeking board approval on the basis that he still owns controlling interest and can do whatever he wants. Some directors try to manage the company and consider suing Tom and Cynthia to gain their way.

In the end, Tom and Cynthia bought back stock from those investors who prevented the ownership group from speaking with one voice. Once that was done, they presented an ownership plan to the board that helped the company expand and diversify slowly, maintain their success, and yield an acceptable return to the owners.

A NONBUSINESS EXAMPLE

The differences between directing, advising, and managing can be difficult to grasp, especially for those who have not sat on balancing boards. A nonbusiness example may help.

Your 11-year-old asks for help reviewing his essay titled "The Assyrians." You know nothing about these ancient people, but want to help. You have three options.

» You can read the assignment to see whether what your child has written is consistent with the assignment, and then ask your child to demonstrate his understanding of the assignment to show he has satisfied the requirements. If you do this, you are directing.

» You can give your child some insight about writing papers, such as stressing the importance of a good introduction and conclusion, and suggesting reference sources that may be helpful. If you do this, you are advising.

» You can do additional research and rewrite the paper to make sure that he gets it right. If you do this, you are managing. You are no longer a helpful third party. You own the results.

In this story, the board is not acting as the balance point. The board is a group of owners who advocate their respective interests. The directors vote to further their interests or frustrate the interests of other owners.

An alternative to the power struggle that ensued would be for the board to act as the balance point—the board should direct the owners to identify their respective values, needs, and goals regarding the business and to come up with a set of values, needs, and goals that will work for all the owners. Some would speculate that the differences within this ownership group are so significant that it is highly unlikely they will come up with a single plan. We agree—if the goal of the work is that the owners agree on a plan where they would all stay as owners. But that is not the goal. The goal is to solve the conflict, and the balancing process offers at least two advantages to solve the conflict.

First, the process will keep the problem where it belongs—in the ownership group. This may limit the effect of owner differences on board performance and keep owners from managing the business. Second, the effort will let all the owners know where each of them stand. This often has a moderating influence on those owners who are more vocal in their criticism when in a smaller group. Involving all the owners will give those who want to sell their share of the business a chance to either influence the other owners or let the other owners know they want to be bought out. Either way, the ownership group will likely be more united when the work is done, and management can then make plans to handle the transition among the ownership group while continuing to operate the business.

KEEPING THE BOARD CALENDAR

One of the easiest and most effective ways for the board to own the process is to establish and follow a board calendar. A board calendar is similar to a project plan, a maintenance schedule, or the yearly compliance activities of an accounting department. A board calendar requires the principal groups in the business system to address certain items at certain times during the year. A board calendar is based on the company's fiscal year and is built around the board's meeting schedule. This master calendar helps bring order to the entire planning process. The board calendar will drive the work of the board *and* the work of the owners and managers. In developing and using a board calendar, the board will allocate throughout the year those items that must be addressed on a regular basis. This guides the activities of the owners and managers and ensures that the board's activities are completed in a timely manner. Since the board holds the owners and managers accountable for their plans, it is reasonable for the board to set the time frames for completion of these items. Of course, the owners and

> **THE BOARD CALENDAR WILL DRIVE THE WORK OF THE BOARD *AND* THE WORK OF THE OWNERS AND MANAGERS.**

managers periodically review the board calendar to make sure that the due dates work for them.

When preparing the board calendar, review the responsibilities of the owners, board, and management outlined in the owners' manual to make sure that the calendar reflects everything that has to be done. The calendar should also reflect the responsibilities of any board committees. While every calendar is unique, a board would typically schedule the following items:

» Receiving, evaluating, and accepting the owners' plan

» Receiving, evaluating, and approving management's strategic plan (or updates)

» Receiving, evaluating, and approving management's annual plan and budget

» Evaluating progress on all plans

» Discussing the results of the prior year including whether the owners' plan was accomplished and whether management's goals and objectives were achieved

» Electing a board chairperson and officers as required

» Evaluating the CEO, top managers, and family members in the company

» Setting compensation for top managers and family members in the company

» Establishing yearly dividend plans

» Evaluating the board and individual directors

» Training, including the training of new board members

» Inquiring about succession and transition plans

» Approving policy manual updates

» Conducting an overall human resources review

» Asking due diligence questions

Chapter 9 covers a list of items to be discussed at each board meeting.

BOARD'S PORTION OF THE CALENDAR

To begin constructing a board calendar, identify the items to be scheduled. Then allocate the items among the regular board meetings so the work is done in a timely manner. If the board uses committees, integrate the activities of the committees into the calendar. For example, the company's fiscal year runs from January to December and the board has four regular meetings per year. This requires that the planning process be completed by December 31; in other words, the owners' plan needs to be accepted and management's plans approved by the end of the year. Consequently, the owners submit their plan in the summer so the board has time to evaluate and accept the owners' plan, the managers have time to incorporate the owners' plan into their plans, and the board has time to review and approve management's plans by the end of the year. Appendix 7.1 presents a sample board calendar showing when to address topics for a company that operates on a calendar year basis.

OWNERS' AND MANAGERS' PORTION OF THE CALENDAR

After allocating the board's responsibilities among its regular meetings throughout the year, expand the calendar to reflect what, and by when, owners and managers must do to be ready to present to the board. This portion of the calendar involves the owners and managers in setting their particular target dates, but the board directs both groups to develop task lists and timelines to complete their work. By including the owners' and managers' tasks and timelines, the board is in a better position to assess the entire planning process and determine whether owners and managers need help in fulfilling their respective functions. Appendix 7.2 shows how to expand the board's portion to include the basic responsibilities of the owners and managers.

The reason we focus on the calendar is that all too often companies begin their planning process at the end of the old fiscal year or just after the beginning of the new fiscal year. The company may be two to six months into the year by the time all plans are accepted and approved. When this happens, it is less likely that management will accomplish its plan and less likely that the owners will feel that their needs and goals are being addressed.

The calendars described in this section are generic. Your calendar will depend on your circumstances and the nature of your business. But every board calendar, if it is well thought out, keeps the board focused on the process and the owners and managers focused on the fundamental elements of the ownership and management plans.

Meeting legal responsibilities

Another important reason for a board to *own the process and not the result* involves directors' legal obligations.

Duty to oversee management

A business and affairs of a corporation shall be managed by or under the direction of a Board . . .

The laws of most states provide that directors have a duty regarding management. Usually, the law doesn't require a board to manage the business to satisfy this duty. It is sufficient if the board oversees management. Most boards hire full-time managers to run the business, thus choosing to oversee management rather than directly managing the business. By balancing effectively, boards can satisfy their duty to oversee management.

Satisfying the legal duty to oversee management is based on owners clearly identifying what they are looking for from the business. An owners' plan that reflects what the owners want as a group and that is consistent, complete, and doable provides the board with a standard for overseeing management. Separating ownership, governance, and management provides a foundation for identifying each group's basic responsibilities, and helps to keep the directors focused on oversight and the owners and managers focused on problem solving. This process reduces the board's tendency to take on problem solving which, as we already noted, increases the risk of the board managing or alienating the owners or managers by being an agent for one group or the other. A balancing

> SEPARATING OWNERSHIP, GOVERNANCE, AND MANAGEMENT PROVIDES A FOUNDATION FOR IDENTIFYING EACH GROUP'S BASIC RESPONSIBILITIES, AND HELPS TO KEEP THE DIRECTORS FOCUSED ON OVERSIGHT AND THE OWNERS AND MANAGERS FOCUSED ON PROBLEM SOLVING.

board is engaged—not as an afterthought or rubber stamp, as is often the case with boards of closely held and family businesses—but as the overseer of the entire process.

Some say the board has to be involved in management because the law requires that the business shall be managed by or under the direction of a board. The following section talks more about the board's legal responsibilities. But here we point out that the law does not require the board to *manage* the business. The board's legal responsibility to *oversee* management gives it the authority to elect the officers to run the business and requires it to ensure that the officers manage the company. The owners can certainly require the board to have a more active management role in the business, and the board has the legal authority to insert itself into management, but the board is not legally required to do so—nor do we believe it to be in the best interest of a business for the company to have two different groups managing the business. The proper role of the board of a closely held and family business is to oversee management by having management under the direction of the board and by acting as the balance point rather than managing the business.

Here are some tips for directors to help them meet their duty to oversee management:

» Make sure that the owners and, particularly, managers provide the directors with all the information needed to properly oversee management. The ability to oversee management includes

- understanding the owners' plan
- understanding management's plan
- understanding fully and completely the doability of management's stated goals, strategies, and tactics
- understanding how the business compares with other similarly situated businesses
- awareness of the primary risks affecting the business

» Make sure management makes available all resources the board may need.

» Make sure that the company complies with the law, corporate policies, and the shareholders' values.

DUTY OF CARE (ALSO KNOWN AS THE BUSINESS JUDGMENT RULE)

A director shall discharge the duties of the position of director in good faith, in a manner the director reasonably believes to be in the best interests of the corporation, and with the care an ordinarily prudent person in a like position would exercise under similar circumstances. A person who so performs these duties is not liable by reason of being or having been a director of the corporation.

The laws of most states provide a standard requiring directors to act responsibly when overseeing management. This standard is often referred to as the duty of care or the business judgment rule. If directors meet this standard, they ought not to be found liable for decisions they make even if those decisions are later found to be detrimental to the business.

Satisfying this legal duty of care is easier when the board is the balance point between the owners and managers. As the balance point, the board requires both these groups to develop plans that the board evaluates based on the standard of acting independently.

Directors may rely on information, opinions, reports, or statements (including financial statements) prepared or presented to them, unless a director has knowledge that the statements are not true. This encourages directors to ask for what they need in order to act as an effective balance point. Also, all directors are presumed to agree to a board decision unless a director (1) objects at the beginning of the meeting because the meeting was not lawfully called or convened and then does not participate in it; (2) votes against an action; or

(3) is unable to vote because of a conflict of interest. This presumption encourages directors to actively participate in decision making and discourages acquiescence to decisions that do not meet the duty of care. As a result, all directors act as the balance point, whether or not they participate.

Though not always easy, the board has the responsibility for taking the high road. If, over time and after attempts to address an issue, managers continue to act against the best interests of the business, the board may need to make changes within management. And if, over time and after attempts to address the problem, the owners are not acting with a unified voice, the directors need to resign.

Here are some tips for directors to help them meet their duty of care:

» Act in good faith. In other words, act in the best interests of the company and the ownership, and not for your personal benefit.

» Make decisions based on what an ordinary, reasonable prudent person would do in a similar position.

» Check your ego, biases, and grudges at the door. In other words, act independently.

» Attend all board meetings and actively participate.

» Review the information received.

» Ask for what you need and ask about what you don't understand.

DUTY OF LOYALTY

The laws of most states also provide that directors have a duty of loyalty to the business. The duty of loyalty generally deals with conflicts of interest and corporate opportunity. Restrictions against conflicts of interests prohibit a director (or members of the director's family) from having a material financial interest with the company unless the material facts of the arrangement are fully disclosed and the arrangement is approved by either the board (or a committee of the board or by the owners) without participation of the person with the conflict. This doesn't apply when the board sets its own compensation. Regarding corporate opportunities, before individual directors may pursue an opportunity, they must make the opportunity available to the company if it is related to the company's business.

Satisfying the legal duty of loyalty is easier when the board is an effective balance point because the board is focused on the process and not the results. By not focusing on the results, directors are less tempted to achieve a particular outcome in which they have a real or perceived interest.

Effective balancing requires that the board act as a third party. Owners will delegate to the board the responsibility to hold the owners accountable only if owners trust that the directors are true to the process rather than to any particular outcome. If the board is not acting as a third party, the owners will likely be aware of this early on and will talk about what to do about the situation.

Here are some tips for directors to help them meet their duty of loyalty:

» Avoid conflicts of interest.

» Disclose and obtain approval of all benefits you receive directly or indirectly from the company (except board compensation).

» Do not participate in business opportunities that relate to the business of the company without disclosure and approval.

CAUTIONARY REMARKS

It is true that if the board is not meeting the owners' needs or the owners' needs have changed, the owners have the authority to dissolve the board. It is common for owners to dissolve the board at the first sign of dissatisfaction. However, before taking such a big step, the owners should ask themselves whether *they* are the problem—whether they have been clear about what they want the board to do; whether they have conducted a board evaluation and given feedback to the board; and whether the board has had a chance to react to this feedback, communicate with the owners, and become a better board. Most boards, especially newly formed boards, need some time to understand the owners' values, needs, and goals, and become effective. Owners should give their board every chance to become effective.

CHAPTER

8

SEVEN EFFECTIVE
BOARD STRUCTURES

Before continuing on, take a moment to conceptualize the basic board process. It may help to take out a sheet of paper and draw out Figure 6.2 (the board's basic balancing function). Then apply it to your own situation. How does the balance power work in your company? Who are the owners, directors, and managers? How well is it working? Think about the answers to these questions, then verbally explain it to someone. You may find that you understand what we've been saying better than you think. Explaining it to someone will convince you of that.

In this chapter, we shift from explaining the overall structure and process of having a balancing board to explaining a specific structure: that of the board. The board structure that you choose results from answering the owners' manual questions, Where is the balance point? How does the balancing process work? and Should our balance point structure or process change? If the answers to these questions are clear, working through how to structure the board is much easier. This chapter addresses how you can assess whether you want a board of directors and what board structure will work best for your business.

THE BASICS

After clients begin to understand the idea of the board of directors acting as the balance point, one of the first questions they ask is about the type of board they should have. The answer to this question is not simple. There is no "best" board structure for all businesses—there isn't even a recommended board structure that works for every business. We identify seven alternative board structures to help business owners decide what type of board will work best for them.

ASSESSING THE BOARD'S PURPOSE

The board structure that is best for a business at any given time is determined by how the owners answer three questions.

WHY DO WE WANT A BOARD?

For a board to work, it must serve a legitimate purpose. A board will not make any meaningful contribution if it exists because it is legally required or because "companies like ours" are supposed to have a board. Chapter 3 explains four situations when a board of directors is necessary.

» when entrepreneurs want to transition to others the day-to-day running of the business

» when owners and managers are different people

» when there are multiple owners

» when entrepreneurs want to sell the business or their stock to others

If entrepreneurs want to transition the management responsibilities to others, the transition plan should clearly identify the location of the balance point, the entrepreneur's role relative to the balance point, and anticipate how the balance point will transition when the entrepreneur no longer wants to perform the balancing function. If owners and managers are different people, the owners should explore the issues, risks, and challenges arising from this situation and ask how a board acting as the balance point between ownership and management can help. If the business has multiple owners, they should consider the issues and challenges arising from this situation and ask how a board acting as a third party can help. If entrepreneurs are selling the business or their stock to others, they should determine how a board of directors would increase the value of the company or increase the probability of payment if the purchase price is paid over time. Owners need to have a thorough understanding of how a board can help before agreeing to form a board.

WHAT DO WE WANT THIS BOARD TO DO?

This includes the related questions, How will this board work with the owners? and How will this board work with the managers? Once the owners agree on why they want a board, they can identify the roles and responsibilities of the owners, board, and managers; how the board will work with the owners; and how the board will work with managers. Using information in Chapters 4 through 7 as a guide, the owners can discuss these roles and responsibilities, raise issues that concern them, resolve those issues, and agree on what they want the board to do.

It is essential to involve all of the owners in these discussions. Since effective balancing requires that the owners speak with one voice, all owners should be part of the process of identifying the board structure. Individual owners can, of course, decline to participate. Those owners who don't participate should receive a written statement of what the other owners agree to so all the owners are informed.

WHAT STRUCTURE WILL THOSE IN POWER ACCEPT AND ENDORSE?

An underlying reality of all closely held and family businesses is that for the transition plan to succeed, those with the power must accept and endorse every element of it. This reality also holds true for the board. In other words, those with the power must commit to

» the need for a board

» the different roles and responsibilities of the owners, directors, and managers

» the structure of the board

» the board process

» the need to support and participate in the process voluntarily and constructively

If those in power can't accept these five requirements, the board as a balance point between ownership and management will likely have a short life. The board usually then becomes merely another body for those in power to command, or the board is discontinued or ignored.

Answering these three questions will help the owners know why they want a board, what the board will do, and what board arrangements are possible. With this information in hand, the owners are able to ask the next question, Which board structure is best for us?

IDENTIFYING THE APPROPRIATE BOARD STRUCTURE

Determining what type of board structure is best is no simple matter. Table 8.1 identifies seven alternative board structures (ABSs) to help owners determine the arrangement that best suits their purposes for a board.

Table 8.1 Seven alternative board structures

ABS 1:	Entrepreneurs get input from individuals they choose
ABS 2:	Entrepreneurs meet with an identifiable group on an as-needed basis to get input
ABS 3:	Entrepreneurs meet with an identifiable group on a regular basis to get input
ABS 4:	An elected group of insiders with legal decision-making authority
ABS 5:	An elected group (having a majority of insiders) with legal decision-making authority
ABS 6:	An elected group (having a majority of outsiders) with legal decision-making authority
ABS 7:	An elected group of outsiders with legal decision-making authority

As you go through the explanations of these structures, remember that when we mention the entrepreneur, we mean the founder in a first-generation business, the owner in a business owned by one person, or the clearly dominant owner; in other words, the person with the power to make balancing decisions.

With an ABS 1, entrepreneurs seek input from individuals they trust and respect. Entrepreneurs are the board of directors and seek guidance whenever they feel the need.

With an ABS 2, entrepreneurs establish a group that meets on an as-needed basis to give input. This would be considered an ad hoc board of advisors—what we'll call an advisory group. Again, entrepreneurs are the board of directors and seek guidance whenever they think input is needed.

With an ABS 3, entrepreneurs establish a group that meets regularly to provide input. This arrangement is considered an advisory group. Entrepreneurs, again, are the board of directors. The advisory group typically provides input on a wide variety of topics, such as goals and plans of the entrepreneur and the company, and helps the entrepreneur make decisions. Sometimes an advisory group is brought together for a specific purpose, such as discussing international expansion or marketing strategies. In either case, the advisory group gives input to the entrepreneur, and the entrepreneur retains decision-making authority and responsibility.

Board structures reflected in ABSs 1 through 3 have several characteristics that are important to remember:

» The entrepreneurs are the board of directors and have the sole authority and responsibility to balance the interests of the owners and managers.

» The input the entrepreneurs receive from other individuals may help them be a better owner, director, manager, and family member. However, the input the entrepreneurs get is just that—input. The entrepreneurs can accept or ignore the input at their discretion.

» Managers, professional advisors, family members, and other individuals can all provide input.

» Having an ABS 1 through 3 does not change the entrepreneur's role because the entrepreneur retains the balancing function.

Table 8.2 illustrates the relationship of the board of directors and an advisory group in ABS 1 through 3.

Table 8.2 ABS 1 through 3

ABS	Board of directors	Advisory group
1	1 person	Different people, meet as needed
2	1 person	Same people, meet as needed
3	1 person	Same people, meet on regular basis

When the entrepreneur (or the person with the power to make balancing decisions) wants to share or delegate the balancing function, ABSs 4 through 7 are appropriate board structures. ABSs 4 through 7 are also appropriate structures when there are multiple owners, when owners and managers are different people, and when entrepreneurs want to sell the business or their stock to others. ABSs 4 through 7 shift the role of balancing to a group. ABSs 4 though 7 are board of director structures.

With an ABS 4, the board is an elected group of insiders having legal decision-making authority. If each director feels free to participate as a director without feeling the need to acquiesce to the person in power, and if the individual in power allows the board process to work without interference, this structure can work well.

With an ABS 5, the board is an elected group with a majority of insiders having legal decision-making authority. An ABS 5 board will benefit from outside wisdom and the board's dynamics will change because it won't be the group of insiders "having our little board meeting."

With an ABS 6, the board is an elected group with a majority of outsiders having legal decision-making authority. An ABS 6 board will lessen the dominance of owners, family members, and managers on the board. The balancing process must be clear and working in order for ABS 6 to be effective.

With ABS 7, the board is an elected group of outsiders having legal decision-making authority. This board has an easier time functioning as the balance point between owners and managers (and acting as a third party with no self-interest in the results) simply because no owner or manager is on the board. It is the best structure for addressing serious power struggles within the ownership and management groups or between these groups. It is also a good structure when entrepreneurs die and their nonactive spouse inherits the business.

Table 8.3 illustrates the mix of insiders and outsiders in ABSs 4 through 7. We used 5 members to make the chart easy to read, not as the number of directors you need. The most appropriate structure depends on what the owners want and will support. And the "appropriateness" of a certain type of board structure may change over time as the goals and support of the owners change.

Table 8.3 ABS 4 through 7

ABS	Total Members	Insiders	Outsiders
4	5	5	0
5	5	3	2
6	5	2	3
7	5	0	5

The seven alternative board structures raise the question of advisory groups and how they compare to boards of directors. The differences between an advisory group and a board of directors are striking. Table 8.4 compares boards of directors and advisory groups.

Table 8.4 Board of directors and advisory group

Board of directors	Advisory group
elected by the owners	selected by the person wanting the advice
specific responsibilities	only responsibility is to advise
legal vote	no vote
accountable to the business and the owners	no accountability

The owners elect a board of directors. This means that the board acts as an official body of the corporate structure. Those wanting advice select an advisory group. This means that anyone can have an advisory group—CEOs, management teams, owners, family members—and the meetings are not part of the legal workings of the corporate structure. That's why we use the term "advisory group" rather than "advisory board."

A board of directors has specific responsibilities—namely the legal duty to oversee management and the duties of care and loyalty. An advisory group's only responsibility is to provide input.

A board of directors has a legal vote. This means that what they decide is official. An advisory group has no legal vote. Advisors just give their opinions.

A board of directors is accountable to the owners and to the business. It is accountable to the business because the law requires the directors to act in the best interests of the company. It is accountable to the owners because the owners elect the directors. This dual accountability can be troublesome. Chapter 6 talks about the tensions that can arise from the dual accountability of a board of directors. An advisory group has no legal accountability. Advisors just do what they think is best.

Both boards of directors and advisory groups can be meaningful, effective, and part of the transition process. The best choice for owners depends on answering the questions, Why do we want a board? What do we want this board to do? and What structure will those in power accept and endorse?

ASSESSING THE APPROPRIATE BOARD STRUCTURE

The most important consideration in determining the appropriate board structure is the role of the person who currently holds the authority to make balancing decisions. In a first-generation business or a business having only one owner or a clearly dominant owner, this person usually functions as the balance point.

THE ROLE OF THE ENTREPRENEUR

Many closely held and family businesses have one individual at the center who holds the power to make balancing decisions. In businesses having this type of person at the helm, the most important consideration when determining the appropriate board structure is the role of the entrepreneur. How does the entrepreneur want to be involved?

As noted in Chapter 3, we do not require or even encourage these individuals to give up their power. In fact, the opposite is true. We encourage them to stay involved, but in a way that allows them to achieve their goals. We also encourage them to control the pace of change, based on their abilities, desires, and interests, and those of their successors. Those individuals holding the balancing power choose how much power and control to transition at any particular time, as well as to whom and how fast.

With ABSs 1, 2, and 3, the entrepreneur is the board of directors and makes all the balancing decisions. With ABSs 4 through 7, all of the board functions, including decision making, transition to a group. Whatever board structure entrepreneurs choose will depend on their plans and comfort level with input from others. What entrepreneurs want and do must come together in order for any board structure to work.

Chapter 3 introduced the idea of the board of one. Entrepreneurs can decide to be the only member of the board even if they seek advice from others, including forming an advisory board. What is essential, though, is for entrepreneurs to realize that they retain the responsibility and sole authority to make board level decisions.

All too often, when entrepreneurs are the sole member of the board, the board process is, at best, casual. A casual balance point may be entirely appropriate when entrepreneurs run the business. A casual balance point, however, will usually not help if entrepreneurs seek to transition all of their management responsibilities or wish to sell the business. A casual balance is usually not effective if entrepreneurs are no longer involved and either the owners and managers are different people or there are multiple owners and they have not worked out (formally or informally) the balancing function. The reason for this phenomenon is simple. In these circumstances, a casual balance point does not adequately prepare or require the managers and future owners or family members to carry out their separate and distinct roles and responsibilities. And a casual balance point is not positioned to help owners and managers work out differences.

Warren's story

Warren founded Custom Steel, a steel fabrications company. Custom Steel's profitability depends on predicting the price of and buying steel. When Warren ran his company, he used his business sense and instincts to buy steel and set prices. When Warren transitioned from management, he required the new president to present his steel projections and pricing conclusions to the board for approval. This action increased the formality of the balance point and helped prepare the new president to handle this task.

THE ROLE OF OTHERS

The next consideration in determining the most appropriate board structure is the role of others. It really boils down to whether entrepreneurs want to involve others or need to involve others to facilitate the change or accomplish their goals. In either case, if the answer is no, ABS 1 is the most appropriate board structure. If the answer is yes, entrepreneurs have two options.

First, others can be involved to give advice (ABSs 2 and 3). After seeking the advice of others on a regular or permanent basis, an advisory group is formed. Involving others in this way allows entrepreneurs to retain the board functions. Even if an advisory group is established, so long as entrepreneurs are the board of directors they will retain all of the balancing functions, and it is important that others understand how those functions are carried out.

Second, others can be involved as members of a board of directors (ABS 4 through 7). Involving others as directors gives the board the legal authority to make decisions (that is, to vote). This is a big step for entrepreneurs because they will be bound by the board's vote. So, in this case, entrepreneurs need to ask, Am I ready to transition control over the balancing decisions? Do I want the group to have legal decision-making power? Am I prepared to be outvoted?

Many entrepreneurs start with an ABS 4 board (all insiders) when first expanding the board of directors. Many entrepreneurs feel comfortable starting the board process with other owners, trusted managers, or family members. This structure works well if entrepreneurs want to have a real board of directors consisting of more than themselves. Expanding the board to a group means that each director is free to participate as a director without feeling the need to acquiesce to the person in power, and the individual in power allows the board process to work without pulling rank.

A problem frequently arises with ABS 4 boards when entrepreneurs don't want the board of directors to be a group. In these situations, entrepreneurs make it clear in direct or subtle ways that their vote is the only one that counts, and that they need to continue as the sole decision maker. The other board members soon come to view themselves as merely advisors, deferring to the entrepreneur. In a closely held business the board usually consist of the entrepreneur (the sole or dominant owner) and all of the other owners or senior managers. In a family business, the board often consists of a strong entrepreneur, a spouse, and their children. Whether overt or indirect, well intended or not, the result is equally damaging—and the result is a board that genuinely involves others is not created or maintained. A board that operates like this is, in reality, an ABS 3 board.

Jake's story

Jake Tominson founded Phoenix Distributions. Jake, his wife, and three children own the company equally. Two of Jake's children work in the business. Linda is marketing director and is slated to succeed Jake as president in two years. Mary works in finance and human resources. John is still in college, but Jake thinks he would be a terrific salesman if he came into the business. Jake put his wife and three children on the board.

Jake sought our help to prepare for this transition from the presidency. When we interviewed the owners, we asked them who sat on the board. "All the owners," they each replied. "So Jake doesn't make all the board decisions?" we pressed. "Oh no, we vote, and a majority vote controls," was the response. We then asked, "Has there ever been a vote that was not unanimous?" No one could recall any. We then followed up with the statement, "So the four other directors could out-vote Jake." Their responses varied from, "We would never do that." "He wouldn't accept that result." "Why would we want to do that?" to "Good heavens, no!"

All the owners of Phoenix Distribution thought they had an ABS 4 board, but in reality they had an ABS 3 board. Jake controlled the board, and at best his family provided input. We went through this exercise to help Jake and his family understand the difference between a board dominated by a single person (an ABS 1 through 3 board) and a board where the vote is truly shared (an ABS 4 through 7 board). If this distinction is not clearly made early on, the owners' will have an inaccurate understanding of how a board of directors with more than one director works.

To have an ABS 4 board, entrepreneurs must commit to shifting decision-making authority to the group and put in place policies that require the group to act as a unit when exercising that authority. For example, entrepreneurs may decide not to vote unless there is a tie. Or to always vote last. Whatever policy is adopted requires entrepreneurs to act with some restraint, since others on the board will have a natural tendency to defer to them. Likewise, the other members of the board need to clearly understand that they are expected to act as directors and not as advisors.

Jake's Story—The Conclusion

Jake saw two significant benefits in short order. His son John and his wife volunteered to lead the owners in developing the own-ers' plan and manual. Linda assumed leadership for the strategic and annual plan, which was great training for her. Mary and the other managers picked up their performance and helped Linda with the plans for the company. These developments gave Jake the opportunity to see how his family worked together as owners and how management could put together and implement plans. The second benefit Jake experienced was an increase in commit-ment and trust among his family members and senior managers because they all were finally assuming meaningful responsibility for the future of the business and learning that they could actually do it by working together.

Entrepreneurs can also empower others on the board by shar-ing control over how the owners and managers are involved in the business. Sharing this control requires that entrepreneurs commit to changing how they controlled the process in the past. Once committed to sharing control, entrepreneurs greatly enhance the probability of achieving the type of change required to achieve their goals. Having this support and assistance can be a great relief for an entrepreneur who up to this point has had to go it alone.

THE ROLE OF OUTSIDERS

Other owners often become more active in the decision-making process when the entrepreneur is ready to involve others. Part of determining the role of others is determining the role of outsiders. At some level, of course, outside input is always occurring. Business owners may read a relevant article in the *Wall Street Journal* or discuss a business issue with golfing partners. But when owners receive the outside input in a continuing advisory capacity or from members of the board of directors, this outside influence becomes less easy to dismiss.

If the owners want to involve outsiders, one question to ask is how they want to structure this input. As noted earlier, owners can choose to receive input from the outside world from an advisory group (ABSs 1 through 3) or from members of a board of directors (ABSs 5 through 7). In either case, involving outsiders requires a willingness to open up and share information with people who are not part of the inner circle.

If owners want outsiders sitting on the board of directors (ABSs 5 through 7), another question to ask deals with the composition of the board—whether it should contain a majority of insiders, a majority of outsiders, or all outsiders. This may seem like an easy question to answer because most owners choose a majority of insiders so that insiders can retain control. However, to answer this question effectively, it is important for the owners to seriously consider the advantages and disadvantages of each choice. They can start by honestly reviewing the following questions:

» Why is a board needed?

» What do we want this board to do?

» What structure will those in power accept and endorse?

The owners can then consider the characteristics that describe a majority of insiders, a majority of outsiders, or all outsiders, and determine which alternative board structure will be best depending on how they answered the preliminary questions.

MAJORITY OF INSIDERS

In ABSs 1 through 3, having a majority of insiders is not a major change because the advisors have no legal authority to make decisions. But with an ABS 5 board (majority of insiders), there is a shift in the voting power of the board, which is different from that of an ABS 4 board (all insiders).

The shift in voting power comes from the fact that an outsider has the same legal power as an insider. This means that outsiders can significantly impact board decisions. For owners who want an outside voice on the board to facilitate change, help accomplish the transition goals, or help the next generation, ABS 5 is a good board structure to use as a starting point.

With an ABS 5 board also comes an increase in the professionalism of board discussions. It becomes less acceptable for old conflicts to dominate the discussions or for the board meetings to have that private "we can do what we want" approach. Outsiders—because they are outsiders—have a way of moving discussions forward, following agendas, and suggesting that the owners address owner issues outside of the board meetings. Outsiders can and should have a positive impact on board civility and general effectiveness.

Here are some situations that may call for an ABS 5 board:

» when the board needs to be a bigger part of the decision-making process

» when the board needs more formality and structure

» when the ownership and management are "home grown" and don't have much business experience outside of the company

» when the ownership group needs help in developing an owners' plan

» when the ownership group recognizes that the company is entering into areas where the owners or managers can't provide all of the needed expertise or guidance

MAJORITY OF OUTSIDERS

With ABS 1 through 3, having a majority of outsiders is not a major change because the advisors have no legal authority to make decisions. But an ABS 6 board (majority of outsiders) has a major impact on the family business. In this structure, the outsiders control the majority of the vote, enabling them to outvote owners, family members, and managers on the board.

Some may question the value of having a majority of outsiders on the board. But having owners, managers, and family members dominate the board can, and often does, present problems. These insiders can compromise the board process and undermine the board's balancing role and its ability to truly direct by demanding that things be done the way they want regardless of the board's legal decision-making authority and its stated position that the board is to act as the balance point.

On the other hand, excluding insiders from sitting on the board has its problems. Those not on the board can undermine the board process by using their power in harmful ways, such as trying to dissolve the board, and creating havoc in the owners' and managers' groups. Again, honest discussion about the positive and negative consequences of having an ABS 6 board is necessary to make good decisions.

Situations that call for an ABS 6 board may include

» when the owners understand that they need a strong push to resolve their issues and develop an owners' plan

» when two or more owners on the board recognize they are dead-locked and force the minority owners to choose sides

» when the owners want an ABS 5 board for the wrong reasons; for example, when the owners want outside expertise to guide their company, but don't want the experts to have any power

» when the transition plan calls for the owners to lessen their control in governance and management issues

» when the next generation in a family business sits on the board, and the senior generation doesn't want the next generation to have the majority of votes

The appropriate mix of insiders and outsiders is a big issue in closely held and family businesses. It leads to the question of whether owners, managers, and family members should be on the board. Closely held and family businesses have demonstrated to us over and over again that the more owners, managers, and family members on the board, the harder it is for the board to be the balancing point between owners and managers, to be a third party with no self-interest in the results, and to maintain the boundaries between ownership and management.

Why? To begin with, the board is not perceived to be a third party. Rather, the board is seen as siding with the owners, or, more commonly, some faction within the ownership group. Or the board is perceived as siding with management or a strong president. Whichever is the case, when others think the board is not acting as a third party, its credibility and effectiveness suffer greatly.

Second, it is more difficult to maintain the boundaries between ownership and management when owners and managers are on the board. If the owners on the board act as owners and not directors, they begin to address and solve owner problems or pull rank at board meetings. They are also more likely to manage from the board seat. If these things occur, the owners' ability to speak with one voice is diminished, if not eliminated entirely, and the likelihood of management having an effective relationship with the board greatly decreases. Likewise, if managers on the board act as managers, they are less able to critique management plans and are less likely to work as a third party on assisting the owners with their owners' plan. Owners on the board who act as owners tend to become advocates for the views of owners, and managers on the board who act as managers tend to advocate management's position. This significantly compromises the board process.

Having a majority of outside directors on the board, on the other hand, tends to lessen the dominance of owners, managers, family members, and buddies on the board, but only to the extent that these outside directors exercise their authority, adhere to the board process, and act as a balance point between owners and managers. Preserving both the third-party nature of a board and the proper boundaries between owners and managers is usually easier with an ABS 6 board.

We acknowledge that entrepreneurs often resist using ABS 5 or 6 boards. Remember, each board alternative has its strengths and weaknesses, as well as risks and rewards. The appropriate board alternative depends on the goals and the comfort level of those in power. Therefore, with any board alternative, the ownership group must address certain issues.

> THE MORE OWNERS, FAMILY MEMBERS, AND MANAGERS ON THE BOARD, THE HARDER IT IS FOR THE BOARD TO BE THE BALANCE POINT BETWEEN OWNERSHIP AND MANAGEMENT, AND THE HARDER IT IS FOR THE BOARD TO BE A THIRD PARTY WITH NO INTEREST IN THE RESULTS.

ALL OUTSIDERS

In case our opinion is still not clear, let us spell it out. The more owners, family members, and managers on the board, the harder it is for the board to be the balance point between ownership and management, and the harder it is for the board to be a third party with no interest in the results. Additionally, the right structure for the board depends on why a board is needed, what the owners want the board to do, and what structure those in power will accept and endorse. Each business must wrestle with these factors and arrive at a conclusion that works best for their circumstances. There is no right or wrong answer for every business.

An ABS 7 board structure (all outsiders) offers the opportunity to mitigate the significant problems that can exist with having owners, managers, and family members on the board. For one thing, an ABS 7 board offers the best structure to address power struggles. An ABS 7 board can help entrepreneurs who are concerned about how their presence influences the involvement of other owners and managers.

In considering an ABS 7 structure, we encourage owners to weigh the advantages of all outsiders against the disadvantages; deciding when, if ever, an ABS 7 board is appropriate; and having an honest discussion about how to make an ABS 7 board work. We frequently hear that an ABS 7 is dismissed because of a particular disadvantage an owner sees. For example, owners often believe they won't be adequately informed unless they are members of the board. But it's possible to establish policies to provide owners the information they need; for example, by having the owners list all the information they want, explain how they want this information analyzed and presented, and specify how often they want the information.

Owners are also protected by creating a detailed and comprehensive owners' plan and evaluating how the company is meeting that plan. In this way the owners can monitor whether their values, needs, and goals are being met. Furthermore, owners have the responsibility (1) to find qualified and competent directors to serve on the board who will make sure the owners are informed, and (2) to evaluate the board as a whole and each director individually. Finally, owners can assemble their own group of advisors to help them understand and monitor any area of concern in the company or industry.

Some people also argue that owners lose control over their business when the board makeup consists entirely of nonowners and nonmanagers. In reality, the owners only give up control of the process and direct approval of management plans. They retain their power by working together to come up with an owners' plan and then ensuring that their values, needs, and goals are addressed. The owners' plan should identify all aspects that the owners believe need to be addressed for them to remain committed as owners for the long term and for the owners to endorse an ABS 7 board. In addition to such common needs and goals as dividends and debt levels, the owners' plan could require management to evaluate perceived risks affecting the owners or to review policies the owners believe conflict with their values. The owners retain control over the structures that establish what the owners, board, and managers are expected to do and how they will work together to accomplish their respective responsibilities. The owners also exercise control by evaluating these structures from time to time, and in particular, by assessing how the board is guiding the process.

Owners often reject an ABS 7 board, in essence, because they are unwilling, unable, or don't understand the need to perform their responsibilities as owners. Owners, either consciously or unconsciously, often avoid or shortcut the work they need to do as owners by requiring that one or more board seats be reserved for owners so they can further their interests and oversee management. This position blurs the boundaries between the owners and board because those owners-directors have a dual purpose: to serve as a director and an owner at the same time. While an owner may certainly wear more than one hat by also serving as a director and a manager, it is critical that the owner does not act with a dual purpose. In other words, an owner-director should act as an owner when part of the ownership group but as a director in board meetings.

Owners—and nonowner managers and professional advisors—resist using an ABS 7 board structure. We aren't advocating an ABS 7 board structure for every business nor are we advocating it as a goal for every business. An ABS 7 board structure, like every other alternative, has its advantages and disadvantages, and we encourage each ownership group to decide for themselves.

Situations that may call for an ABS 7 board are

» when strong owners transition from running the company and realize that they won't be able to stay out of management and don't want others to take over too quickly

» when there are two or more owners who understand from their past performance how destructive they would be to the board process if they were on the board

» when there are two or more owners—one who leads the management team and others who aren't employed in the company

» when there are two or more owners, all employed in the company—one who is president and the others report to the president

» when the next generation needs a lot of leadership development and management training, and the senior generation is not the group to provide this training and development

» when an entrepreneur unexpectedly dies and a nonactive spouse inherits the business

Owners need to decide where they want to go (the succession plan), what is the best way of getting there (the transition plan), what type of structure to start with, and how the balance point should change over time. In other words, the owners should decide where to start on this board transition plan, how far they want to transition, how fast and for what purpose or end goal. Owners must discuss which levels are appropriate and when. They always control the answers to these questions. No one board makeup is right for every business and no one structure is wrong.

9

SELECTING AND ELECTING DIRECTORS

In Chapter 8, we identified the preliminary questions that owners must answer in preparation for establishing a board:

» Why do we want a board?

» What do we want this board to do?

» What structure will those in power accept and endorse?

Although we have said this before, it is important enough to say it again. If the owners do not discuss and agree on the answers to these questions, any formal board structure will be flawed. The owners should take their time to fully and honestly answer these questions. Hurried discussion leads to a poorly performing board, disgruntled owners, or a weak commitment from those in power.

After answering these questions, and after deciding to have a balancing board, the owners need to agree on how to select and elect directors. Remember, owners who are organized, specific, and purposeful will have an easier time putting the board together.

SELECTING CANDIDATES

Clients frequently ask how to find people to sit on a board. In a sense, the answer is similar to finding a competent executive. The company develops a clear job description; identifies expectations; describes the experience, skills, and personal attributes they seek; and then puts together a plan to find candidates. Owners should answer the following questions as they prepare to select directors:

» What do we expect from the board as a whole?

» What do we expect from our individual directors?

» What personality characteristics do we want our directors to have?

» What skills and experiences do we want represented on our board?

» Who should be excluded from consideration?

» What board composition do we want?

EXPECTATIONS FOR THE BOARD

"What do we expect from the board as a whole?" addresses a fundamental need of the owners. If the owners don't agree on their expectations for the board, it is likely that some owners will be dissatisfied with the board's participation or performance. Common expectations of a balancing board include

» Acting as a third party with no self-interest in the plans or in any particular decision that is approved.

» Holding senior management and owners accountable for fulfilling their respective responsibilities. This includes asking the questions that need to be asked.

» Striving for consensus among the directors. True consensus is only reached when directors have the opportunity to present their views and concerns. Good boards encourage listening to all opinions, especially minority opinions.

» Acting as a group in all the directors do. This means that directors do not work "underground," levying criticism or forming plots. Rather, they voice disagreements and concerns inside board meetings and deal with them in a constructive manner. It also means that once a board makes a decision, all the directors support that decision and contribute to its success. This is especially true with owners, managers, or family members on the board who may not have voted in favor of the decision. If a director cannot publicly support and contribute to the success of any particular decision the board makes, the director should attempt to change that decision through more discussion. If that fails, and the director cannot support the board's decision, the director should consider resigning.

» Evaluating themselves as a board. An effective board is able to critique itself and present its findings to the owners. We understand that self-interest often trumps self-evaluation. However, an effective board acts as a third party even when evaluating itself.

» Committing to training and development. A board should never be closed to learning new skills or ways to make itself more effective. A closed board is an arrogant board. An arrogant board eventually ceases to act as a third party and, instead, directs its energy to promoting or protecting its own interests rather than the interests of the owners and business.

EXPECTATIONS FOR THE DIRECTORS

"What do we expect from our individual directors?" is also critical because each director's performance affects the overall performance of the board. If the owners don't define their expectations for director performance, the directors (or the board collectively) will create their own expectations, which may or may not be acceptable to the owners. If these expectations are not acceptable to the owners, then time, energy, and money will be spent communicating and discussing these expectations and, quite possibly, directors may have to be changed. Common expectations of directors include

» Acting as a third party with no self-interest in the plans or in any particular decision that is approved.

» Attending scheduled board meetings. Directors need to show up to demonstrate their commitment.

» Coming prepared for meetings. Many directors come to meetings unprepared. They haven't thought about the issues. They haven't read their packets before the board meeting. Their plan, apparently, is to just say what they feel. This behavior demonstrates a complete lack of respect for the owners and the board process.

» Supporting the board structure and process. This means understanding the balance point concept and agreeing to work within the parameters of the process. It also means striving to ensure that the owners' plan and management's plans are in balance, and reconciling any differences between the respective plans.

» Acting as part of the team. This means helping the board as a whole to be effective and professional. It does not mean building exclusive and private relationships with specific owners or managers.

» Acting with courage. This means saying what needs to be said, doing what needs to be done, asking the tough questions that need to be asked, and making the tough calls that need to be made.

» Showing compassion and respect when dealing with owners, managers, and the other directors.

» Being available for special meetings if necessary. Often boards call special meetings to discuss matters that can't wait for regularly scheduled meetings. A director should participate in these discussions, either in person or by electronic communication.

» Monitoring their performance as directors. This means doing an honest self-evaluation. It also means that if directors cannot meet all the owner's expectations, they should resign and not hang on until action is taken to remove them from the board.

CHARACTERISTICS OF A DIRECTOR

Above and beyond their business experience, directors bring character to the board. This is usually described as ethics, integrity, common sense, and so forth. Common characteristics of a director include

» Displaying a true interest in the company and the owners (or the family of a family business)

» Displaying a true interest in being a director

» Displaying a sense of fairness

» Displaying a willingness to listen to all sides of an issue

» Displaying curiosity and the ability to ask questions

» Voting for what they think is right, even if others disagree

» Displaying an appreciation for and understanding of the dynamics of owning and operating a business

» Making a commitment to understand the business

» Being willing and committed to putting self-interest aside

» Serving for reasons other than just for the compensation

QUALIFICATIONS OF AN INSIDE DIRECTOR

If the owners have decided on ABS 4, 5, or 6 (see Chapter 8), the qualifications of an inside director are, by and large, the characteristics of a director. The owners can use the list of characteristics above to evaluate themselves, managers, and family members. However, two other characteristics are critical when considering an insider for the board. First, the insider must have the owners' trust. Without that, accusations of bias, unfairness, or collusion may occur. If this happens, the credibility of the entire board comes into question. Second, insiders must be able to withstand any accusations of bias, unfairness, or collusion while maintaining their credibility with the owners and management.

Being an insider on a board is not always an enviable position. It is our experience that almost all business owners, presidents, CEOs, and some family members automatically assume they will be on the board. Evaluating or discussing the merits of any particular insider rarely happens. Two key ideas emphasized in this book are having good discussions before making decisions and making sure the decisions are integrated into the transition plan. Choosing insiders as directors is no exception.

When evaluating the merits of having an insider on the board, owners should consider

» their ability and commitment to act as the balance point between ownership and management

» their other-centeredness

» their acceptance by those in power

» their understanding and comfort with the risks and rewards of serving on the board

» their maturity as evaluated by their task performance in other areas of life

» their willingness to be held to the same standard as an outside director

» their willingness to accept the owners' expectations for performance

Note that insiders do not have to be on the board to participate in the board process. Managers, for example, can present information at a board meeting but not be on the board. Owners should ask themselves about the value is of having a particular individual on the board rather than just making presentations from time to time. Similarly, owners can ask to attend board meetings without being on the board. Again, the question is about the purpose of having this owner on the board rather than just visiting from time to time.

QUALIFICATIONS OF AN OUTSIDE DIRECTOR

In choosing outside directors, owners need to keep in mind answers to the questions about why the owners want a board and what they want the board to do.

For example, a majority owner wants a buddy on the board because the person "thinks, decides, and acts like me." This owner advocates strongly for this specific person. However, in answering the question "Why do we need a board?" the owners decide that they want a strong person to challenge the "homegrown" thinking of the majority owner. After reminding the majority owner why the other owners want a board, the majority owner withdraws the buddy from consideration. If this ownership group didn't go back to the basic question about why they wanted a board, it is very likely that the buddy would have been on the board and there would have been conflict in the owners' group.

The answers to the questions about why the owners want a board and what the board's functions will be lead to developing director qualifications. Sometimes the answers point to general qualifications the owners would like the directors to have. In other cases specific qualifications will emerge. As a starting point, each outside director should have at least one of the following qualifications:

» a specific area of expertise; examples include skills such as strategic planning, financing, accounting, marketing, sales, human resources, R&D, and so forth

» a specific experience; examples include experience in diversifying, acquiring, or replicating a business; serving as a director in a family business that has gone through a succession plan; or serving as a director in a related business that has gone through a growth plan like the one the owners expect their company will go through

» a specific image; examples include experience as a community leader, an industry expert, or a networking specialist

EXCLUDING INDIVIDUALS FROM CONSIDERATION

Professional advisors should not serve on boards of directors. Many businesses place their advisors on their board because the advisors have a good relationship and history with the company or the owners. Owners also choose them because they are regarded as trusted advisors. However, there are many reasons not to have them on the board.

» Professional advisors often represent or serve specific owners or managers; for example, the principal owner's personal attorney or accountant. Asking professional advisors to be a third party serving the best interests of all the owners, the managers, and company may be hard—if not impossible—for them to do. In some cases, it may be a direct conflict of interest.

» Professional advisors may have a bias, conscious or unconscious, against specific owners after years of working with one owner. This also compromises their ability to act as a third party.

» Professional advisors may have intimate knowledge about one or more of the owners that they cannot ignore when making decisions.

» Professional advisors may prevent the board from effectively evaluating plans because of their board membership. For example, a company's outside CPA served on the board. The company considered buying a new building and needed to do a cost-benefit analysis. The CPA offered his firm, and the company accepted. When it came time for the board to discuss and evaluate the analysis, the person on the board with the best financial expertise to evaluate the analysis was the one who put the analysis together. The board accepted the analysis. This director was not a third-party evaluator of his own analysis. In essence, he deprived the board of the ability to effectively evaluate the plan.

» Professional advisors may not have the expertise that is needed even though they may have exposure in many different areas. For example, the business attorney in a company with significant intellectual property issues may understand the business but may not be proficient in intellectual property law. Rather than getting a specialist, the board defers to the attorney on all legal matters. The attorney may be caught between keeping the work and recommending that the board go to a specialist.

Personal friends or buddies of senior managers or owners should not serve on the board of directors. These individuals may have the attributes and qualifications of a good director. They may even be fair-minded people with good intentions. However, with few exceptions, they will not be able to act as third parties. They will, with few exceptions, align with their friends.

Finally, the company's banker, creditors, customers, and competitors should not serve on the board of directors. This group of potential directors will, with rare exceptions, be more concerned with their own needs and goals rather than the needs and goals of the owners and the business.

DETERMINING BOARD COMPOSITION

"What structure will those in power accept and endorse?" The answer to this question consists of several subtopics that all relate to the board's structural arrangements.

SIZE OF THE BOARD

There is no rule of thumb for board size. The closest thing to a rule would be having an odd number of directors to prevent tie votes. But this is not required.

The discussion on size of a board should always begin with a review of the answers to the fundamental questions presented earlier. It should then focus on three points.

1. How many owners, managers, and family members will be on the board? Once the owners have decided on the board structure they want, the options are often reduced. For example, in an ABS 6 structure (where outsiders are the majority), the number of insiders will be less than the number of outsiders. So if three insiders will be on the board, the board must have at least seven directors (three insiders and at least four outsiders). In an ABS 5 structure (where insiders are the majority), the board must have at least five directors (the three insiders and as many as two outsiders).

2. What qualifications and expertise do the directors need? The qualifications the owners want often point to a specific size. For example, if a company is very sophisticated in all areas of its business and industry, but lacks expertise in expansion and growth, the owners may decide they need an expansion specialist and someone who has helped another business grow. In this case, the owners need two outsiders.

3. What size board will those in power accept and work with? As with any critical decisions the owners make, the commitment of those in power is necessary for any size board to work.

We are often asked about the optimal size board to facilitate good discussions among all members. In our experience, groups larger than seven members have a harder time building cohesiveness and getting all participants involved. But there are no absolutes, and the answer for you depends on how you answer the fundamental questions for having a board.

TERMS AND TERM LIMITS OF THE DIRECTORS

Terms and term limits are decisions that depend on the board's purpose and expectations. We make no generalizations, but we can describe how owners have looked at these issues.

Owners tend to establish specific terms in the following situations: when owners feel they are just beginning the board process and want the most flexibility in determining its membership, when owners may not be effective as board members, and when family members use their board experience as a learning process. Owners tend to elect directors for an unlimited term (no departure date) when they understand that the majority owner (or those in power) wants an ABS 4 board consisting of owners, key managers, and family members and sees no reason to change it in the future. Sometimes owners just ask others to be on their board; terms and term limits are never discussed. It is another thing that entrepreneurs just do.

Terms are typically one, two, or three years in duration. Two- or three-year durations are preferred because it takes time for directors to learn how to act as the balance point. Longer terms also reflect a commitment of the owners to the board process. Terms of one year force the owners to reevaluate the effectiveness of directors or make it easier for the owners to change directors without having to evaluate them and confront any real issues. One-year terms may also reflect a lack of commitment to the board process.

Many companies stagger terms so not all directors are up for reelection in any one year. For example, in a case of five directors, one may have a two-year term, two may have a three-year term, and two may have a four-year term. Staggered terms are often used in an attempt to preserve the board's continuity; it is often the case that the preservation of the balancing board process and training of directors are easier if new directors are phased in gradually.

Term limits restrict the number of years or terms that a director may serve on the board. Term limits are usually specified when

» owners know that they want to add new perspectives to the board in the future to meet their changing needs and goals or those of the company

» owners feel the current board is getting stale

» owners determine that lifetime membership is not a good thing

» owners want family members to have future opportunities to serve on the board

» there are more family members who want to serve than there are board seats

Term limits are not recommended when the majority owner (or those in power) wants an ABS 4 board consisting of owners, key managers, and family members and sees no reason to change it in the future.

Term limits are typically three to five terms depending on the length of the term. Each position on the board does not have to have the same term limits. Again, it depends on the owners' goals and needs and the level of continuity needed to establish an effective balance point.

SELECTING DIRECTORS

We suggest the owners agree to follow a specific process in selecting directors to serve on their board. The following steps outline a process that works well, but ownership groups should modify the process to suit their particular situations.

STEP 1: IDENTIFYING POTENTIAL CANDIDATES

The first step in selecting directors is to agree on a process to identify potential candidates. One process that works well is for the owners to establish a search committee to find potential candidates. This committee presents the owners with a list of individuals whom the committee believes meet the selection criteria. The owners will then review the list and remove any names representing a conflict of interest or a conflict with an owner and otherwise narrow the list to the requested number. The remaining names become the list of candidates.

We are repeatedly asked where to find candidates. Our best answer: by networking. We ask the search committee to prepare an inquiry letter briefly describing the skills, experience, and personal characteristics that the owners are looking for, as well as describing the board process and the company. The committee sends the inquiry letter to contacts of the owners and company who may know of the type of people described in the letter. Often these referral sources include the company's attorney, accountant, and other key service providers, along with respected friends and personal services providers for one or more of the company's owners, directors, and managers. Remember, you are not looking at these referral sources as potential candidates themselves—and don't be shy in telling them so. Let them know that you are asking if they know of anyone who meets the criteria and who they believe would be a good director. Search firms can also help in this process. Appendix 9.1 presents a sample letter for seeking referral for an outside director.

STEP 2: SELECTING ACTUAL CANDIDATES

The owners then decide who will meet with the potential candidates—all the owners or a committee representing the owners.

The owners (or a selection committee) select one or more individuals to initially contact each of the potential candidates. The purpose of the call is to explain what the owners are doing, how the candidate's name surfaced, and to ascertain whether the candidate is interested in serving as a director. If yes, an interview is scheduled with each potential candidate.

The owners (or the selection committee) put together a prospective packet to give to candidates before their interviews. The packet should contain the following items (dictated by what information the owners are comfortable in sharing):

» a statement of why the owners want a board, what the owners want the board to do, and how the board is to work with owners and managers

» the type of board structure the owners have identified

» the owners' expectations for the board and directors

» the desired skills, experience, and personal characteristics the owners are seeking

» the owners' plan

» a summary of the company

» a summary balance sheet, income statement (actual and projected), and a three-to-five year historical financial profile

» any current strategic and annual plans

» a description of the owners and their stock percentages

» any prior decisions about director compensation and limitation of liability

» a letter explaining why the owners are considering this person

The purpose for this packet is to give candidates an idea of whether they will make a good director. The packet will also let candidates know how well the ownership group is developed, organized, and functional. The packet also reminds the owners of the type of person they are looking for to serve as a director.

Is it appropriate to ask candidates to sign a confidentiality statement before sending them the packet? Owners address their concerns about confidentiality in many different ways. Generally the solutions fall in one of three categories. First, owners contact the referral source and obtain more information about the candidate's trustworthiness. Second, the scope and depth of what is included in the packet is narrowed to reduce the owners' confidentiality concerns. Finally, if reasonable, owners ask candidates to sign a confidentiality agreement. The best solution depends on the owners, the particular candidate, and the circumstances. Owners need to be reasonable, remembering that most (if not all) of the potential candidates have no interest in benefiting themselves with information you give them. And, of course, your concerns about confidentiality are natural as you begin to open the company to outsiders, but these outsiders will eventually need to know a lot more than what is in the packet you give them.

Sometimes the search committee wants additional information before meeting with a candidate. If so, they can request that candidates send a résumé and cover letter. This is not always a good idea, though. Checking with the referral source will help determine whether or not this request is appropriate. If so, we think a good résumé includes a candidate's business experience, board experience, and special skills as a director. A good cover letter addresses why the candidate wants to serve on boards, includes the candidate's philosophy of what makes a good board, and describes situations in which the candidate could be helpful as a director.

During the interview, owners evaluate the candidates and make sure the candidates understand their role and what is expected of them.

The owners should explain the selection process and timeline. Worksheet 9.1 provides a list of questions to help prepare for the interview.

After interviewing the candidates, those owners involved should present their recommendations to the entire owner group. Owners need to decide how many candidates they want and what they decide will depend on the circumstances at the time. For example, with three open slots to fill on the board, does the search committee have to find three candidates or more than three to give the owners a choice? Most owners and family members we work with identify one potential candidate for each opening, knowing they can go back to the list of names if a potential candidate withdraws or is removed from consideration for any reason.

The owners who can vote then elect the directors, specify their terms, and then notify all candidates of their decision. Remember, there is usually no rush to put a board together. Owners should not feel pressured to settle for candidates because of an artificial deadline.

COMPENSATION FOR DIRECTORS

Directors should be paid. Payment tells directors their participation is valued. The fees reflect how seriously the owners take the board's role and the directors' responsibilities. Payment also makes it easier to hold directors accountable as the balance point between ownership and management.

Nonpayment, on the other hand, tells directors their involvement is not valued and their responsibilities are more informal or ad hoc. It makes a statement about the owners' commitment to the board process. Also, if someone is willing to serve on the board as a volunteer, it may indicate that the director is going to advise and not direct, or that they want to be an agent of an individual owner or manager.

In closely held and family businesses, the owners generally determine the type and amount of pay with input from the directors (and management if there are budget issues). Legally, though, the board can determine its own compensation if the owners give them this authority and it is not considered a conflict of interest. Here are some guidelines to consider in determining the type and amount of compensation to pay directors of closely held and family businesses.

TYPE OF PAY

The company pays directors' fees—payments for meeting time, preparation time, and all reasonable expenses. The most common forms of director fees are a yearly amount (retainer), an hourly or daily amount, a per-meeting amount, or a combination of these three. Each of these methods works. Two factors determine which method is best: the amount of work the owners expect each director to do and the nature of the work.

If you expect the director to do a lot of work, an hourly rate is preferable. If you expect a set amount of work (for example: four board meetings per year, two committee meetings a year, and one hour of preparation time for each hour of meeting time), consider either an annual retainer or a standard meeting fee.

If the work is especially sensitive to maintain business and family integrity, an hourly rate is preferable, because the director will be involved in more sensitive work. If you don't expect the work to be particularly sensitive to the owners, managers, or family members, consider either an annual retainer or a standard meeting fee.

The idea is not to get the best directors for the lowest price, nor is it to pay as little as you can. Remember, these are individuals you have chosen to fulfill the critical role of being the balance point between ownership and management.

Other ways to compensate directors include stock or stock options, phantom stock (a contract right to receive payments based on the changing value of the actual stock), life insurance or other types of insurance, and fringe benefits. Each of these options comes with potential problems. In a closely held or family business, offering stock, stock options, or phantom stock plans increases the chance that a director will be motivated to make short-term decisions that maximize profit or otherwise make decisions that are in line with the director's personal needs. If this occurs, the director will find it hard to act as a third party with no self-interest in any particular plan or result. In a family business, stock or stock options are usually contrary to the long-term goal of keeping ownership in the family. Finally, company liquidity issues arise when giving directors stock in a closely held and family business. In this situation, the company generally has to make available the cash needed to buy shares so liquidity decisions the directors make can affect the business. These liquidity issues have two potentially significant impacts. First, the company's plans must include the repurchase of shares owned by directors. Second, as stated above, care is warranted to ensure that directors don't vote in favor of plans that include the retirement of their shares.

Offering insurance or other perks tends to motivate directors to stay on the board as long as possible, thereby potentially extending their term beyond what might be appropriate. This also inhibits directors from being a third party with no self interest in any particular plan or result.

The essential question to ask when determining the method of compensation is how the type of compensation might affect the director's ability to act independently. The answer to this question should point you to the most appropriate payment method.

AMOUNT OF PAY

The question of how much to pay a director is a complicated one. Owners need to keep in mind that this is not a place to cut corners. Compensation should always cover reasonable expenses directors incur to attend meetings. This includes reimbursement for mileage (if driving) or airfare (if flying). If directors come from out of town, lodging and meals should be covered. Compensation should also cover preparation time as well as meeting time. Ultimately, the amount of compensation is a combination of the value owners and managers believe they are getting, what the company can afford at the time, and the directors' level of satisfaction in continuing to act as the balance point.

Here are some of the factors affecting the compensation decision:

» Will the board be an advisory board or a board of directors? The pay for advisory board members should be less than that for directors because the members are only advising. We think the compensation for advisors should be 50 percent or less than what a director receives.

» What do you want the directors to do?

» How many board meetings and committee meetings will there be each year?

» Are there likely to be special meetings?

» How much time will a director need to get ready for a meeting?

» How many training sessions will the directors be expected to attend?

» What are the risks involved in being a director? Are there any circumstances and challenges affecting that risk? For example, the size of the company might have an impact. The larger the company, the more is at stake and the more the directors should be paid. Other examples include the likelihood of mergers and acquisitions, succession challenges, and inexperienced management. In each case, directors should receive higher pay.

» What are the directors' qualifications? The more qualified the directors are, the more they will expect to be paid. Experience can be a factor in paying more for a director but often experience doesn't guarantee that they are qualified.

» What are the directors' roles and responsibilities? For example, the chairperson usually has significantly more responsibilities and should receive higher pay. This is true for committee chair-persons too.

» What business possibilities or financing might come to the company through the directors?

» How much can the company afford?

After reviewing the factors involved in determining compensation, figure out what is reasonable compensation for the work expected of the directors and figure out what you can afford. Here are some ways to help determine the amount of director compensation.

» Ascertain the compensation of directors on other boards of comparable companies. This information can be obtained by talking to other business owners and directors and from surveys that are available to the public.

» Discuss compensation with candidates (before they are elected) and your directors (after they are elected). Ask them what they consider reasonable compensation to be, particularly after they have served on the board for a while. We typically hear directors comment that serving on a board that functions as a balance point is much different than service on other boards of directors.

» Base the compensation on the compensation of the company's president or CEO. To do this, begin by determining a base rate. A base "day" rate is determined by dividing the CEO's or president's base compensation (excluding bonuses and perks) by the number of days they work. For example, if the president receives an annual salary of $200,000 and works 250 days per year, the base day rate is $800. A base "hourly" rate is determined by dividing the CEO's or president's base compensation (excluding bonuses and perks) by the number of hours they work. For example, if the CEO receives $200,000 and works 2000 hours, the base hourly rate is $100.

» Use the base rate to determine fees for directors based on the projected work involved. For example, if you expect to have six meetings a year (four board meetings and two committee meetings), with each meeting lasting a half day, and directors preparing one hour for each hour of meeting time, then the resulting fee would be $4,800 (meeting rate of $800 x 6 days [each "day" = 4 hours of meeting time + 4 hours of preparation time] or hourly rate of $100 x 8 hours [meeting and preparation time] x 6 meetings). This amount is the director's fee, not including expenses. This method works well unless the CEO is grossly overpaid or underpaid. As always, use your best judgment when following this method.

» Base directors' fees on either a per-meeting rate or a retainer (an annual amount paid in a lump sum or more frequent, smaller amounts). Directors can receive extra compensation if they are asked to contribute more than initially expected. The extra amount can be paid by the hour, day, or meeting using the appropriate formula.

PAYMENT FOR INSIDERS

The final decision the owners need to make is whether inside directors should receive as much as outside directors or even be paid at all. Some say no—if the insiders are clearly employed at the company. They say that these insiders already receive regular payments.

We disagree. When insiders are directors, they are supposed to act independently. They are supposed to be the balance point between ownership and management. They are not supposed to act as owners or managers. They are supposed to provide the duties of care, loyalty, and management oversight. Paying insiders separately for these duties holds them accountable to act like directors and to direct in the same way as the outsiders do. It lets them know, in no uncertain terms, the expectations the owners have of them.

SUMMARY

All the preparation you do will pay off. You will structure a board to meet the owners' goals and current needs. You will clearly know the kind of person you are looking for and why. You will be able to communicate your goals, needs, and expectations to prospective board members. And the owners' group will speak with one voice.

10

CONDUCTING EFFECTIVE BOARD MEETINGS

K nowing the board's purpose, determining its best structure, understanding what it is going to do, and choosing appropriate directors will give you peace of mind and a solid plan to go forward. But that isn't enough to ensure that your board will be effective. As you have seen in Chapters 1 through 8, having a balancing board is complex. For you and the other owners, it requires having

» *commitment,* not compliance. Those in power must really understand what having a balancing board means to their business and commit to it. It also means that those not in power take part in the discussions so they support having a balancing board and don't feel forced into it.

» *clarity,* not confusion. Owners are clear about why they want a board, what they want the board to do, and how they want the board to work with owners and managers. No one should have to guess.

» *courage,* not cowardice. Owners must be resolved to stay the course even if some of the issues get dicey or some of the decisions seem questionable.

As long as the owners' values, needs, and goals are clear and the board follows the process established by the owners, the board should have the authority to make tough decisions. Owners who take authority back from the board (or hint at doing so) just because they don't get their way on an issue demonstrate a lack of leadership that will affect the success of the business and the integrity of the entire owners' group.

This chapter discusses how to ensure that board meetings will be effective. This is the nuts-and-bolts chapter. In it, we will discuss the four criteria for having effective board meetings:

» developing the role of the chairperson (and those of other leadership positions on the board)

» preparing agendas

» conducting meetings

» training directors

DEVELOPING THE ROLE OF THE CHAIR

The board chairperson has a critical role in the effectiveness of a balancing board. The chairperson's three main responsibilities are

» to act as liaison between the board and the owners and managers

» to guide the board in fulfilling its responsibilities

» to prepare for, preside over, and facilitate board meetings

We will separate the chairperson's duties by describing what they do before, during, and after a board meeting. As you will see, the chairperson is not an honorary position nor should it automatically be assigned to the owner with the most shares. This position requires time, patience, communication skills, and a great deal of courage.

CHAIR'S DUTIES BEFORE A MEETING

Before a board meeting, the chairperson prepares the agenda. This involves working with the CEO well before the meeting to ensure a well-thought-out and timely agenda. This may also require the chairperson to check with the owners, particularly when the board is evaluating the owners' plan. Preparing the agenda also involves ensuring that the agenda is designed to help the board to direct and not manage.

For example, instead of just adding to the agenda the topic of deciding whether a large customer should get a 10 percent volume discount, the chairperson should ascertain from the CEO whether this issue has a significant financial or strategic aspect, or greatly affects the completion of the annual plan or the owners' plan. If it doesn't, the chairperson should probably tell the CEO to make the decision and perhaps include it in a report to the board. If it does, the chairperson should put the item on the agenda. We discuss preparing the agenda in much more detail below.

The chairperson prepares the resolutions to be voted on at the meeting and sends those resolutions to the directors so they know what is expected of them at the meeting. These resolutions should be sent out as early as possible to allow for director feedback, requests for clarification, objections, and accuracy checks.

The chairperson prepares or approves packets of information to be sent to the directors well before the meeting. Directors need this information early so they have ample time to prepare for the meeting. All too often, directors will tell us that they get the information the day before the meeting.

The chairperson seeks input from the directors about the information they received. For example, they may need clarification about financial items and would like their questions addressed at the meeting. This helps focus the discussion so the time spent at the board meeting is controlled and productive. Often a board spends most of its time on financial statements, which look backward, and not as much time discussing items that look forward.

The chairperson also makes arrangements for the meeting (location, food, A/V equipment, etc.), and ensures that the accommodations are comfortable and conducive to the meeting. The chairperson determines who should and should not attend the board meeting. The chairperson often works with the CEO or owners to make such decisions.

CHAIR'S DUTIES AT THE MEETING

Chairpersons facilitate the meeting. They understand and use a director's unique skills, ensure that all directors have the opportunity to speak, and draw out those who are quiet. They ensure that questions are asked and answered, and they get the minority opinion on the table. They help create a "safe" environment where directors are not concerned about privacy or confidentiality issues. They ensure that everyone is clear about the board's role as directing or advising, and step in when the board starts managing. They record decisions or directions made by the board. And they also strive to make the meetings enjoyable.

Chairpersons also ensure that the board moves through the agenda with efficiency and flexibility and keep track of the time. They call for votes on written motions and resolutions and make sure that all directors know exactly what they are voting on. They identify issues that are surfacing and need to be addressed (or that underlie the issue at hand), and determine how the board should respond to these other issues. They lead the directors in representing and promoting owners' values and give feedback to directors who aren't acting in accordance with the owners' values. Above all, chairpersons lead the directors to act as the balance point, consistent with the owners' manual, and ensure that the board owns the process and not the results.

CHAIR'S DUTIES AFTER THE MEETING

After the board meeting, chairpersons follow up on issues that arose in the meeting but were tabled, glossed over, or inferred. They list issues to talk about at the next meeting and provide that list to the CEO or owners, as appropriate, for consideration. They evaluate how the meeting went and what changes might be necessary. They monitor the progress of the owners' plan and management's plans. They review the minutes of the meeting, make corrections, and ensure that the board minutes are distributed.

Chairpersons maintain the policies and procedures that help the board and directors fulfill their responsibilities. The policies and procedures should be in writing and included either in the owners' manual or a board manual.

Chairpersons know what is going on with the owners and work at maintaining a good relationship with all owners and appropriate family members. They know what is going on with the CEO or president and work at maintaining a good relationship with the senior managers. And they regularly monitor whether they, as well as the rest of the directors, are acting independently.

To chair a balancing board requires dedication and commitment. It requires chairpersons to learn how the owners want the board to operate and then teach other directors how to act as a balance point. Chairpersons must be guided by the owners' definition of the board arrangement and effectiveness, as well as their own sense of excellence and fairness. They must walk the fine line between having more detail or fewer details, staying on task or deviating from the agenda, advising or directing, confronting or letting go, continuing discussion or tabling a topic, and so forth. The chairperson's role is not about power. It is about accountability and service. Pick your chairperson well.

THE ENTREPRENEUR AS THE CHAIR

Some entrepreneurs want to be the chairperson of the board but don't want to take on all the duties of that position. They want to set meeting agendas, but they don't want to prepare the agenda or do any of the paperwork for it beforehand. During the meeting, they want to concentrate on getting their points across, but they don't want to facilitate discussion. After the meeting, they are interested in following up on any issues important to them, but they don't want to do the paperwork or work with specific board members. These examples are typical of entrepreneurs in general and in practice will be consistent with their style.

When the entrepreneur wants to be the chair, but doesn't want to do the work, the role of facilitator and administrator can be given to another member of the board. This other member, though not the chair, could be considered a vice-chair, the meeting chair, the facilitator, or just the director with additional responsibilities. Someone must handle facilitating and administrating duties—but it doesn't have to be the chair.

BOARD SECRETARY

The secretary of the board may or may not be the secretary of the company. They are two different roles. One is an officer of the corporation, and the other is a board duty assigned by the owners, the chairperson, or the board. The secretary of the board takes the minutes of the meetings and submits them to the chair, drafts resolutions, sends notices to directors, and performs other administrative functions as the board or chairperson may determine. If the secretary of the board is also the secretary of the corporation, the secretary certifies proceedings and documents and maintains the corporation's minutes book. The secretary of the board attends the board meetings and reads the resolutions to be voted on. Unless the secretary is a director, the secretary does not participate in discussions or voting.

COMMITTEES

A committee is a group of volunteers that the board asks to perform specific tasks outside of the board meeting. Typically, a committee consists of all directors, but that doesn't need to be the case. A committee usually reports to the board and helps the board make decisions, although the board can delegate decision making to the committee.

Committees are an effective way to divide the work of the board among the directors (and perhaps others). Typical committees include an audit, review, or finance committee; management evaluation, compensation, hiring, or human resource committee; board evaluation committee; and a nominating committee. Other committees are formed as needed and exist as long as they are needed.

If a board establishes committees, most of the arrangements described in this book relating to the effectiveness of the board will also apply to committees. Remember, committees' effectiveness promotes or distracts from the board's effectiveness. Here are some observations that will help you develop and maintain an effective board committee arrangement, and thereby an effective board.

» The owners' manual should define why each committee is necessary, what each committee does, how each committee relates to the board and how the board relates to each committee, and the general structure and composition of each committee.

» The board's calendar should include tasks of each committee.

» Each committee should meet and determine how it needs to organize itself to accomplish its responsibilities.

» Each committee should elect a chairperson or leader to carry out functions similar to the board chair. Committees are extensions of the board. As such, each committee should view itself as operating as the balance point. Each committee should realize that it is responsible for the process and not for solving owner problems or management problems.

» Each committee should operate independently, acting as a third party and being other-centered.

PREPARING AGENDAS

The quality of meeting agendas directly relate to the effectiveness of the meeting. If the agenda is confusing, unclear, vague, and unfocused, the meeting likely will suffer. The time and effort spent preparing a clear, relevant, and focused agenda pays off significantly in relation to the meeting's outcomes.

An agenda for a board meeting should include

» a list of topics in the order they are to be discussed (including those items that are part of every board meeting)

» a short description of each agenda item and what action is expected from the board (initial discussion, brainstorming, advising, voting, etc.)

» a summary of key questions or issues for each agenda item

» the estimated time for discussion and action on each agenda item

» a list of guests attending the meeting for the item and an explanation of why they are coming

TOPICS FOR EACH MEETING

The board should develop an agenda form listing topics to be included at each board meeting, as well as topics that occur during fixed times throughout the fiscal year (determined by referring to the board calendar). The topics should also reflect unforeseen circumstances requiring board involvement. These items typically appear on the agenda of most every board meeting:

1. The directors check-in and general announcements.

2. Minutes from the last board meeting.

3. The CEO's summary report describing the general status of the business, and including significant, unanticipated events—both positive and negative—that affect the owners' plan or management's plans, and any changes to or ideas about management's plans.

4. Reports from specific departments summarizing accomplishments since the last board meeting and anticipating activities through the next period as the board may request or require.

5. A summary of assignments and due dates before the next board meeting.

6. The financials, including the balance sheet, profit and loss statements, budget analysis year-to-date, budget analysis against the plans, an explanation of any significant changes to any plans, and the chief financial officer's summary explanation. A one-page summary of the company's vital signs is helpful and tends to keep the discussions at the appropriate level.

7. A check-out, review of the next meeting date, an overview of the general focus for the next meeting, and a short evaluation of the current meeting. Sometimes the meeting is followed by social time.

Appendix 10.1 presents a sample board meeting agenda that follows this general outline. Appendix 10.2 presents another format based on the three primary groups: owners, managers, and board. Appendix 10.3 explains the agenda, and may be helpful to include with the board packet to help train your directors.

We cannot overstate the importance of having the agenda clearly state what action the board is expected to take regarding each of the substantive agenda items. Actions can be generally divided into four categories: directing, advising, information gathering, and reviewing. We discuss each of these items in more detail below.

DIRECTING

These are key issues facing the business where management's solution requires approval from the board. Such issues require the board to act as a balance point.

> For example, management learns that its primary competitor wants to buy a patent for a proprietary product that could significantly improve the quality of its manufactured goods and, in turn, increase its competitive advantage. The management team believes it can make a bid for the patent and secure its purchase because the company's distribution channels offer greater potential return for the patent owners. However, buying the patent would require the company to match the competitor's price and, more significantly, to accelerate the projected conversion of its manufacturing process by five years in order to meet expected demand. This could happen if the company increases its debt and reduces distributions to owners. The change would also result in revamping the company's workforce because many of the long-term employees would not make the shift to the new manufacturing processes. Bottom line, the CEO doesn't believe the company could slowly convert; the company has to do it now.

> The board agenda explains the issue and management's proposed solution. It also summarizes the approval requested from the board. At the meeting, the CEO explains how the solution affects the owners' plan, management's strategic and annual plans, and the company as a whole. The board evaluates the solution to see whether the CEO remains true to the owners' values, needs, and goals; stays on plan; and has a realistic implementation plan. If management's plan changes the owners' plan, the board also ascertains whether the owners should become involved.

This process accomplishes three things: (1) it lets senior management manage and the directors direct; (2) it ensures that the owners' plan and values are in the forefront of the CEO's mind; and (3) it gives the board the opportunity to evaluate the CEO.

We suggest that each board agenda include at least one item requiring the board to direct either owners or managers. This reminds the directors that their primary responsibility is to act as the balance point, and own the process, not the result. It also reminds the owners and managers that they are to solve problems and come to board meetings with solutions that the board can evaluate.

ADVISING

At certain times, the CEO and management team want advice from the directors on key issues facing the business. CEOs may bring concerns or issues to the board before presenting them to their management team. Or they may just want to hear from directors having unique skills or experiences. Also, owners may want advice from directors from time to time. We recommend that items requiring the board to advise be separately noted on the agenda to avoid lumping them in with matters where the board directs. This clarifies the difference between advising and directing. It also lets CEOs know that they can come to the board for help before presenting solutions to problems or issues.

INFORMATION GATHERING

The board may want senior management to report on certain matters that will help the board better understand some specific part of the business. Examples are competitive analyses, updates on environmental or government regulations, and next-generation leadership development.

REVIEWING

The board also may want to regularly or periodically review specific items such as the financial results and other indices that inform the directors about management's and the company's performance according to plans. The board needs to monitor the company's financial situation and progress. And the CEO needs to know that the board is watching the numbers and assessing achievement of the plans.

Two common problems arise for boards when reviewing these types of matters. First, boards often spend too much time on the numbers. For many boards, reviewing financial statements takes up most of the board meeting. When boards spend too much time on financial matters, the CEO perceives that to be the only real priority and begins to manage the company differently. If this happens, the original purpose of the board or the owners' values may be compromised.

Second, boards often drive their review down to the smallest detail. For example, a board begins discussing the rising costs of general administration and ends up discussing whether the purchasing manager is spending too much money on long-distance phone calls. When boards focus on too much financial detail, they lower the quality of their discussions. They usually begin to offer advice, or worse, to manage. This also tells CEOs that they won't have as much discretion in running the company as they hoped, or lets them know that they don't have the board's trust.

These consequences all seriously damage the relationship between the board and management, and generally cause ongoing conflicts. A fine line exists between overseeing the finances and managing the finances. That is why the board should make that distinction up front.

To deal with these concerns, senior management can provide relevant financial information to the board chairperson before the board meeting. The chairperson sends this information to the directors before the meeting and asks them what financial items they want to discuss at the meeting and why. The chairperson then determines the level of detail necessary. Only those financial items directors identify before the meeting are discussed. Again, the goal is not to get bogged down in the financial detail, but rather to focus on key issues as they relate to the company going forward, and to require directors and management to be prepared.

Here are some suggestions for preparing board meeting agendas.

» Prepare an agenda form including topics that need to be on each meeting agenda. A form can remind those putting together the agenda to think about what might be needed at the meeting in order for the board to act as the balance point and otherwise fulfill its responsibilities.

» Specify the time allotted for each agenda topic. This helps the chairperson manage the discussion and keep the directors on track.

» Identify for each topic what action, if any, is expected from the board. For example, a report may require no action from the board. Some topics might require the board to advise, and other topics might require the board to direct.

» Use Worksheets 6.1 and 6.3 (discussed in Chapter 6) to help owners and managers determine what to present and how to present it to help directors act as the balance point when evaluating that particular presenter's information.

SENDING OUT INFORMATION

Directors should receive the meeting information packet at least ten days before the meeting's date because owners expect directors to be prepared for the board meeting. To do this, directors need to review the information in advance. It is reasonable to expect directors to set aside some period of time prior to each board meeting to review the information sent out in advance, but it is unreasonable to expect them to set aside the afternoon or evening prior to the meeting for review. Giving directors as much time as is reasonably possible to review the information prior to the meeting shows respect for their service. The information sent to directors should include at least the following:

» the meeting agenda

» resolutions to be reviewed and voted on at the meeting

» minutes of the prior meeting (if not already sent)

» supporting material related to the agenda items, including the worksheets described above

CONDUCTING MEETINGS

With an agenda in hand that clearly states the goal for each item and the expectations about how the board will allot its time, the chairperson is prepared to conduct the meeting. The skills of conducting a good board meeting are similar to the skills of conducting any meeting. A good chairperson keeps the board on task; makes sure meetings begin and end on time, and knows when to veer off the agenda and when to cut off nonrelated discussion. A good chairperson watches for people who dominate the discussions; understands and deals with directors who give ultimatums or use power plays (for example, a director who says "I'm going to leave the board if you don't vote my way"); and understands personal leadership styles, strengths, and weaknesses (for example, chairpersons who let people talk incessantly or are overly dominating need to be aware of and guard against such tendencies).

Additionally, a good chairperson

» Ensures that the board spends most of its time directing; that it doesn't manage; and when it advises, it knows that it is doing so.

» Monitors the level of detail. Often boards like to dig into the smallest details (as they do when they are managing). The chairperson understands there are times for great detail but they should be purposeful and directed, and makes that judgment call.

» Encourages those with minority viewpoints to speak out. Sometimes this is hard when the chairperson supports the majority viewpoint.

» Watches for personal biases.

» Decides what is a confidential discussion and when it should be kept out of the minutes.

» Understands that it is difficult to be a facilitator and a participant. As participants, chairpersons may become passionate about a subject or frustrated with other board members who don't share their opinions. If chairpersons become consumed by the discussion, they cannot facilitate the meeting. As facilitators, chairpersons may get caught up in clock watching, detail watching, encouraging minority opinions, and so forth, and not fully express themselves. If chairpersons become consumed by facilitation, they will not participate effectively. This dilemma is often the hardest part of being a chairperson. Good chairpersons must be able to be a participant-facilitator, evaluate their own behavior, be a contributing member, and generally control the meeting.

Chairpersons develop their own style in managing a meeting. It is helpful, however, to have some consistency in managing the discussion, particularly when making decisions where differences exist among the directors. Appendix 10.4 provides a list of semiformal procedures that can be used to help run a meeting.

MEETING MINUTES

Minutes should be taken at each board meeting. The chairperson ensures that someone takes the minutes, completes them after the meeting, and sends them to the appropriate parties. The chairperson can assign a permanent secretary among the directors, rotate the duty among all directors, or bring in someone to take the minutes. Employees of the company (excluding owners and family members) should not be board secretaries. (Even a loyal employee with twenty years of service who "knows everything anyway" should not be the secretary of the board.) The employees should not know details of confidential and sensitive information that directors discuss. Examples of such discussions include closing a plant, terminating an officer of the corporation, determining owner distributions, and changes to the owners' plan.

What the minutes should contain is based on the owners' need for information. If the owners have no opinion on the matter, the chairperson should decide what goes in the minutes and the level of detail. Minutes typically contain the following information:

- » Who was at the meeting, including when people arrive and leave.

- » Where the meeting was held.

- » When the meeting started and ended.

- » Notice of the meeting.

- » All decisions by the board, including who made the motion, who seconded it, and how the individual directors voted (especially if there are any dissenting votes).

- » A summary of the discussions and the reasons underlying the actions taken. This is always a judgment call. The minutes need to maintain a balance between recording enough information to explain the board's decisions to the owners and recording every utterance. Additionally, some of what goes on in a board meeting is confidential and should stay that way.

- » Information about the next meeting, including those matters to be addressed at the next meeting.

» A list of the assignments including who will do them, by when, and what the person should do with the assignment once completed.

Appendix 10.5 presents a form that you can follow when writing up meeting minutes. The agenda can serve as a good format for the content of the minutes.

TRAINING DIRECTORS

Many directors believe they don't need training. They see themselves as excellent businesspeople with experience and wisdom. This makes them good businesspeople, but not necessarily good directors. Others believe they have sufficient board experience and therefore don't need training. Most board experience does not include acting as a balance point, owning the process and not the result, acting as a third party with no self-interest in any particular decision, directing but not managing, or understanding how to direct owners. Board training is an essential part of developing an effective board.

The owners have the ultimate responsibility to ensure that the board is well trained and working as the balance point. The chairperson, though, has the primary responsibility for the board's training. This doesn't mean that the chairperson has to do the training, but rather ensures that training is provided.

There are four aspects of board training: ensuring that the directors understand the owners, the owners' manual, and the owners' plan; the company; their role in the board process; and the importance of board evaluation and training.

UNDERSTANDING THE OWNERS

The best way to make sure that the directors understand the owners is to give them a packet of basic information, a "director's notebook," and to discuss the materials with them. This packet should include the current owners' manual and plan; a list of the owners and the stock they own; a statement of the board's role and the desired board process; any shareholder control agreements, voting agreements, or buy-sell agreements; the current board policies (including terms and term limits); codes of conduct; and board structure. Directors may have received some of this information in their prospective director packet. If so, provide them with the remaining information. Appendix 10.6 lists some of the items that might be included in this director's notebook.

New directors should spend time with the owners (or owner representatives to the board) and the chairperson to discuss and understand these items to get a better sense of the owners' values, needs, and goals. A new board should have these discussions together.

UNDERSTANDING THE COMPANY

The best way to make sure that the directors understand the company is to give them another packet of basic information to study and understand. This third packet should include materials describing the company and its industry; the company's current strategic plan, current annual plan, and current budget; annual financial statements for the past two years and the year to date; the articles of incorporation and bylaws; and minutes of prior board meetings and board committee meetings for at least the last two years.

New directors should spend time with the chairperson and senior management to discuss and understand these items to get a better sense of the company's general business and operations. A new board should have these discussions together.

UNDERSTANDING THE BOARD PROCESS

The best way to make sure that the directors understand their role in the board process is for an owner, the chairperson, or an outside consultant, acting as a trainer, to discuss the board acting as the balance point and to provide exercises (using issues that are clearly relevant and timely) to let the directors experience what it is like to perform the balance function. Directors need to understand the concepts of acting as a balance point, owning the process and not the result, ignoring self-interest in decision making, and being other-centered. Conducting exercises with the directors helps them to focus on asking questions and providing analyses rather than giving answers. The chairperson should also steer discussions away from giving answers and, instead, give feedback to directors on how well they are acting independently. Appendix 10.7 contains a suggested overview for initial board training.

The best way to make sure that directors understand the importance of regular board evaluations is to include in their packet a copy of the board evaluation forms and the prior two years of board evaluations, or a summary of the board evaluations written by the chairperson.

New directors should spend time with the chairperson to discuss and understand these items to get a better sense of how important good director performance is. A new board should have these discussions together.

UNDERSTANDING THE IMPORTANCE OF BOARD EVALUATION AND TRAINING

Many owners are uncomfortable evaluating their board for these reasons:

» owners feel that directors are intelligent, well intentioned, and should not have to be told how they are doing

» owners don't like giving negative feedback

» owners know that the board is not doing a good job but don't want to "make waves"

Evaluating the board is critical for it to effectively function as a balance point. Owners and managers trust that directors will find the balance between their respective plans. They expect directors to be third-party participants and not agents of any particular group. They expect directors to be fair, open-minded, and thorough in their interactions with owners and managers. If the board is not doing a good job, the balancing process can break down and conflicts will erupt in the owners group, in management, or between these groups. This is exactly what owners and managers expect a balancing board to prevent.

Evaluating the board is also an opportunity for owners and managers to formally express their opinion on how the board is handling the balancing process and these opinions need to be heard. Board evaluation is a great opportunity for course correction and improving the balancing process.

Board evaluations should be done annually, much like management does an employee's annual performance review. And like employee evaluations, if significant issues arise, the appropriate groups should deal with them on a timely basis.

We recommend four separate evaluations of the board (see Figure 10.1):

- » owners evaluate the board as a board
- » managers evaluate the board as a board
- » directors evaluate themselves as directors
- » directors evaluate the chairperson as the chair

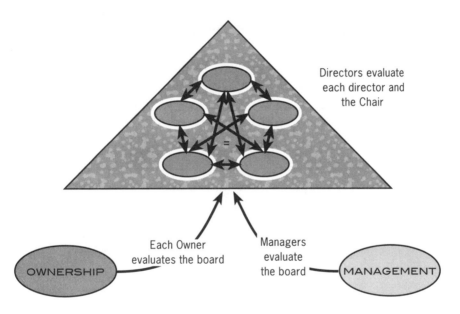

Figure 10.1 The evaluation process

Owners evaluate the board on how effectively the directors understand and perform the balancing function. Ask each owner to evaluate the board. Often, owners perform these evaluations anonymously although they may adopt a policy that the evaluations are not confidential. Typically, owner evaluations start out confidential but become public during the course of discussions when addressing problems. Worksheet 10.1 provides a sample evaluation form for owners to use to evaluate the board.

Managers also evaluate the board on how effectively the directors understand and perform the balancing function. Typically, managers who evaluate the board include the CEO, president, any senior managers who have attended board meetings, and others whose input the owners or the chairperson find helpful. Managers perform these evaluations anonymously and give them to the owners; chairpersons may also receive the evaluations to use as a basis for training and developing the board. Worksheet 10.2 provides a sample evaluation form for managers to use to evaluate the board.

Directors evaluate each other on how well they understand and perform the balancing function. Directors also evaluate chairpersons on how well they perform their responsibilities. Again, directors perform these evaluations anonymously, and give them to the owners because the owners are ultimately responsible for having an effective board. Chairpersons may also receive the evaluations to use as a basis for training and developing the board. Worksheet 10.3 provides a sample evaluation for the directors to use to evaluate each other. Chairpersons' evaluations should be communicated to them so they can improve their performance as chair. Worksheet 10.4 provides a sample evaluation for the directors to use to evaluate the chair.

CHAPTER

11

THOUGHTS FOR PROFESSIONAL ADVISORS

This chapter is directed to professionals who work with closely
held and family businesses in transition and who want to help
owners, directors, managers, and family members work effectively through the complex and challenging issues that exist during
transition. These ideas are relevant whether you are an accountant, attorney, banker, coach, business consultant, family business consultant,
individual consultant, leadership consultant, management consultant,
organizational consultant, team development consultant, financial
planner, insurance agent, investment banker, psychologist, strategic
planner, therapist, trust officer, venture capitalist, or any other service
provider working with businesses in transition.

Business owners might be tempted to skip this chapter. But if
you read it, you will understand three very important things: (1) you'll
learn how professionals you work with see your situation and ap-

proach your company; (2) you'll discover that you can have a voice in the roles your individual professionals play; and (3) you'll have a better idea of how to evaluate the professionals' performance. After all, it's their job to help you get to where you want to go.

THE BASICS

Numerous professional services are available to a business in transition. However, all professional advisors should ask these basic questions: What help is needed? Am I providing that help? What help can other professionals already involved provide? What other professional assistance might be needed?

This chapter offers general thoughts; we do not intend this to be a definitive discussion on the topic. The discussion does not criticize how professionals work with businesses in transition. We want to help professionals by encouraging them to discuss how they work with businesses and clients facing transition challenges. The more that all professionals (including us) can learn about what services a business transition client needs and how we can attend to that need, the more our clients will benefit. We hope this chapter makes a positive contribution to any thinking that evolves from an honest analysis of these matters. As we invited business owners to do in the Introduction of this book, we invite you, the professional, to take from this chapter what you think will help and leave the rest.

OUR ROLES AND RESPONSIBILITIES

As professional advisors to businesses, we assess our roles and responsibilities with clients at the beginning of our engagement, and periodically evaluate our work during and after the engagement. Most professionals act similarly, knowing that the roles and responsibilities of any professional can change over time and as circumstances change.

It's particularly helpful to evaluate our roles and responsibilities as professionals when we work with a business in transition; that is, a business experiencing change of such a nature that the systems, structures, and processes in place to own and operate the business (e.g., to make decisions and get the work done) will alter in some manner. In four distinct transition situations, change to the existing systems, structures, and processes is likely. Those four situations include

» when entrepreneurs want to significantly change their involvement in the business

» when owners and managers are different people

» when there are multiple owners

» when entrepreneurs prepare to sell the business or their stock

It's especially important to evaluate our roles and responsibilities as professionals when we are working with a business in transition because (1) the needs of a business in transition change; (2) a successful transition may require additional professional services; and (3) our clients may look to us for overall guidance and we need to know how to respond. An example may help illustrate these points.

North Metallic Manufacturing's story

Joe and two employees from Joe's previous employer, Frank and Tom, founded North Metallic Manufacturing more than thirty years ago. It was a successful partnership from the start. Joe actively developed new products and ran operations. Frank led the sales efforts, and Tom headed up administration, including finance and human resources. Joe was clearly the leader of the business, not because he owned 60 percent of the company, but because everyone liked him—he had impeccable ethics, he worked harder than anyone else, he kept tabs on the entire operations and, most importantly, he got results. North Metallic grew into a leading manufacturing company with several proprietary products and recently surpassed $120 million in annual revenues. The company now enjoys a solid reputation of producing quality products, providing top-notch service, and doing business the right way.

Joe just turned sixty-five. He told himself that when he reached that milestone he was going to transition out of management and spend more time with his wife (who has some health problems) and his eight grandchildren. He also thought about what would happen to the company after he transitioned. Joe wants his daughters to benefit from the company. He plans to pass his shares equally to his three daughters, who would then own the company. Joe believes he has a solid management team in place who can run the business so his daughters won't have to do anything except accept dividends that can help them financially. He wants his daughters to begin receiving that financial benefit sooner rather than later.

Joe's daughters worked in the company while growing up, but they all went to college, got married, and now have families and careers unrelated to the business. Harry, married to Joe's youngest daughter, mentions to Joe that he'd like to come into the business. Joe always thought Harry was a good marketing person that the company could use—and possibly Harry could even run the company. For now, though, Joe plans to promote Pete to president to run the company so Harry can achieve some of his other goals.

Pete is forty-two, has an MBA, and worked for Joe for eight years. He is second in command of the finance group. While Joe never graduated from college, he values education, knowing that his business needs people more highly trained than he if it is to remain viable. Joe thinks Pete is the right person to take over Joe's role for several reasons. Pete works hard, everyone likes him, and Pete doesn't think he needs to do it all. Joe has some concern about Pete's youth, but feels he is bright and has a knack for getting things done. Joe also likes Pete because of his financial background. Joe knows that one of his own weaknesses is the lack of finance knowledge. Joe hasn't always trusted Tom's judgment and believes that the business needs more financial depth than Tom currently provides.

Joe talked to Frank and Tom about his plans. Both seem to agree with whatever Joe wants. When the company celebrated its twenty-fifth anniversary, Joe remembers Frank and Tom telling him that they were honored to have been part of "Joe's company" and they thought they would be retiring and selling their shares back to the company when they turn sixty-five. (That would be another five years for Tom and eight years for Frank.) Since then, Tom's daughter joined the company and is doing superbly in sales (according to Frank anyway), and Frank's son, who worked every summer and school break at the company doing whatever some-one his age could do, is in his second year in college, majoring in finance and accounting.

Joe thinks Pete will be the person to lead the management team through the expansion plan Joe just completed with help from his managers, Frank, Tom, and a strategic planner. The plan is aggressive, and over the next five years will require hiring about half as many workers as the company now employs and launch-ing two new product lines. But the plan is clearly doable in Joe's mind. It's just that he doesn't believe he is the person to lead the effort, nor does he believe he has the energy, although he won't admit either to anyone other than his wife.

Joe's transition involves three of the four distinct transitional cir-cumstances we identified. First, Joe plans to significantly change his involvement in the business. He has kept tabs on the entire operation since the company was formed and is the one who got results. Clearly Joe is at the center of North Metallic. Joe is consulted on all of the decisions he thinks are important. Joe's transition raises the question about whether he will remain at the center of everything or whether he will transition the responsibility to run the company to Pete and other members of the management team. What will Joe's role be after Pete's promotion? What responsibilities will Pete and Joe have? Will Pete have the authority he needs to do his job? What concerns will Joe have that need to be addressed? What concerns will Pete, Tom, and Frank have that need to be addressed? What kind of assistance generally might be needed to help everyone affected by Joe's transition?

Second, when Joe promotes Pete to run North Metallic, owners and managers will consist of different people for the first time. Theoretically, Joe will not be responsible for running the business. He wants Pete and the other managers to pick up those management responsibilities. So how will Joe keep tabs on the entire operation if he isn't involved in running the company? How will he make sure that Pete gets results, and more importantly, the right results? How will Pete know what results he is supposed to get? Who will be Pete's boss? How will Pete respond to Frank and Tom, owners who are still actively employed, and how will he respond to Joe? What concerns will Joe have that need to be addressed? What concerns will Pete, Tom, and Frank have that need to be addressed? What kind of assistance generally might be needed to help everyone affected by this part of the transition?

Finally, North Metallic has multiple owners. Joe, Frank, and Tom were owners from the beginning, and their respective roles as owners and managers just worked out naturally. Frank and Tom basically defer to Joe because he is the guy that really makes things happen and they trust him. Joe involved Frank and Tom because he appreciates their support and trust, and their values, needs, and goals were similar to his own. There just wasn't any conflict—they all got along. But now, when Joe transfers ownership to his daughters, the ownership group will expand to include multiple owners, some of whom are not employed in the business. What will Joe's daughters do as owners? What will they do when they own all of Joe's shares? How will Frank and Tom relate to Joe's daughters as owners? How will Pete respond to Joe's daughters as owners? What concerns will Joe have that need to be addressed? What concerns might need to be addressed for Tom and Frank, for Joe's daughters, for Pete, for Frank's son, and Tom's daughter? What kind of assistance generally might be needed to help everyone affected by this part of the transition?

Joe is clearly in transition. And, as we pointed out earlier, when business owners like Joe are in transition, everyone is in transition. "Everyone" includes the business, North Metallic Manufacturing; its other owners, Frank and Tom; Pete and other members of management; and even Joe's family and possibly members of Frank's family and Tom's family. As the example illustrates, transitions such as Joe's raise a number of questions and suggest the need to assess how the current system, structures, and processes will serve the business and its people in the future and what changes, if any, are needed.

Given Joe's transition and the number of questions it raises, what is the role of the professionals who are working with North Metallic? Let's start with the basic questions each of these professionals can ask.

» What professional services do North Metallic and its owners and managers need in light of Joe's transition?

» Which of those services can I provide?

» Which of those services can other professionals already working with North Metallic best provide?

» Which of those services should other professionals provide?

The answer to these questions entails a two-step process. The first step involves understanding what services are needed when a business is in transition. The second step involves assessing who can provide those services.

WHAT SERVICES ARE NEEDED

The types of services professionals can provide to businesses in transition, such as North Metallic, are probably as varied as the number of professionals offering services generally. There are many ways to categorize and evaluate those services. We distinguish between two types of professional services: core discipline services and integration services. Businesses in transition need both *core discipline* services and *integration* services. The importance of these services are not relative to each other; that is, core discipline services are not more important than integration services and integration services are not more important than core discipline services. We deliberately did not further label these services to minimize confusion or misunderstanding and to lessen the perception that one type of services is more important than another type.

CORE DISCIPLINE SERVICES

Generally speaking core discipline services are services that directly reflect professionals' core discipline, enhanced by their unique skills, knowledge, and experience. Professionals provide these services to the business; to one or more owners, directors, managers, or the business as a whole; and perhaps to family members, particularly when working with a family business. Businesses need core discipline services whether or not they are in transition.

Examples of core discipline services are abundant: an attorney preparing wills, an accountant preparing audited financial statements or tax returns, a planner helping develop and implement a strategic plan, and a consultant helping an ownership group or family improve their communication.

Core discipline services are important to businesses generally, but they are particularly important to businesses in transition. Here are some examples of some of the core discipline services North Metallic and its people may need.

» Whatever changes Joe's transition requires must comply with applicable law, regulations, and legal agreements. For example, Pete probably needs to be formally elected president to have the authority to run the business as Joe wants. Bank documents may need reviewing to make sure that Joe's plan to leave management will not violate any covenant with the bank. Since Joe is going to be relying on other people to run the company (he will no longer have his hand on the pulse of the business), Joe may want Pete and the other key managers to sign employment agreements with retirement incentives to increase the chance they will stay with the company, as well as noncompete arrangements to decrease the negative effect of having a key manager leave. Pete may want an employment agreement to protect him from what he perceives as an increased risk that he gets the right results for Joe. Frank and Tom may want to revisit the buy-sell agreement to address their concerns about Joe's shares passing to his daughters. Frank and Tom may also be thinking about making some of their shares available to their children who work at North Metallic.

» Laws may adversely impact a business that is (or will be) in transition if these laws are not addressed by well-thought-out plans. For example, transfer taxes are due on Joe's transition of ownership to his daughters. If Joe doesn't plan properly, the transfer tax may become a significant cash flow burden that falls on the business at a time when the business isn't in a position to pay the tax.

» A business in transition, and its owners, directors, and managers, need a variety of products and tools professionals provide. North Metallic's cash needs for expansion may require additional or renewed loans or lines of credit, refinancing to tap existing equity or reduce interest expenses, or adding investors. Joe already uses a strategic planner to help guide management in putting together a long-term plan; but external market forces might require additional planning, such as marketing, production, and sales plans for the new products. Life insurance may be useful to provide liquidity to Joe's estate to pay taxes on shares transferred when

Joe dies. Life insurance can also provide liquidity to North Metallic if Joe, Pete, or another key manager dies, or to fund some of the management team's retirement benefits. Joe will likely want reports that allow him to monitor the business, and he

CORE DISCIPLINE SERVICES ARE CRITICAL TO HELPING A BUSINESS IN TRANSITION. THEY SHOULD NOT BE IGNORED.

may want these reports reviewed by the company's accountants. Internal challenges may require finding, training, and educating new hires; development to help the management team work effectively without Joe; and development of individual skills to help the new leaders rise to the next level. All this in addition to keeping the company's systems up to date (technology, manufacturing, purchasing, delivery, R&D, engineering, and human resources).

» Businesses in transition and their owners, directors, and managers may also benefit from developing additional knowledge, skills, and experience offered by professionals. Improved decision making and communication can enhance performance and planning; leadership development or individual coaching can remove barriers to productivity; and team development may enhance a group's ability to generate and implement plans.

Core discipline services are critical to helping a business in transition. They should not be ignored.

INTEGRATION SERVICES

Integration services are harder to describe than core discipline services. Generally, integration services involve assessing and perhaps changing the systems, structures, and processes by which the business is generally owned and operated, decisions are made, and the work gets done. Integration services involve the independence and interdependence of the key groups working directly with the ownership and operations of the business. More specifically, integration services involve identifying the roles and responsibilities of each of the principle groups involved with the business; how those principal groups work together; the structures, policies, and procedures each group needs to carry out its respective role and responsibilities; and the knowledge and skills needed to carry out roles and responsibilities; testing the arrangements by the principal groups; and evaluating and changing the arrangements as necessary. Integration services not only focus on the specific and distinct roles and responsibilities of the primary groups involved with the business, but also ensure that each group has the authority to fulfill its responsibilities and is accountable for the work they are supposed to do. In other words, integration services ensure that all groups work together, coordinate their plans, and progress toward successful transition.

A business in transition needs integration services. Integration services do not replace core discipline services; they are additional services.

Integration services are important to businesses in transition, and should not be ignored. But understanding integration services is difficult. Let's look at how integration services could help North Metallic.

Joe's transition plan has him moving from the center of everything. It makes Pete the center of management and leaves Joe as the center of everything else (whatever that is). Eventually the ownership portion of Joe's "everything else" will transition to his daughters. When this happens, can Joe still be involved with the company? Could North Metallic still benefit from Joe's involvement? Can he have a role if he is not an owner and the center of everything? If the answer to any of these questions is yes, how will Joe be involved? What will he do? How will he relate to Pete and other members of management? How will he relate to Frank and Tom? How will he relate to his daughters as owners? And how will all these individuals (as well as the other employees, customers, vendors, bankers, etc.) relate to Joe?

Integration services involve looking at what Joe does at the center. This includes identifying the functions Joe performs while holding everything together. If Joe is truly the center of everything important that happens at North Metallic, then Joe must be performing the key functions of management, ownership, and governance because these are the only three functional groups within every business.

Integration services ensure the existence of a plan to transition all of Joe's key functions in a way that is good for Joe and good for the company.

> Since Joe wants to transition his management functions first, this means he wants to retain his ownership and board functions. So what has to happen for this to occur? One change involves Joe ensuring that Pete knows what Joe, Frank, and Tom are looking for as owners. North Metallic's current arrangements don't need a structure or process to do this because Joe does it automatically as the primary owner and manager. Pete needs to know what Joe, Frank, and Tom are looking for from the company so that Pete understands how to manage the business. This is critical for Pete because he will be evaluated on whether he delivers what Joe and the other owners want. Which then raises the question of accountability. With Joe in charge, the company didn't have to provide any structure or process to make sure Joe, Frank, and Tom got what they wanted from it. Joe makes sure that the owners get what they want, or, if the company can't provide what the owners want, Joe talks to Frank and Tom and together the owners make adjustments. Joe ensures the interests of the owners and business align, or are in balance—and the proof that he does this well is that Frank and Tom trust Joe to do the right thing, and he does. Since Joe will no longer occupy the center of everything, the system needs to provide a way for Joe to hold Pete and the rest of management accountable for delivering on the values, needs, and goals of the owners.

> What happens when Joe transfers all of his ownership to his daughters? Then Joe will no longer be involved in ownership, but he still may be integral to ensuring that North Metallic delivers on

what the owners want. And, even if Joe is not involved, Pete still needs to know what the owners want from the business. Integration services assess changes to the current arrangements that may be required for the owners to deliver to Pete what they want as owners. Since the ownership will involve Joe's daughters and his daughters are not employed in the business and don't know Frank and Tom as well as Joe does, some structure and process will likely be needed to get all of the owners to agree on their values, needs, and goals, and about how they are going to work together as owners. Whatever arrangement is put in place can't rely on Joe doing this work for the owners; the owners will need to do this work themselves. When Joe, Frank, and Tom were the only owners, they had a sense about what they could reasonably expect the business to provide because they worked in the business. Joe's daughters don't have this luxury. And Joe's daughters will eventually own legal control of the company. Some people might think that Joe's daughters could then get from the business whatever they want because they have legal control. But what if North Metallic can't provide what they ask? Some structure and process is needed to ensure that what the owners ask for is doable.

Integration services involve looking at what changes are needed to facilitate Joe's objectives in the short term and the long term. Initially, the focus would be on the immediate change; that is, Joe's transition from management. But whatever changes occur to address the short term should also be consistent with the changes needed for the long term (when Joe's daughters own all of Joe's shares). Integration services look at the systems, structures, and processes of management, ownership, and the board and determine what changes to the current arrangements are required to successfully complete the transition.

PROVIDING NEEDED SERVICES

Professionals themselves are the only people who can truly assess what services they can or cannot provide. Surely others may have opinions, but professionals are in the best position to determine what they can provide and whether they want to do so.

Once the groups involved understand what services are needed for a business in transition, the next step involves determining whether you can and want to provide those services. If so, great—go for it. Become knowledgeable in providing the services the best you can. If you can't or don't want to provide the services, don't, but you should help the business find someone to provide the services it needs. It isn't helpful for you to identify services that the business needs, decide you can't or won't provide them, and then fail to point out the need, thus letting the transition falter for lack of appropriate help. Here are a few examples to help illustrate this.

> John, North Metallic's attorney, has extensive estate planning experience. When Joe approaches John with his transition ideas, John correctly describes ways that Joe can transfer his ownership to his daughters while reducing the tax burden on the transfers. John talks to Joe about buy-sell issues that will affect Joe, Frank, and Tom, as well as Joe's daughters, and recommends reviewing and updating the buy-sell agreement. John suggests that Joe update his will to ensure that his estate plan is consistent with his transition goals. Because he is the company's attorney, John also appropriately offers the following advice: Joe should resign as president; the board should elect Pete as president; the owners need to rethink who should sit on the board; the company should consider putting employment agreements in place for Pete and other members of the management team; and the company's financial documents need to be reviewed to make sure that there are no loan covenants contrary to Joe's plan.

All of John's suggestions are sound and reflect core discipline services that are needed. Even if John believes that the services he provides are all the services that are needed, he should still ask what else may need to be addressed. If John understands the dynamics and complexity of transition work, he can respond in one of three ways:

» Do nothing, perhaps believing that Joe or others will cross that bridge when they come to it.

» Assume that the services he provides will adequately address those dynamics—so he should lay out his plan and present it to Joe, explaining how it addresses the concerns.

» Point out the dynamics and complexity of transition work to Joe, and suggest that a professional already working with North Metallic address these items (if John believes an existing professional can provide that service) or he can suggest looking for another professional.

What is the right choice?

Joe discusses his transition plan at length with Norm, North Metallic's accountant. Norm has been with Joe, Frank, and Tom since they started the company. Norm consulted with dozens of clients like Joe over the years because they are all Norm's age and Norm has been their accountant for most of their business careers. Norm asks a number of questions and has plenty of good, sound, practical advice. He helps Joe and his wife make financial projections to assess their cash needs. He confirms what John told Joe about the tax impact on transferring shares to his daughters. And Norm also has several ideas for reducing the company's tax burden.

Norm asks a number of questions about Pete and the management team, pressing Joe about how competent they are to run the business, especially to execute the new plan. He also quizzes Joe about the role Frank and Tom will have in the business and what they think about being owners with Joe's daughters, particularly with each of them having a child working in the business. Norm asks about Harry, Joe's son-in-law, joining the business. Joe thinks they are all good, probing questions. Joe thinks the management team is ready to transition. They carried a large load the past five years with the previous plan and did a terrific job at putting the new plan together. Joe explains that Frank and Tom support his transition plan, and will keep an eye on the management team for Joe. As far as Frank's son and Tom's daughter, Joe explains that they are doing well, and making a good living. Joe responds to Norm's inquiry about what Frank and Tom think about being owners with his daughters by explaining that his daughters are not going to be running the business; they are just going to be owners—Pete and the management team will run the business. Besides, Joe says, a buy-sell agreement lets Frank and Tom sell their ownership anytime they want. Joe thinks he has convinced Norm that everything is in place. Still, Norm cautions Joe to stay involved with the business because, as Norm explains, Pete is young; costly mistakes can be made quickly; and the business wouldn't be the same without Joe.

Norm confirms that his office can review the company's finances on a regular basis to give Joe some comfort, and that he will let Joe know if they see anything unusual. Norm reminds Joe that his office does all the tax returns for the owners and the business and also reviews the company's financial statements for the bank, so that he can make sure that the numbers all line up.

Norm reiterates that he and his office will continue providing the core discipline services currently available and will make an extra effort to confirm that everything is in order. Joe feels great knowing that the company's long-time accountants will continue watching the finances, and, at least in the short term, watch them a little closer. Norm's probing questions also seem very sound. Norm correctly has concerns about Joe's transition plan, relating primarily to management's ability to operate the company without Joe's daily presence and to Frank's and Tom's acceptance of the plan, and he brings those concerns to light. It gets Joe thinking, and Norm, perhaps not totally convinced, advises Joe to stay involved with the business.

Advising Joe to stay involved is probably terrific advice. Most businesses benefit from the continued involvement of the key founder who transitions from management as Joe proposes to do. But, could Norm do anything else besides advising Joe to remain involved? What does staying involved mean? How does Joe stay involved and still let Pete and the management team run the company? And if Joe stays involved, how will he ever find time to spend with his wife and grandchildren? And how will Joe's involvement help Frank and Tom? Doesn't that send the wrong message—that you can't ever retire? Norm is on the right track with his questions and concerns. Norm raises integration services issues when he correctly identifies that Joe's transition will alter existing key players' roles and responsibilities and raise questions about authority and accountability. While correctly identifying the concerns, Norm could suggest that Joe and he, along with perhaps others (like John, Frank, or Tom), find a professional to help them identify how to address these concerns and how Joe can transition as he wants.

Joe really likes Tim, the professional consultant who helped with the latest expansion plan. Joe mentions his transition plan to Tim during the planning process, but they didn't talk much about it at the time. Now, having heard Norm's concerns, Joe goes to see Tim to specifically talk about his transition. Tim doesn't think Joe's transition will affect the plan at all. Tim points out that all of the external indicators supporting the plan, including market demands, competitive forces, and financing, are as favorable as ever, and those factors aren't going to be affected by Joe's transition. Tim also explains that the internal factors are positive. He points out that the R&D people seemed capable of developing the products needed for the two new lines the plan calls for. Frank and his team can launch the new products, and the purchasing, manufacturing, and shipping systems Joe implemented are well above average, even for a company the size of North Metallic. Tim thinks the management team, though young, has sufficient skills to implement the plan. Tim reminds Joe that the planning includes an annual review of progress on the plan so Tim will be in a position to give Joe feedback if he sees anything that doesn't work.

Certainly Tim is correct in saying that Joe's transition will not affect the external factors. But will the internal factors change? Tim doesn't say. He thinks the existing people can implement the plan, but is that belief based on how well the people performed in the past when Joe was active in management? Is Tim's conclusion based on his assessment of how well those people will do if Joe isn't around regularly? Is the difference significant? Is it possible that Joe's presence makes the people underneath him perform better than they might perform if he isn't present? If so, can Pete have the same influence? As with John, if Tim doesn't know whether internal factors may be affected by Joe's transition, he should at least ask about what else may need to be addressed. If Tim begins to see that internal factors can negatively affect implementation of Joe's transition plan, Tim can respond in several ways:

» Do nothing.

» Suggest reviewing the plan, and making adjustments to take into account what the people can do without Joe's daily presence.

» Explain that he thinks Joe's transition will reduce the effectiveness of the remaining personnel and suggest seeking additional help to lessen or avoid this result. Tim may still conclude that the expansion plan will need changes, and suggest that Joe seek help in assessing how his transition will affect the people who will have the responsibility to manage the company.

What is the right choice?

Joe seeks out Jane, a licensed psychologist who helped in the past with some communication challenges. Some members of the management team had difficulty adjusting to Joe's dynamic style, and Jane effectively helped Joe and the managers make adjustments that improved how they all worked together. Jane helped Joe write up some of his goals around the twenty-fifth anniversary, and she coached him on how to talk to Frank and Tom about what he wants to do. Jane even helped Joe and his wife intervene with their middle daughter when she was heading for divorce and perhaps alcohol treatment. Jane's communication skills helped Joe and his wife get their message across to their daughter, and she actually appreciated their intervention.

Jane sees right away that Joe's transition will change the way decisions are made in the company and how the work gets done. She explains how the communication patterns and decision making, at least on significant matters, run through Joe. Joe's transition from management, and Pete taking over Joe's position to run the business, clearly require changes to how decisions are made and communicated. Jane also suggests that Joe communicate his plans to Frank and Tom in the right way. She expresses concerns about what Frank and Tom might hear, or read into Joe's transition, what their new roles will be, and how management will respond to them now that Joe won't be around regularly. Jane suggests that she work with management about how they will communicate with each other and make decisions when Joe is no longer involved in management. She also thinks it a good idea to work with Pete and Joe on how they will communicate—about what information Joe wants to receive from Pete and how often, and how they will work out differences. Finally, Jane thinks she can help Joe communicate his transition ideas to Frank and Tom to ensure they hear them correctly and accept them.

Again, Jane's advice is sound and reflects core discipline services that are needed. Even if these are all the services that Jane sees as necessary, she should still ask about what else may need to be addressed. But does Jane really believe that communication and decision making are the only part of the existing system that need changes as a result of Joe's transition? Does Jane really think that the work she proposes will address all of the concerns stemming from Joe's transition plan? If so, then Jane should explain how her work will address the concerns, lay out her plan, and present it to Joe. If not, Jane can raise some of her concerns or ideas about what else within the existing system may need to be addressed to adequately prepare for Joe's transition.

Having listened to John, Norm, Tim, and Jane, Joe begins to doubt whether he has covered all the bases. Rather than change his plans and ignore his gut instinct, he seeks a referral for someone who helps people like Joe transition in their company. Through networking and referrals, he meets Cynthia, and asks for her views. Cynthia explains that his transition will likely change how everything happens in the company because Joe is involved in everything. His transition will alter the roles and responsibilities of himself and Pete, Frank, Tom, and probably many others in upper management. She stresses the importance of clearly identifying everyone's new roles and responsibilities so there won't be any questions about who is supposed to do what. She tells Joe that it is important that he transition authority to those who will have his old responsibilities. Cynthia says nothing is more frustrating than having the responsibility, but not the authority, to do something, particularly if you are going to be held accountable. She points out the need to determine how Pete and the management team will know what Joe wants them to do and how they will be accountable for the results. She asks about who will be on the board and what the board will do, stresses the importance of giving the board a real role. (This is news to Joe because he only thought of the board whenever John said the directors needed to sign something.) Cynthia suggests that the ownership systems, structures, and processes will need changes to prepare for Joe's daughters becoming owners. And she asks questions about how Frank and Tom will transition their stock to their children (who will then become owners). Joe doesn't understand all of what Cynthia says, but he does come away with the realization that his transition will have a greater impact on everyone than he first imagined, and that the impact not only affects management but also ownership.

Cynthia's feedback reflects the integration services that Joe's transition needs. And, it is helpful that Joe hears about these services. But what is Cynthia's responsibility if she is hired? Obviously, it is to deliver the best integration services she can. But the advice Joe receives from John, Norm, Tim, and Jane about the core discipline services is also sound. Does Cynthia have any responsibility to ensure these core discipline services are delivered as well? And what if Cynthia could deliver some of the core discipline services, for example, the communication development Jane spoke about—what responsibility does Cynthia have to involve Jane in providing these services? What responsibility does Cynthia have to ask Joe if any other professional working with North Metallic could provide some of the services she can? And, will Cynthia answer these questions differently if she thinks Joe and North Metallic will benefit more if other professionals are involved?

If Joe asks Cynthia how the company could benefit by involving more professionals, and thus incurring more costs, one response is that coordinating the different parts of the transition plan is essential to a successful transition. Also, the company's regular professionals will better understand the company and the individuals involved so, besides continuing their core discipline services, they can help implement the agreed-upon changes and spot whether the key people return to their former ways. This illustrates that professionals who provide integration services also have responsibilities related to core discipline services and the professionals who provide those services.

SUMMARY

This chapter raises more questions than answers when it comes to providing professional services to businesses in transition. That is partly because in our experiences there *are* a lot more questions than answers. Keeping the examples in mind, and based on our experience, here is a summary of our thoughts on the roles and responsibilities of professionals to companies that are in transition:

» Businesses in transition need two types of professional services: core discipline services and integration services.

» Core discipline services relate primarily to the professional's core discipline. These services usually focus on a specific topic, concern, activity, or result, and involve one or more people specifically associated with the topic, concern, activity, or result. Businesses not in transition often need similar services.

» Integration services coordinate the systems, structures, and pro-cesses of the three principal groups in every business (ownership, management, and the board) by recommending and implementing changes to the existing arrangements that will ensure a successful transition.

» The importance of both types of services are not relative to each other; that is, core discipline services are not more important than integration services and integration services are not more important than core discipline services—although the needs of the business, owners, directors, managers, and family members associated with the business will suggest which work is the highest priority.

» Professionals who provide core discipline services have a minimum responsibility to

- understand integration services, why they are needed when businesses are in transition, how they differ from core discipline services, and who can provide them.
- assess what integration services they (the profession-als) can and want to provide.

- consult with businesses in transition about the need for integration services.
- remain involved to ascertain that the integration services delivered are consistent with the core discipline services provided and are otherwise consistent with what the professionals know to be the values, needs, and goals of the owners and the business.

» Professionals who provide integration services have a minimum responsibility to

- understand the core discipline services currently provided to a business, who provides those services, and what other core discipline services are needed.
- involve the professionals who provide core discipline services so they understand the integration services and deliver their core discipline services in the context of the integration services.
- assess what core discipline services they (the professionals) can and want to provide.
- consult with businesses in transition about the need for core discipline services, and coordinate those services with the integration services.
- remain involved to ascertain that the core discipline services delivered are consistent with the integration services provided and are otherwise consistent with what the professionals know to be the values, needs, and goals of the owners and the business.

» Allow "What is in the client's best interest?" to be your guide in determining how to provide professional services to clients in transition.

» Keep an open mind about the services a business in transition may need.

» Remember, there is likely more than enough work to go around, if everyone shares.

Professionals who work with businesses in transition often encounter complications because of the numerous and diverse issues in the businesses and the need for many different services. In one way or another, transitions affect not only the business but everyone who is an owner, director, key manager, or family member. The work involves individual values, needs, and goals; group values, needs, and goals; and the business's values, needs, and goals. It involves laws of governments and the laws of human nature. Because of the complexity, working with businesses in transition often requires involving professionals with different skill sets, depending on the issues that surface and the skills of the professional doing the business transition work. And involving different professionals adds to the complexity of the work. We hope this chapter helps professionals address some of the complexities added by their involvement so they, in turn, can focus on solving the transition challenges.

12

CONCLUSION

One reason we wrote this book for closely held and family business owners is that many of you told us you are not comfortable planning your personal transition and the succession of your company. The idea that it is time for you to let go and get on with the rest of your life is foreign to you. You dedicated your life to the business and don't see the wisdom in letting go. When presented with the offer to move on, you often decide you aren't ready to retire—that going from the one who does it all to just an owner is too drastic a move.

We hope our book addresses your concerns. And now we hope you realize how understanding the balance point is critical to your succession and transition process. We hope that you now are able to answer these key questions involved in any transition of a business:

» How do business owners transition to a new role yet stay involved?

» How can business owners continue to use their power to guide the company if their role is changing?

» How do owners who are not managers stay legitimately involved with the business so they feel that their interests are protected?

» How do multiple owners let managers know what they want from the business without having to "manage the managers"?

The book began with three basic ideas: (1) all closely held and family businesses have a balance point; (2) all closely held and family business owners should know where the balance point is in their company and how the balance point works; and (3) all closely held and family business owners should understand when to transition the balance point.

Two more basic ideas have been inherent in our book: (4) all succession and transition plans should include a plan for the balance point; and (5) all strategic and annual planning should be done with the balance point in mind. This way ownership, the board, and management can transition together. When ownership, the board, and management are in sync, the transition usually succeeds.

Most business owners whom we have worked with have taken the balance point concept and moved their transition forward in some major way. We believe that because you see how understanding the balance point protects your interests, the well-being of your business, and the interests of your family, you will integrate it into your succession planning. We believe that because you understand that an effective balance point helps you meet your needs and goals, you will integrate it into your transition planning. And we believe that because you see that an effective balance point helps you prepare for a smooth transition, helps you determine your role in the transition process, helps you determine how fast or slow you transition, and helps you determine how much control to give up and when to give it up, you will take action.

Business owners are a resourceful group. They will assess the risks, do what they think is right, and then assess the results. We want you to assess the balance point concept, integrate it into your thinking, take action, and assess the results. We believe good things will happen.

GLOSSARY

The following terms are used in connection with common business entities. Many of these terms have specific legal implications, the full effect of which is not necessarily reflected in the definitions used here. Check your state law for clarification, and address particular legal questions to a lawyer experienced in business law, family businesses, or succession law. Words in SMALL CAPITALS are defined elsewhere in this list.

advisory group. A group of people selected (not elected) by the person wanting advice. An advisory group has no decision-making authority or responsibility and no voting authority. An advisory group does not replace a board of directors; in other words, a board of directors continues to have authority and responsibility even when an advisory group exists.

annual plan. A plan for an entity that covers the entity's fiscal year and describes various tactics that management will follow to implement the entity's STRATEGIC PLAN. An annual plan usually includes budgets.

articles. A document filed with the secretary of state to legally form a corporation or a limited liability company. Corporations file articles of incorporation and limited liability companies file articles of organization.

balance point. The place where the balancing gets done; also, who is doing the balancing.

1. Another name for a board of directors that does the balancing functions we describe in this book. For example, "the balance point makes sure that" (the board makes sure that) or "the entrepreneur's role as the balance point" (the entrepreneur's role as the board).

2. Refers to the individual doing the balancing. For example, "the entrepreneur is the balance point" (the entrepreneur himself or herself wants to do the balancing) or "who will be the balance point?" (who will make the balancing decisions?)

balancing. The act of integrating owners' interests and managers' interests in the company.

balancing board. A board of directors who integrate the often competing interests of owners and managers. A balancing board works with the owners and managers to help each group fulfill their respective responsibilities.

beneficiaries. People or entities receiving assets distributed from a trust either directly or for their benefit.

board members. Individuals elected to serve on a board. Members of a corporation's board of directors are referred to as directors, members of a limited liability company's board of governors are referred to as governors, and members of a partnership board are referred to by whatever term is used in the partnership agreement.

board of advisors. See ADVISORY GROUP

board of directors. A group of people (not owners or managers) elected by a company's owners who have decision-making authority, voting authority, and specific responsibilities. Corporations have a board of directors, limited liability companies have a board of governors, and a partnership board is referred to by whatever term is used in the partnership agreement.

buy-sell agreement. A contract typically between the company and its owners regarding the transferability of the ownership interests in the company.

bylaws. A document providing general structures and procedures relating to ownership, ownership interests, the board, officers, and similar matters.

closely held corporations. Corporations whose stock is not registered under federal security laws.

conflicts of interest. Conflicts between the private interests and the official responsibilities of a person in a position of trust. For board members, the term generally describes the relationship they have to the entity versus the actions they may take to serve their interests.

corporations. Entities organized for profit and incorporated under or governed by state laws. See also CLOSELY HELD CORPORATIONS; C CORPORATIONS; PUBLICLY HELD CORPORATIONS; S CORPORATIONS

C corporations. A corporation that has not filed an election to be taxed as a subchapter S corporation under the Internal Revenue Code. C corporations are taxed under subchapter C of the Internal Revenue Code, hence the term "C corporation." Often referred to as a regular corporation. See also S CORPORATIONS

directors. Members of a corporation's board of directors.

due diligence. Prudent actions taking place after careful investigation of facts and conditions.

duty. The responsibility one person has to another person. See also FIDUCIARY DUTY

entity. An arrangement created by law that has independent legal significance such as a corporation, limited liability company, or partnership. "Independent legal significance" means that the entity is considered to have its own legal identity (similar to a person), with the capacity to conduct business; buy, own, sell, and lease property; sign contracts and other instruments; sue and be sued; and take other actions to conduct its business.

entrepreneur. The person who is the driving force and significant decision-maker within a company—not necessarily the creative innovator of new products, services, and businesses. This person is also sometimes referred to as founder or owner/CEO.

family business. A business in which one or more members of a family have a significant ownership interest and significant commitments toward the company's overall well-being.

family council. Typically a group consisting of the entire family (as defined by the owners or the family) or a chosen decision-making body consisting of a smaller group of family members. The family council's main role is to address the business of the family and family involvement issues. Each family council is different and develops unique reasons for existence and methods of operation. Each family council will have unique areas to address. The family council is distinct from the ownership group. The ownership group is limited to family members who own stock. The family council can include owners and nonowners. While this distinction may be obvious, it is important because many of the family council's decisions need approval from the ownership group before the decisions become part of the owners' plan and owners' manual.

fiduciary duty. An obligation that one person has toward another person as a result of his or her position or authority. Board members' obligations or duties generally include acting in good faith, acting in the manner they reasonably believe to be in the best interests of the business, and acting with the care that a prudent person in a like position would exercise in similar circumstances. A board member who performs these duties or obligations is not liable for the board's action or failure to act.

fiduciary responsibility. The responsibility of an individual or entity to exercise reasonable judgment and prudent oversight in any actions taken. It requires application of due diligence.

founder. See ENTREPRENEUR

governors. Members of a limited liability company's board of governors.

indemnification. A person's or entity's obligation to protect another from a specified loss or to reimburse another for a specified loss; often includes costs to defend against the loss. Entities typically indemnify their board members; that is, entities secure members of the board from loss in the event of a lawsuit and defend them in the lawsuit.

insiders. Usually those members of a board who are owners or managers.

limited liability company (LLC). A type of company that offers its owners the advantage of limited liability (like corporations) and partnership-like taxation, in which profits are passed through to the owners and taxed on their personal income tax returns.

limited liability limited partnership. A limited partnership that has filed a statement under state law to qualify as a limited liability limited partnership. This status provides limited liability to the general partners of the limited partnership.

limited liability partnership. A general partnership that has filed a statement under state law to qualify as a limited liability partnership. This status provides limited liability to the general partners of the partnership.

limited partners. See PARTNERS

managers. The individuals who oversee day-to-day activities and who are responsible for the planning process of the company. They are hired by the business, not elected by the board. May include officers, directors, and owners.

member control agreement. An agreement among members of a limited liability company that may define roles, responsibilities, policies, procedures, and structures of the company. The agreement must be signed by all current members of the company as well as those who have agreed to contribute capital. It usually supersedes contrary provisions in any other company document and possibly state law. See also SHAREHOLDER CONTROL AGREEMENT

members. Owners of a limited liability company. See also PARTNERS; SHAREHOLDERS

membership interests. The members' proprietary interests in a limited liability company. See also PARTNERSHIP INTERESTS; SHARES

officers. Individuals elected by a board and who have been delegated specific responsibilities by the board or by law; usually those individuals with the responsibility to oversee the general operations of the entity. Common titles include chief executive officer (CEO), president, chief financial (CFO), treasurer, chief operating officer (COO), vice president, and secretary. May also include directors, owners, and managers.

outsiders. Board members who are not owners, managers, or family members.

owner/CEO. See ENTREPRENEUR.

owners. Individuals or entities who own the equity interest in an entity. A corporation's owners are called shareholders, a limited liability company's owners are called members, and a partnership's owners are called partners.

owners' manual. A document describing the roles and responsibilities of the owners, managers, and board; the owners' structures, policies, and procedures; the board's structure; guidelines for how the board works with owners and managers; and such other arrangements as the owners agree to include in the manual. These arrangements are usually not legally enforceable. If provisions found in the owners' manual are to have legal effect (either because the arrangements supersede state law or are otherwise to have binding effect), those arrangements are typically included in legally enforceable agreements or other documents, such as shareholder control agreements, member control agreements, bylaws, operating agreements, or buy-sell agreements.

owners' plan. A plan put together by the owners of an entity that describes the values, needs, and goals that the owners have as a group.

partners. The owners of a partnership. The partners of a general partnership are typically referred to as general partners. The partners of a limited partnership include one or more general partners and one or more limited partners. In a limited partnership, the management and control are vested with the general partners; limited partners often have no management or control and may vote only on limited decisions, if any at all. See also MEMBERS; SHAREHOLDERS

partnership interests. The partners' ownership interests in a partnership. A general partnership has general partnership interests. A limited partnership has general partnership interests and limited partnership interests. Either of these entities may also have partnership interests referred to by other names in the partnership agreement, such as preferred partnership interests or partnership interests designated by classes. See also MEMBERSHIP INTERESTS; SHARES

publicly held corporations. Corporations whose stock is registered under federal security laws.

quorum. The number of a individuals in a group that must be present for the group to act on a particular matter.

S corporations. Corporations that have filed an election to be taxed under subchapter S of the Internal Revenue Code. This type of taxation generally results in the corporation's income being taxed to the shareholders rather than to the corporation. See also C CORPORATIONS

shareholder control agreement. An agreement among shareholders of a corporation that provides for certain roles, responsibilities, policies, procedures, or structures of the corporation. The agreement usually must be signed by all of the current shareholders, and often supersedes contrary provisions in any other corporate document or state law. See also MEMBER CONTROL AGREEMENT

shareholders. The owners of a corporation. See also MEMBERS; PARTNERS

shares. The units, however designated, into which the shareholders' stock in a corporation are divided. See also MEMBERSHIP INTERESTS; PARTNERSHIP INTERESTS

stock. The shareholders' ownership interest in a corporation. If the corporation has only one class of stock, it is referred to as common stock. If the corporation has different types of stock, they are usually referred to as common stock and preferred stock. Common stock may be either voting stock or nonvoting stock; the only difference is having the right to vote. Preferred stock has those rights set out in the documents creating the preferred stock, which may include preferred rates of return, preference on distributions and liquidations, and the right to vote in certain cases.

strategic plan. A plan for an entity that covers an agreed-upon period of time and addresses goals and strategic concerns relative to the entity and its business. It's designed to accommodate the owners' plan and is approved by the board.

succession plan. A plan that describes the owners' goals for the succession of their company. Such goals may include selling or giving the business to one or more owners, family members, managers, employees, or third-party investors. They may include going public or liquidating the company. Often used synonymously with TRANSITION PLAN, but we think it is important to distinguish between the two.

transition plan. A plan that outlines what has to happen to realize the owners' succession goals and how they will be accomplished. So if the succession plan is to sell or give shares to family members, none of whom will work at the company, the transition plan identifies what needs to happen to make this work and how those events will occur. Often used synonymously with SUCCESSION PLAN.

trust. An arrangement established by a donor, settlor, or grantor by which a trustee (a person or entity) is directed to hold, administer, and distribute assets for a beneficiary (another person or entity). The trust arrangement may be either revocable (it may be changed or terminated by the donor) or irrevocable (it is permanent and cannot be changed). The trust arrangement may be either *inter vivos* (created during the lifetime of the donor) or testamentary (created following the death of the donor).

TABLE OF APPENDIXES

APPENDIX 1.1

USING THESE PRINCIPLES IN OTHER CONTEXTS

Chapters 1 through 10 explain how all closely held and family businesses can benefit from using a balancing board. This section briefly describes how the balancing concept can be used in

» companies with a large number of owners

» limited liability companies

» family limited partnerships

» cooperatives

» public companies

» nonprofits

COMPANIES WITH A LARGE NUMBER OF OWNERS

One question we often hear is whether the balance point idea works for companies having a large number of owners. Our answer: Absolutely, but large ownership groups do present unique challenges.

First, the more owners there are, the harder it is for them to speak with one voice. Everything is harder. There are more people involved, more meetings and documents needed, more problems to hear, more differences to resolve, more personal dynamics to address, and so on. Getting everyone to speak with one voice is harder, but possible.

Second, the more owners there are, the greater the potential benefit if they can speak with one voice. Companies benefit if the ownership group is unified, and are hurt if there is dissension within the owners' group. At a minimum, individual owners need an opportunity to express their own values, needs, and goals, especially when the differences that exist within the ownership group are large and getting larger. When individual owners do not get this opportunity, owner conflicts are more likely, and managers are more likely to feel like they serve many masters.

Here are some suggestions for developing and implementing the balancing concept with a large ownership group:

» Give each owner the opportunity to be involved. You can't force owners to participate, but you can invite all of them to do so, and eliminate retaliation against those who don't participate.

» Identify at least one value, need, or goal that all of the owners can agree on at the outset. Find at least one thing that can be used to build a commitment among a large enough group of owners to begin the work that owners need to do.

» Create a process that the owners can support that will guide them through the planning outlined in this book. It is critical that they agree on a planning process before beginning. Use the large group to identify issues and agree on solutions, and smaller workgroups to identify alternatives and implement agreements.

» Here is one process that works well with large owner groups. Form four groups—ownership, board, management, and coordination. The ownership, board, and management groups each work through issues relating to owner- ship, the balance point, and management, respectively. Each group appoints a chair to facilitate the group's process. The coordination group (which ideally includes the chairs of the three work groups and at least one other owner who would serve as chair) oversees the work of all the groups.

» Enroll the owners in the process. Get them to understand their challenges, identify possible solutions, and create solutions that they believe best address the issues based on their unique ownership group and business.

» Allow owners to test the results and make changes as necessary. Implement the balance point concept—don't leave it on the drawing board. To test the system, owners, managers, and the board need to follow the owners' man- ual, put the plans together, and allow the board to act as the balance point. The process must also allow the owners, managers, and the board to adopt changes so the system can respond to unexpected or unique circumstances that may arise.

» Engage the services of one or more consultants experienced in working with large ownership groups. Involve the trusted advisors of the owners and the business so that the consultants and advisors have full access to each other. Give the consultants (with input from the owners and advisors) the responsibility for helping the owners develop the system and let the owners (with input from their advisors and consultants) retain responsibility for the results.

Some examples might help explain these ideas. In a closely held business with many owners, a facilitator or owner-representative can find out who wants to be active in developing an owners' plan, who wants to vote on the plan, who only wants to have an explanation of the plan, and who doesn't want to be involved at all. Dividing the owners into the four groups will help the facilitator or owner-representative assess the kind of coordination needed to develop a single owners' plan for all owners.

In a family business with different family groups, divide the ownership group into smaller family groups. Have each small group develop their owners' plan. Then invite representatives from each family group to integrate their individual plans into a single owners' plan.

The other question we commonly hear is whether there is an ownership group too large for this process. Our answer: no. We don't believe the size of an ownership group prevents it from developing a process to implement the principles described in this book. An ownership group may not be able to follow a process to implement these principles, but that's not because the ownership group is too large. If there are no significant conflicts among the owners, they should continue to do what they have been doing. If significant conflicts occur among the owners or between owners and management, their options are limited. The ownership group can either develop a process to work through the issues, or continue to do nothing and let owners take matters into their own hands. Doing nothing seems the more risky option.

> THE SIZE OF AN OWNERSHIP GROUP [DOESN'T] PREVENT IT FROM DEVELOPING A PROCESS TO IMPLEMENT THE PRINCIPLES DESCRIBED IN THIS BOOK.

LIMITED LIABILITY COMPANIES

Most owners choose a legal entity known as a corporation through which to conduct their business. The corporation may be either a C corporation or an S corporation—the only difference being how the corporation is taxed. All corporations have owners (shareholders), a board of directors, and managers (officers elected by the board and managers often chosen by the officers).

This book reflects the ownership, board, and management arrangements of corporations. Another legal entity offering some significant advantages over corporations and gaining popularity is the limited liability company or LLC.

While the principles in this book can apply to LLCs in the same way as they do to corporations, the ownership, board, and management arrangements of an LLC can be made quite different than those of a corporation. For example, some state laws presume that LLCs will not have a board. In these states, if the owners want a board, they must include the necessary provisions in the documents establishing the LLC. Other states presume LLCs will have a board unless the owners decide otherwise. Some states also presume that the owners will manage the LLC, thereby eliminating a separate management group and vesting management responsibilities and authority in the owners. Other states presume that the LLC will have a separate management group but allow the owners to change this arrangement in the formation documents.

Owners need not shy away from using LLCs because of the flexibility to modify board and management arrangements. In some instances, the added flexibility may be advantageous. And the ownership, board, and management arrangements of any LLC can be tailored so the principles of this book can apply and the advantages of the LLC retained. It will be important, however, to make sure legal counsel is involved so the documentation for the LLC properly reflects the intent.

FAMILY LIMITED PARTNERSHIPS AND FAMILY WEALTH MANAGEMENT

Family limited partnerships (FLPs) are another type of legal entity that has increased in popularity. FLPs have for years been used to transfer family assets from one generation to another. Their use increased significantly after the Internal Revenue Service ruled that ownership interest transfers among family members are not aggregated for transfer tax purposes. In other words, the IRS says that Dad can transfer all the shares in the family business to his five children equally, and each 20 percent ownership interest will be valued separately for gift, estate, and generation-skipping transfer tax purposes. Separately valuing each ownership block (20 percent in the example) allows its value to be discounted because it does not represent control (thereby giving rise to a minority interest discount) and is not marketable (a lack of marketability discount).

The explosion in using FLPs to transfer property at a lower tax cost has resulted in the transfer of substantial wealth to younger generations. Many families are now in the wealth-management business, which raises the same type of transition challenges facing families that own a business together.

This book can help a family develop and implement a system that allows them to use an FLP to continue ownership of the family wealth and secure the anticipated tax savings while avoiding many of the pitfalls commonly associated with collective ownership. But two specific issues common to FLPs need to be addressed.

The first issue relates to distinguishing between ownership and management. We emphasize the importance of owners and managers having separate and distinct roles and responsibilities. But it is often difficult in an FLP arrangement to identify the managers and understand what the different types of owners can and cannot do. For example, FLPs that are limited partnerships locate management in the hands of certain owners—the general partners. These FLPs also have two different types of owners, general partners and limited partners, and limited partners usually have only passive involvement. This gets even more confusing given the many different legal entities that can be used as an FLP. Notwithstanding, any FLP can be structured to support the use of the arrangements we discuss in this book, but the documentation or entity structure may need to be modified.

The second issue relates to locating the balance point. We suggest that every business has a balance point, and that the balancing function be located in a board of directors when the person with the balancing authority wants to transition out of management, when there are multiple owners and they have not worked out a way to share the power, and when owners and managers are different people. Usually all three of these situations will exist in every FLP.

For example, the balancing function in an FLP is initially done by those who created it—usually Mom and Dad. One or both of them, so long as they are living, make sure that the interests of the owners and the managers align. They usually do the alignment by identifying the interests of the owners and directing management to act consistent with those interests. But what happens when Dad and Mom pass away? They are no longer able to be the balance point. Their children (and perhaps grandchildren and spouses) own the FLP but only one or two owners have some management responsibilities. And there usually isn't a plan for who received Dad's and Mom's authority to identify the owners' interests and align them with the interests of those owners in management.

> EVERY FLP CAN BE STRUCTURED TO HAVE A BOARD.

Parents will often spend considerable time thinking about who should own and manage the FLP when they can't, but often spend little effort on planning for the transition of their balancing authority. Without some plan, however, someone of the next generation usually tries to duplicate how Dad or Mom did it, and these efforts are often not accepted or appreciated by their siblings.

We think it is critical for the owners of FLPs to spend just as much time planning for the transition of the balancing authority as they do with transitioning ownership and management. We also think the ideal place to locate the balancing authority is in a board of directors.

Creating a board with an FLP is sometimes difficult. FLPs that are partnerships don't have boards, and FLPs that are limited liability companies may or may not have a board. However, every FLP, whether it is a form of partnership or limited liability company can be structured to have a board. It just may take some additional planning.

COOPERATIVES

A cooperative is a legal entity formed to market or process products by patron members or to provide products, supplies, and services to its members. So cooperatives conduct business just like corporations. Common examples are cooperatives that market or process agricultural products raised by their members or cooperatives that provide electricity, water, phone, or other utilities to their members.

Chapter 2 describes four circumstances where it is essential to clarify and formalize the balance point of closely held and family businesses. Cooperatives have at least two of these four situations: cooperatives always have multiple owners and not all of the owners are managers. As a result, the principles in this book pertain to cooperatives.

But unlike corporations and other legal entities, cooperatives have specific requirements regarding ownership, governance, and management. These requirements vary from state to state, but the following gives a sense of the unique arrangements:

» All or a significant portion of the owners must be people who are doing business with the cooperative—often called patrons or members. Owners have a variety of voting and financial rights established by law or agreement based on the amount of business the owner does with the cooperative and other factors.

» Owners must always be represented on the board, and often a majority of the directors must be owners.

» Management is usually vested in the board except to the extent the board delegates its management authority to officers the board elects.

A goal of these requirements is to protect owners. This goal is certainly warranted since the livelihood of cooperative owners is tightly associated with the success of the business. The assumption underlying these requirements, though, is that the way to protect owners is to require their involvement in ownership, governance, and management. But this mandatory involvement can be a source of conflict.

For example, owners of cooperatives always wear more than one hat. They are owners and they are the cooperative's main suppliers or customers. This dual role can be a source of conflict among owners or between owners and the business.

Another example is the requirement that the board include owners (and often a majority of the directors must be owners). This mandate can have at least two consequences. It encourages an owner-director to act as an owner (protecting and promoting the interests of the owners) rather than as a director, which can limit the benefits to owners and managers from effective governance. In addition, it can narrow owner input to the extent that those owners sitting on the board are not speaking for all the owners. Failure to identify the values, needs, and goals of the owners as a group can create dissension in the ownership group because owners not on the board often don't have a way to voice their opinions. This in turn can lead to incomplete management plans because management is not hearing from all the owners.

> ALL BUSINESSES ARE BETTER SERVED IF THE FUNCTIONS OF GOVERNANCE AND MANAGEMENT ARE SEPARATE.

A third example relates to vesting management in the board. A common source of conflict between boards and management occurs when boards manage rather than direct. Requiring the board to manage the business (except to the extent the board delegates management) tends to institutionalize this potential conflict. We believe all businesses are better served if the functions of governance and management are separate so management can focus on running the business for the owners' benefit and the board can focus on ensuring that the interests of the owners and the businesses align.

The potential conflicts arising from this particular legal arrangement (cooperatives) are not unlike the conflicts that exist within closely held and family businesses. Privately owned businesses usually include owners on the board and in management. The only difference is that owners of cooperatives have fewer options to help resolve potential conflicts than do owners of corporations because the functions of ownership, governance, and management cannot be made entirely independent. And this means that the principles in this book are particularly applicable to cooperatives.

PUBLIC COMPANIES

We introduced the idea of a balancing board in Chapter 2. We explained that a balancing board integrates the values, needs, and goals of the owners as a group with those of the managers. The balancing process involves the owners identifying their collective values, needs, and goals, and presenting their plan to the board for evaluation and approval. The balancing process continues with management developing plans for the company that respond to the owners' plan; they present their plans to the board for evaluation and approval. If the owners' interests are not aligned with the managers' interests, the board "balances" the competing interests. The remainder of our book explains how this balancing process works.

We are not suggesting that the balancing process described in our book applies to public companies in the same way and to the same extent as it does to closely held and family businesses. Significant differences between public and private businesses clearly prevent this possibility. However, public companies can benefit from discussing the principles involved in the balancing process and how these principles can address challenges unique to public companies. So, the question is whether public companies could benefit from a balancing board as we describe.

The balancing process differs between public and private businesses in at least three ways. First, if a public company has a balancing board, the role owners play in the balancing process will be different. The nature of the ownership group in public companies is much different from that of closely held and family businesses. Public companies typically have more owners coming from widely diverse backgrounds. These two factors make it improbable (if not impossible) that all the owners will work together to identify the values, needs, and goals for the owners as a group as we suggest for private businesses.

The commitment of the owners is also different. Usually, owners of public companies can easily sell their interests on the public markets. This ability to exit ownership quickly and efficiently with little burden on the company arguably shifts more balancing opportunities (and hence balancing responsibilities) to owners. In other words, owners of a public company (not the board) can determine whether management is running the business in a way that meets their specific values, needs, and goals. If it does, the owners will remain owners. If not, they will sell. Government regulations are designed in part to make sure the public receives timely and useful information allowing all existing and prospective owners to make such decisions on a fair and equitable basis.

> **PUBLIC COMPANIES CAN BENEFIT FROM DISCUSSING THE PRINCIPLES INVOLVED IN THE BALANCING PROCESS.**

Boards of both public companies and private businesses evaluate management and management's plans. We suggest that boards of private companies evaluate based on three basic criteria: Is management responsive to the owners' values, needs, and goals? Are management's plans and actions thorough, well thought out, and consistent? (Specific questions to ask in the evaluation process are found in Chapter 6.) Do the managers operate the company based on board-approved plans?

Boards of public companies evaluate management's plans and actions in ways similar to those of boards of private companies. And boards of public companies certainly evaluate management by how well they achieve their plans.

However, when boards of public companies set goals, expectations, values, guidelines, and ethical or other standards, we think they go beyond what balancing boards in private companies do. They take on the owners' role by directing management to work under their parameters.

We do think that public companies with effective governance can approximate the balancing function and find ways to create pseudo-owners' plans. Three examples illustrate this point.

» The nature of the ownership group of some public companies may support the owners coming together to describe their values, needs, and goals as a group. This may be possible because the group's size is such that it can create a structure and process to receive meaningful input from individual owners to develop an owners' plan. Or one or more of the entrepreneurs may still be involved, and they could take the lead in identifying the significant values, needs, and goals they have as owners. Either of these options can be extremely helpful to a board attempting to identify a core set of values, needs, and goals by which to balance the interests of management.

» The directors could develop a structure and process by which representative owners hold cost-effective and productive meetings to identify a set of values, needs, and goals for the owners as a group. This structure and process might be similar to arrangements management has used for years to solicit input from their employees.

One advantage of these arrangements is that the board can focus on directing the representative owners' group to come up with an owners' plan, and on directing management to develop plans consistent with the representative owners' plan. The board would also be following governmental regulations requiring that boards and managers solicit and respond to broad owner input.

» In a third alternative, the directors act as owners. To effectively separate governance and management, directors may benefit from structuring one or more meetings at which they identify values, needs, and goals that they believe reflect the ownership group of their company. The board will then direct management to integrate these values, needs, and goals into their plans for the business.

Some of the other principles underlying an owners' plan for private companies may also benefit public companies. For example, creating a written document containing the board's goals, expectations, values, guidelines, parameters, ethical standards, and so forth for management (and reviewing it at least annually) offers the same advantages as for private businesses. Those advantages include

» having a greater chance that management will understand what is expected of them

» having a greater chance that directors will understand where they, as individuals, stand on the important issues

» having a written document that will guide the board when evaluating management's plans and proposals (directors won't have to identify these values, needs, and goals each time they are asked to approve management's decisions)

» easily identifying and understanding differences between directors and management and thus increasing the chance for collaboration

» providing a clear record of what directors believe is in the best interests of the business that will guide their actions as directors

We realize this section does not answer many other valid questions and concerns about applying the principles we discuss in this book to public companies. We only want to suggest that public companies may benefit from an honest and vigorous dialogue about the extent that the principles (as opposed to the structures and process) might apply to public companies.

NONPROFITS

In nonprofit companies, owners are a foreign concept. Nonprofits usually have a board and perhaps committees, management, employees, and volunteers, but no owners. Sometimes entrepreneurs act like owners or benefactors who fund the nonprofit with working capital, but there are no owners in the traditional sense. Some nonprofits have members who may act as owners.

Without owners, there is no owners' plan for the board to balance with management's plans. Without owners, the board doesn't have a balancing role at all. They own the result and the process. The board's role is to use their best judgment and make decisions in the best interests of the nonprofit.

The concepts in this book would apply to a nonprofit if all of the following conditions are met:

» the entrepreneurs or benefactors take on the role of owner and identify their values, needs, and goals for the nonprofit

» the nonprofit designates who will act as the owners

» the designated owners want to work together as a group

» the nonprofit's bylaws clarify the roles and responsibilities of these owners, the board, and management

» the board gives up its traditional power in favor of a balancing role

» directors are chosen and evaluated on their performance or potential performance as well as their financial contribution to the nonprofit (in other words, becoming a director is not a reward for contributing to the nonprofit)

We don't think that these conditions are easily met. However, if a nonprofit is committed to the balance point concept, they should attempt to satisfy these conditions before implementing the concepts in this book.

APPENDIX 4.1

TABLE OF CONTENTS FOR OWNERS' MANUAL

The following topics touch on the fundamental questions an Owners' Manual should address. Use these as a guide—modify and create the headings, topics, and organization that you think work best for your situation. The fundamental questions appear in Worksheet 4.1.

1. Purpose of the Manual

2. Commitments and Timelines

3. Expectations of Owners, Directors, and Managers

4. Owner Arrangements

    a. Owners' responsibilities

    b. How owners will treat each other

    c. Development of owners' plan

    d. Owner positions

    e. Owner meetings*

    f. Decision making*

    g. Arrangements regarding ownership interests*

5. Board Arrangements

    a. Composition*

    b. Board responsibilities

    c. Directors' qualifications

    d. Directors' terms*

    e. Election of directors*

      f.   Succession and filling vacancies*

      g.   Board positions*

      h.   Meetings*

      i.   Evaluation and compensation of officers

      j.   Directors' compensation

      k.   Committees*

6.   Management Arrangements

      a.   Composition*

      b.   Responsibilities

      c.   Strategic plans

      d.   Annual plans

      e.   Decision making

7.   Explanation of the Planning Process Involving the Owners, Board, and Managers

8.   Amending the Manual

9.   Appendixes

* These items are usually also included in the bylaws, shareholder control agreement, voting agreement, or other documents having legal effect.

APPENDIX 4.2

PUTTING TOGETHER AN OWNERS' PLAN

An owners' plan lets the board know the values, needs, and goals of your owners as a group. There are many ways to develop an owners' plan. Whatever way you use should reflect the needs of your owners' group and be acceptable to all participants.

Use this guide to develop your owners' plan. It is designed to help owners come up with a process that all the owners will support, clarifies how owners are involved, and allows owners to make decisions based on consensus.

1. Develop guidelines that participants will follow in putting together their owners' plan; that is, ensure that they all play by the same rules. Consider the following issues:

    a. The plan must work for everyone.

    b. It must reflect the values, needs, and goals of all the owners.

    c. The owners are *not* deciding what the company can or cannot do—that is the job of management and the board.

    d. The owners are *not* making decisions for the company—they are creating a plan that must go first to the board for approval, then to management, and then back to the board.

    e. How are the owners going to decide what goes into the plan? Consider having them make decisions by consensus—where individual owners may not get what they want, but must ask and answer, Can I live with this decision knowing that we will review it in a year?

    f. If individual owners do not participate then they give tacit approval to the plan the other owners develop.

2. Ask the owners to identify and write down their individual values, needs, and goals in advance so they come to the meeting prepared.

   a. Send an explanation of what the owners are to do before the meeting and what they will do at the meeting.

   b. Write out questions that may prompt them to think of their values, needs, and goals applicable to particularly important topics. Topics for questions may include their willingness to be in business together, their desired financial returns, their retirement needs, and other information on risk, distributions, compensation, and so forth.

   c. Provide guidelines for owners to consider when thinking about their values, needs, and goals for the company. Guidelines may include instructions such as, "How you answer these questions depends on your own personal situation" and "Your response is your own perspective. The goal is to come up with something that works for all the owners." Here are some guidelines relating to a discussion about the financial return owners are wanting from the business:

      i. Consider your own resources in assessing your financial needs and goals.

      ii. Consider your short-term financial needs and long-term financial goals. For example, consider amounts to supplement living expenses, pay education or medical expenses, pursue different careers, and fund retirement.

      iii. Assume that *all* things are possible when you answer the questions. Remember, solutions may come from management or from the ownership group. You can't plan if you don't figure out what you are trying to accomplish.

3. At the owners' meeting, each owner should explain their values, needs, and goals. Then consolidate individual responses into a single response that all of the owners can accept. The following is a suggested process.

   a. Each owner has a sheet of paper hanging on the wall in front of the room with the headings "Values," "Needs," and "Goals." Each writes out their responses under the appropriate headings. This process works best when owners think about their values, needs, and goals before the meeting. This process also works best when every owner attends the meeting. If an owner is not at the meeting, ask them for their responses in advance.

     i. Give each owner the opportunity to explain their responses. If an owner is not present, consider asking them to have another owner explain their responses.

    ii. If agreeable to all, give owners the opportunity to ask questions of each other in order to understand their positions. But note that this is not the time to engage in disagreement or debate. Owners do not have to answer a question if they choose not to.

   iii. When asking questions, be tolerant of differences, and be prepared to listen to understand and accommodate everyone's concerns.

   iv. Continue until all owners have had the opportunity to explain their values, needs, and goals and respond to questions.

b.   Hang a new sheet of paper on the wall.

     i. Ask the group to identify those values, needs, and goals that they all share. People often don't use the same words, but will express the same idea. Gather and modify responses to come up with a single value, need, or goal that is acceptable to everyone. Write this statement on the new sheet.

    ii. When values, needs, or goals are not shared by everyone, ask the group to indicate their support for a response, and then whether they can live with the response that has the most support. Give those who object the opportunity to explain how they would change the response in order to support it. Continue this discussion until the group comes up with a response that all participants support. Then write the response on the new sheet of paper.

c.   At the end of this process, the owners will have a common position.

4.   If individual owners find they cannot agree on any particular value, need, or goal, they should begin discussions that either lead to agreement or the sale of their stock.

APPENDIX 4.3

TOPICS FOR THE OWNERS' PLAN

The following is a list of topics that you may want to consider including in your owners' plan. Clearly every owners' plan doesn't need to address all or any of these topics. Consider having your owners brainstorm their own list of topics to consider.

1. Values the owners want the company to reflect. Consider employees, customers, suppliers, vendors, community, competitors, family of employees, and so forth. Stories can help identify the underlying values. Think about what you are committed to as a way to identify values.

2. Financial information the owners want from the company. Consider audited financials; sales, operating profits, and net income numbers and comparisons to prior years and to plan; assets, liabilities, and net worth numbers and comparisons to prior years and plans; bank and other finance ratios comparing actual numbers to set ratios; economic indicators the owners consider to be key to assessing the financial health of their particular business; and so forth.

3. Risks and concerns the owners have for the business.

4. Debt guidelines for the company.

5. Personal guarantees of owners.

6. Distributions the owners want for tax purposes.

7. Distributions the owners need for nontax purposes.

8. Distributions the owners want for nontax purposes.

9. What the owners are looking for from the company.

10. What the owners want to see included in management's plans for the company.

11. Owners' positions on business factors important to them. Consider growth, profitability, debt, market focus, diversity, research and development, geographic locations, and so forth.

12. Sustainability of growth and profits.

13. Employment opportunities for owners.

14. Employee well-being and benefits.

15. Image of the company in the community and among employees.

APPENDIX 4.4

SAMPLE VALUES, NEEDS, AND GOALS IN OWNERS' PLAN

OWNER VALUES

We will make sound business decisions based on our strategic vision.

We want strong financial performance to enable longevity of the company.

Employees have opportunities to advance their skills and position with recognition for their accomplishments.

We want to be an asset to the community by actively participating in charitable activities.

We will be an ethical company, doing the right thing, and not participating in activities with others that are not right.

OWNER NEEDS

Stock valuation will be calculated and communicated to shareholders annually.

Distributions to pay income taxes on company earnings attributable to owners.

We will meet as shareholders at least once per quarter.

The company must grow its annual profits at a rate of 7 percent.

We will have a viability plan for the company by the end of the year (20__) that details what the company will do if the president cannot be active.

OWNER GOALS

We will sustain an average annual growth rate of 12 percent over the next five years.

We will give 5 percent of our pretax profits to charity.

We will be the preeminent provider of our service in the country within ten years.

We will have a management team that does not include owners and that can successfully carry out the owners' plan.

We will have career development plans for every employee.

APPENDIX 7.1

BOARD CALENDAR

This is a simple calendar for scheduling the primary responsibilities of a balancing board. The calendar is based on a calendar year.

AUGUST

» Discuss owners' plan; resubmit in September if necessary

» Discuss general succession and transition matters

NOVEMBER

» Discuss annual plan, updates to strategic plan and budgets; resubmit in December if necessary

FEBRUARY

» Discuss results of prior year's plans

» Review bonus and dividend issues for the prior year

» Evaluate the CEO, president, and other senior management as required

» Ask legal due-diligence questions

» Set compensation for the officers, dividend plans, and bonus arrangements for the next year.

MAY

» Evaluate the board

» Elect new directors as required

» Elect a board chairperson and officers as required

» Train board as needed

» Conduct a human resources review

APPENDIX 7.2

BOARD CALENDAR WITH OWNER AND MANAGEMENT ACTIVITIES

This is a calendar for scheduling the primary responsibilities of a balancing board and including the primary responsibilities of the owners and managers. The calendar is based on a calendar year.

	Owner	Board	Management
Jun	Work on owners' plan		
Jul	Finalize owners' plan Elect directors		
Aug	Present owners' plan to board	Discuss owners' plan; resubmit in September if necessary Discuss general succession and transition plans	
Sept			Receive owners' plan Work on annual plan, updates to strategic plan, and budgets
Oct	Review owners' manual Education		Receive owners' plan Work on annual plan, updates to strategic plan, and budgets
Nov		Discuss annual plan, updates to strategic plan, and budgets; resubmit in December if needed Consider year-end compensation or bonus issues	Present annual plan, updates to strategic plan, and budgets
Dec			

Jan	Review prior year results Review management's plans		Review prior year results Consider compensation and bonus policies
Feb		Discuss results of prior year's plans Review prior year bonus and dividend issues Evaluate the CEO, president, and other senior management as required Establish compensation, dividend policies, and bonuses policies for senior managers Ask legal due-diligence questions	
Mar			
Apr	Evaluate the board Begin work on owners' plan		
May		Evaluate the board Elect new directors as required Elect a chairperson of the board and officers as required Do board training	

APPENDIX 9.1

SAMPLE LETTER SEEKING OUTSIDE DIRECTOR REFERRAL

Dear _____:

I am writing you as you were referred to me as someone who may know of an individual with the qualifications we are seeking to have represented on our board of directors.

ABC Company is a distributor of electrical products. The company has annual sales of $35 million, employs 90 people, delivers 14 percent to the bottom line, and enjoys a long-term banking relationship. The company is owned equally by three individuals, all of whom work in sales. Adam Smith is the company's president and board chair, but he intends to retire in three years. Ben Jones is to succeed Adam as president and Chuck Johnson is to serve as board chair.

The owners intend to establish a working board of directors. The board will provide direction and accountability for the president and the management team, promote accountability among the owners, oversee the balancing of the interests of the owners and the business, provide fresh ideas, and provide an outsider's view.

The board will consist of Adam Smith and three outside directors. We would very much like a referral of anyone who you believe would make a good director, who has an interest in serving as a director, and who meets the expectations and possesses the qualifications enclosed. We would appreciate it if you would have the person contact me directly or provide me with contact information that I can use to connect with them.

We very much appreciate your time and attention to our request.

Best regards,

_____

Adam Smith, President of ABC Company

enc.

The expectations the owners have for their directors (including themselves):

»   Understands the dynamics of owners also being employees

»   Values the separation of ownership and management

»   Values accountability

»   Acts independently

»   Is discerning

»   Prepares for and attends scheduled meetings

»   Supports the board structure

»   Acts as a unit and not through independent relationships with any particular manager or owner

»   Acts with courage to do what the board is supposed to do (in other words, says what needs to be said, does what needs to be done, asks tough questions, and makes tough calls)

»   Holds the president, management team, and the owners accountable for doing what they are supposed to do

»   Is compassionate and respectful in dealing with the owners, board members, president, and the management team

»   Is available for special meetings in person, by phone, or by some other manner if the situation arises

»   Monitors themselves so if they can't meet all the expectations of the directors, they will resign

Skills and experience

»   Is currently an owner or manager of a closely held business and has been for at least fifteen years

»   Possesses at least two of the following:

    -    Was president, but not an owner, of a business

    -    Experienced in product distribution

    -    Experienced in the electrical product industry

    -    Was actively involved in growing a company past $70 million in revenue

    -    Experienced with doing business in Mexico and Brazil

- Assisted in preparing a strategic plan looking out at least three years and developing annual plans to implement the strategic plan
- Experienced in general business finance
- Owned a business with others
- Was involved in the transition of an entrepreneur from the role of president

APPENDIX 10.1

BOARD MEETING AGENDA #1

[NAME OF COMPANY]

BOARD MEETING AGENDA

Date: _____ and Time: _____

Location: _____

    I.   *Introduction & Check In*

        A.   Call the meeting to order

        B.   Announcements

        C.   Approval of prior minutes

    II. *CEO summary report*

    III. *Items Requiring Action from Board*

        A.   [Insert topics]

        B.   [Insert topics]

    IV. *Items Requiring Advice from Board*

    V. *Reports/Information*

    VI. *Financial Review*

    VII. *Closing*

        A.   Evaluation of meeting

        B.   Next meeting

        C.   Summary of who needs to do what, by when

        D.   Adjournment

APPENDIX 10.2

BOARD MEETING AGENDA #2

[NAME OF COMPANY]

BOARD MEETING AGENDA

Date: _____ and Time: _____

Location: _____

1. *Check In (15 min.)*

    A. Announcements

    B. Review the agenda

    C. Comments, suggestions, changes, concerns about the agenda or meeting

    D. Approve minutes of last board meeting

2. *President's Summary Report (30 min.)*

3. *Owner Matters (30 min.)*

    A. [Insert topics]

    B. Owners excused so board can consider what directions may be needed

4. *Management Matters (90 min.)*

    A. [Insert topics]

    B. Managers excused so board can consider what directions may be needed

5.   *Board Matters (60 min.)*

    A.   [Insert topics]

6.   *Closing (15 min.)*

    A.   Critique of this meeting

- What do you think worked well at the meeting?
- What do you think didn't work well at the meeting?
- What are you thinking about as you leave the meeting?
- Do you have any agenda items for the next meeting?

    B.   Date, time, and location for next meeting: _____

    C.   Summary of who needs to do what before the next meeting

    D.   Adjournment

Explanation of agenda items follows in Appendix 10.3.

APPENDIX 10.3

AGENDA EXPLANATION

CHECK IN

In this section of the meeting the directors may express any concerns; present new questions; and review the meeting agenda, making additions or subtractions as necessary.

OWNER MATTERS

This portion of the meeting gives owners the opportunity to present their owners' plan to the board and make any other requests. Owners can use Worksheet 6.1 (Board Accepting Owners' Plan) and Worksheet 6.2 (Board Processing Owners' Requests) to present their issues.

At the completion of this section, owners will be excused and the board will review the minutes to identify outstanding issues and determine what, if any, direction will be given to the owners.

MANAGEMENT MATTERS

This portion of the meeting provides management the opportunity to present the strategic plan, annual plan, any updates to these plans, and other matters that the executive team, CEO, or directors want the board to consider. The board expects management to inform the board of any deviations from plans, explain the cause, and make recommendations for board approval. This portion of the meeting also provides the board the opportunity to assess the work of management.

Management can use Worksheet 6.3 (Board Approving Management's Plans) and Worksheet 6.4 (Board Processing Management's Requests) to present their issues.

At the completion of this section, management will be excused and the board will review the minutes to identify outstanding issues and determine what, if any, direction will be given.

BOARD MATTERS

This portion of the meeting gives the board the opportunity to continue discussing issues presented in either of the earlier sections of the meeting to determine whether further direction is required. The board will also process issues related to the board's responsibilities as outlined in the shareholders' manual, owners' plan, or board calendar. Board members may contact the chair to place items on the agenda in advance of the meeting. The chair will ensure that items remaining from prior meetings or the board calendar appear on the next meeting agenda.

APPENDIX 10.4

SEMIFORMAL MEETING PROCEDURES

1. Determine whether there is a quorum.

2. Call the meeting to order.

3. Read the agenda; ask for additions and changes, if necessary.

4. Approve minutes of previous meeting.

5. Discuss agenda items. For items requiring a formal vote, first make a motion and second it.

6. Call for discussion.

7. Repeat the motion; write it out if necessary.

8. Vote and record the vote count by number.

9. Summarize the meeting. Move items to the next meeting if needed.

10. Summarize assignments, duties, timelines, new agenda items, next meeting date.

11. Adjournment.

APPENDIX 10.5

SAMPLE MINUTES FOR BOARD MEETING

A meeting of the Board of Directors of ABC Company, a [state] corporation, was held at ____[location]_____, on __[date]_____.

Those Directors present included _____. Also present were _____.

Notice of the meeting was properly given to all of the directors as required in the corporation's bylaws. The meeting was called to order at ____[time]____. ____[name]____ chaired the meeting, and __[name]_____ served as secretary of the meeting.

[Insert topic—single resolution adopted]

[Insert summary of discussion]

Upon motion duly made and seconded, the following resolution was adopted by all of the of directors present at the meeting [If adoption wasn't unanimous, state: The following resolution was adopted by the directors present at the meeting by a vote of __to __]:

RESOLVED, that [insert what the Board decided]

[Insert topic—multiple resolution adopted]

[Insert summary of discussion]

Upon motion duly made and seconded, the following resolutions were adopted by all of the directors present at the meeting [If adoption wasn't unanimous, state: The following resolutions were adopted by the directors present at the meeting by a vote of __to __]:

RESOLVED, that [insert what the Board decided]

FURTHER RESOLVED, that [insert what the Board decided]

Adjournment

There being no further business coming before the Board, the meeting was adjourned at ____[time]_____.

Respectfully submitted,

_____

APPENDIX 10.6

DIRECTOR'S NOTEBOOK

It's helpful to give each director a notebook containing information the director will need at board meetings. Here are some suggestions of what you may want to include in a Director's Notebook.

1. Table of contents

2. Directories

    A. Mailing addresses, phone and fax numbers, and e-mail addresses for the company, owners, directors, and key managers

    B. Organizational chart for the company

    C. Ownership interests of the owners

3. Board calendar

4. Current owners' manual

5. Current owners' plan

6. Current strategic plan

7. Current annual plan and budget

8. Most recent board minutes (agendas, minutes, and handouts)

9. Current internal financials statements

10. Latest annual audited financial statements and management letter

11. Company documents

    A. Articles of incorporation

    B. Bylaws

    C. Shareholder minutes

    D. Directors & Officers insurance policy or summary

    E. Buy-sell agreement, shareholder control agreements, voting agreements, etc.

12. Notes and miscellaneous information

APPENDIX 10.7

BOARD TRAINING IDEAS

This section outlines a training session for directors. Tailor the topics to reflect the specific learning objectives needed for your board.

1. *Introductions*

2. *Explanation where the owners are at and how they got there*

    Explain the owners' succession goals for the business, what the owners are doing, and what they want the board to do to help them accomplish their goals.

3. *The Board is the balance point*

    Explain balancing (the act of integrating the actions of both the owners and the managers). Offer examples of the owners' interests and managers' interests and discuss whether these interests are the same or different. Discuss the roles of owners, managers, and board when the interests of the owners and managers are not the same.

4. *The Board owns the process, not the results*

    Review the responsibilities of the owners, board, and managers as described in the owners' manual.

    Review the process by which owners present their plan to the board for review, and the process by which managers present their plans to the board for review.

    Consider asking the directors to list some of the problems, challenges, or issues they might expect to see in the business and identify which group (owners, board, or managers) has primary responsibility to solve the matter. Identify what the other groups need to do.

5. *Independence*

    Owners tend to accept and managers tend to support the process so long as they trust the board to be independent. Explain what the owners mean by independence.

    Consider asking the directors to discuss what independence means to them and (1) why they think an independent board is helpful to the owners and the managers; (2) what can cause the board to lose its independence; and (3) what can happen if the board loses its independence.

6. *Legal duties*

    Explain directors' duty to oversee management, duty of care, and duty of loyalty. Explain how the directors are protected from liability.

7. *Board organization*

    Review the contents of the Director's Notebook. Ask what documents or other information the directors might want to include in the notebook.

    Include the board calendar, the meeting agenda form, director compensation arrangements, committee arrangements, future meeting dates, and so forth.

TABLE OF WORKSHEETS

QUESTIONS FOR OWNERS' MANUAL

The following questions will help you complete your owners' manual. Use these as a guide—modify and create questions and exercises that you think will best work for your situation. A sample Table of Contents for an Owners' Manual is found in Appendix 4.1.

1. What are we hoping to accomplish with our business?_____

   _____

2. Why are we owners together?_____

   _____

3. What do we expect from each other as owners?_____

   _____

4. How do we want to treat each other?_____

   _____

5. What will we do as owners?_____

   _____

6. What level of participation do we expect from each of us as owners? _____

   _____

7. How do we want to make decisions as owners? _____

    _____

8. What will we do if we can't agree on a major issue? _____

    _____

9. How will we resolve differences among ourselves as owners?_____

    _____

10. What is our voting arrangement and when will we make decisions by voting? _____

    _____

11. What rules do we want to guide us in our meetings? _____

    _____

12. How often do we need to meet to do our work as owners?_____

    _____

13. When do we want to meet? _____

    _____

14. Where do we want to meet? _____

    _____

15. Who will create the agenda for our owner meetings? _____

    _____

16. Who will lead our meetings? _____

_____

17. What positions do we as owners appoint or elect to get our ownership work done?

_____

18. Is a board needed? If so, why? If not, why not? _____

_____

19. What do we want this board to do?_____

_____

20. How will this board work with owners? _____

_____

21. How will this board work with the managers? _____

_____

22. What type of board structure do we want to use?_____

_____

23. What do we expect from each director?_____

_____

24. What do we expect from our management?_____

_____

25. What should the roles and responsibilities of management be? _____

_____

26. Who can be owners? _____

_____

27. Who do we *not* want to be owners? _____

_____

28. When can we sell our ownership interests? _____

_____

29. How will the sale price be determined? _____

_____

30. How and when will the purchase price be paid? _____

_____

31. When can we buy more ownership interests? _____

_____

32. Who can we transfer our ownership interests to? _____

_____

33. Who can we *not* transfer our ownership interests to? _____

_____

34. What policies do we want to have about family members working at the company?

_____

35. How will spouses be involved?_____

_____

36. How will children be involved? _____

_____

37. How will we amend this manual? _____

_____

38. How often will we review this manual? _____

_____

SELECTING A FACILITATOR

Use these guidelines to help you find a professional to facilitate your business transition. Modify them as you think will work best for your situation.

GUIDELINES FOR SELECTING A FACILITATOR

» Be clear in your mind about where you, as an owner, are with your business and where you want your business to go. Remember, you are looking for someone who can help you and your business meet unique and often difficult transition challenges.

» Choose people from referrals to interview, and preferably have other owners interview them too.

» Choose a professional who is able to work with you, the other owners, key employees, and your other advisors. This person must understand, empathize with, and truly want to help you through the transition difficulties.

QUESTIONS FOR EACH OWNER TO ASK BEFORE INTERVIEWING A FACILITATOR

Evaluating self

Why do I want to use a professional? _____

_____

What are my goals? _____

_____

What am I willing and not willing to do differently right now? _____

_____

Evaluating the project

What type of transition is my business facing? _____

_____

What are the goals of the work? _____

_____

What do I want the professional to do?_____

_____

What do I see as my role? _____

_____

Evaluating the professional

Describe the "wrong" person for the job._____

_____

What are the key factors that will determine whether I hire this advisor? _____

_____

Will answers to my questions give me the insight I need to choose a suitable advisor?

_____

QUESTIONS FOR POTENTIAL FACILITATORS

Understanding the business in transition

What does working with a business in transition mean to you? _____

_____

How will you build an understanding of how owners work through a transition?_____

_____

How will you build an understanding of the relationship between the owners, the board, and the managers of a business in transition?_____

_____

Team concept

How will you build and promote collaboration with other advisors serving our business? _____

_____

Describe the optimal working relationship between you and the other professionals serving our business._____

_____

Describe your role as a professional who helps businesses in transition._____

Trust, sensitivity, empathy, compassion

How do you begin earning trust with a client? _____

_____

When a business faces a transition similar to ours, how and when will you help the owners determine what issues they need to address? _____

_____

How will you show sensitivity and empathy?_____

_____

What does compassion mean to you? What role does compassion play in a project?

_____

Additional considerations

Can you provide enthusiastic references from businesses similar to ours? Please provide contact information. _____

_____

Do you have experience with clients whose businesses are at least as complex as ours? Please give examples. _____

_____

Do you feel you are suited to the role we need you for? Why?_____

_____

INDIVIDUAL OWNER'S VALUES, NEEDS, AND GOALS #1

This form may help you identify your individual values, needs, and goals. Owners can modify it by including topics or questions unique to their ownership group. See Worksheet 4.4 for an alternative. Use Appendix 4.2 to help compile responses from all the owners and to develop an owners' plan.

Name:_____

Date:_____

_____

Values	Needs	Goals
Values are the basic principles driving all planning, decision making, and behavior. Values are the principles, standards, morals, ethics, and ideals that are most important to the owners, individually and as a group. Values typically include statements about integrity, honesty in business dealings, personal relationships, compliance with laws and regulations, and confidentiality.	Needs are what the owners want from the business, and what they do not wish to change or lose. Needs typically include information about the company's performance, proof that management is doing its job, defined debt and risk levels or tolerance, how to facilitate open and honest communication among owners and executives, and defined boundaries between owners and management.	Goals are owners' long-term wishes. Goals typically include return on investment, growth parameters, image in and connections to the marketplace and community, long-term involvement as an owner, and stewardship.

My Values

My Needs

Family	Estate Plan	Personal Assets/ Wealth	Business

My Goals

Family	Estate Plan	Personal Assets/ Wealth	Business

My Financial Needs and Goals

Year	20__	20__	20__	20__	20__
Nontax distributions I need in the following years, if any, for living expenses	$_____	$_____	$_____	$_____	$_____
Nontax distributions my financial plan anticipates me receiving in the following years to meet my goals	$_____	$_____	$_____	$_____	$_____
The amount I am looking for from the company in today's dollars to meet my financial goals after considering my other assets (assuming that I don't sell my shares in the business)	$_____				
If I don't have confidence that my financial goals will be met, I anticipate the need to sell my shares in the business in the following year or years	20__				

INDIVIDUAL OWNER'S VALUES, NEEDS, AND GOALS #2

As an owner, what are your values, needs, and goals? Use the following statements and questions to guide you in coming up with your individual values, needs, and goals. Or use other questions and exercises that will work best for your situation (for example, see Worksheet 4.3). Use Appendix 4.2 to help compile responses from all the owners and to develop an Owners' Plan.

About myself

1. How I define the business: _____

   _____

2. What the business means to me: _____

   _____

3. A story that captures what the business means to me is _____

   _____

4. The three most positive things about this business are _____

   _____

5. Three things that must be fixed for me are _____

   _____

6. Here is how I want others to look at the business: _____

   _____

7. I like being an owner because _____

    _____

8. My hope for owning the business is _____

    _____

9. Here is how I *am* involved in the company right now: _____

    _____

10. Here is how I *want to be* involved in the company right now: _____

    _____

11. Here is how I want to be involved in the company in the year 20___: _____

    _____

12. My responsibilities as an owner are _____

    _____

13. My responsibilities as a manager are _____

    _____

14. The benefits of being an owner are _____

    _____

15. My concerns about being an owner are _____

    _____

About the other owners

16. A story that captures what my other owners mean to me is _____

_____

17. My expectations of my other owners are _____

_____

18. What I want all of the owners to take away from the experience of owning the business together is _____

_____

19. What I am willing to do for my other owners is _____

_____

20. What my other owners don't understand about me is _____

_____

21. What I most want to avoid in all of us owning the business together is _____

_____

About my family as owners

22. Do I want my children (or other family members) to work at the business? Why or why not? _____

_____

23. If yes, what I want from the experience of owning the business together with my family is _____

_____

24. What I don't want from the experience of owning the business together is _____

_____

About my financial matters

25. Would I invest in the company if I didn't work here every day? Why or why not?____

_____

26. Based on my financial needs goals and my own resources, how much money do I need from the business for living expenses, retirement, and inheritance? Do I know? Do the other owners know? Will I have enough? How do I know? (Use the table below to estimate the amounts needed.)

Year	20__	20__	20__
Nontax distributions I need in the following years, if any, for living expenses	$_____	$_____	$_____
Nontax distributions my financial plan anticipates me receiving in the following years to meet my goals	$_____	$_____	$_____
The amount I am looking for from the company in today's dollars to meet my financial goals after considering my other assets (assuming that I don't sell my shares in the business)	$_____		

27. Based on receiving the distributions agreed upon by the owners, I may to need to sell my shares in 20____. Explain why: _____

_____

28. How long do I want to continue in active full-time management? _____

_____

29. How is life at work now? _____

_____

30. Should this business continue to exist? Why or why not? _____

_____

Other considerations

31. What things matter most to me and why? List them in the order of importance, the most important being listed first, and explain their importance. _____

_____

32. What was I hoping for when I obtained stock in the company? _____

_____

33. What did I expect my life to be like at work after I obtained stock? _____

_____

OUTLINE FOR A STRATEGIC PLAN

Use this simple outline as a guide when putting together a strategic plan for your business.

I. Four basic questions

    A. What are the owners' values?

    B. What are the owners' needs?

    C. What are the owners' goals?

    D. What are the "can't wait" issues that need to be resolved now?

II. External analysis

    A. Customer/client analysis

        1. Who are the buyers of our products/services?

        2. Who are our largest buyers?

        3. What potential customers can we identify?

        4. What motivates a customer to buy?

        5. What objectives do customers seek?

        6. Are customers satisfied with the current products or services?

        7. What problems do our customers experience?

        8. What are the unmet needs of our customers?

    B. Competitor analysis

        1. Who are our major competitors?

        2. What is their size, growth potential, and profitability level?

        3. What are their strengths and weaknesses?

        4. What is their current business strategy?

5. What is their future strategy?

6. What is their cost structure?

7. What is their pricing structure?

8. What are their business affiliations?

9. What is the history of their reaction to our tactical moves?

C. Industry analysis

1. What are the product or service life cycles?

2. What are the increasing and declining markets?

3. What are the industry trends?

4. What are the threats to growth in the industry?

D. Market analysis

1. What are the new technologies?

2. What are the influential governmental regulations?

3. What are the buyers' cultural and psychological trends?

III. Internal analysis

A. How well has our past performance and strategy worked?

B. What are our current strengths and weaknesses?

C. What are our current financial constraints and freedoms?

D. What is our current image in the marketplace?

E. How well are our values and principles internalized in the company?

F. What are the current issues that affect the development and implementation of this plan?

IV. Goals

A. Growth

B. Profit

C. Market position

D. Image in the marketplace and community

E.   Organizational culture

F.   Transition of management

V.   Diversification, acquisition, and replication

A.   What are our goals?

B.   What is our timeline?

VI.   Products and services to be offered

VII.   Research and development

VIII.   Pricing

A.   What should our pricing philosophy and strategy be?

B.   What margins do we want to hold and for which products or services?

IX.   Staff requirements

A.   Executive

B.   Managerial

C.   Support staff

D.   Labor force

E.   Outside resources and professionals

X.   Financial plan

A.   Assessment of current financial needs

B.   Short-term financing

C.   Long-term financing

D.   Allocation of profits

E.   Capital needs

XI.   Monitoring systems

A.   Budgets

B.   Cash-flow projections

C.   Forecasting schedules

D.   Budget discipline and reporting

XII. Organizational plan

    A.   Organizational chart

    B.   Job descriptions

    C.   Personnel policies

    D.   Performance expectations of our employees

    E.   Training and development

    F.   Performance evaluation

    G.   Improving culture

    H.   Retaining quality employees

XIII. Physical location

    A.   How effectively are we using our current facilities?

    B.   What kind of space will we need or want?

XIV. Sales and marketing

    A.   What is our current approach to sales?

    B.   Should our sales approach change? How?

    C.   What is our current approach to marketing?

    D.   Should our marketing approach change? How?

XV. Operations

    A.   Improving internal efficiencies

    B.   Reducing workflow issues

    C.   Improving internal communication

    D.   Improving quality

    E.   Improving on-time delivery

XVI. Plan approval

    A.   What is the best way to get this plan approved?

    B.   What are the political and family considerations?

    C.   What is the basic strategy to implement this plan?

OUTLINE FOR AN ANNUAL PLAN

Use this outline as a guide when putting together an annual plan for your business.

    I.   What part of the strategic plan will we focus on this year?

    II.   What are our objectives for this year?

    III.   How are these objectives consistent with the owners' plan?

    IV.   Are these objectives doable?

        A.   Company analysis

        B.   Departmental analyses

        C.   External analysis (see strategic plan)

    V.   What is the implementation plan for each objective?

        A.   Break down each objective into bite-sized pieces

        B.   Timelines

        C.   Accountabilities and key people involved

        D.   Measurements (how to evaluate the results)

        E.   Plan B if this plan is not working

    VI.   Budget preparation

        A.   Capital expenditures and depreciation

        B.   Cash flow analysis

        C.   Department budgets and expenditures

        D.   Debt financing plan

BOARD ACCEPTING
OWNERS' PLAN

When owners present their owners' plan (or any updates to it) to the board, they need to clearly state what they want from the board. The board needs to evaluate the owners' plan (or updates) in its role as a balance point. The board chair, working with the owners, fills out the informative items. Each director considers the evaluation section before the meeting.

Board Meeting Date: _____

Action Requested by Board:
Acceptance _____ *Advice* _____ *Information* _____

Brief description of the owners' plan:_____

_____

_____

What are the owners expecting from the board regarding the owners' plan?_____

_____

_____

Evaluation by each director:

1. Does the owners' plan speak for all of the owners? _____

    _____

2. Is the owners' plan clear? Do I understand it? Does something seem confusing or out of place? _____

    _____

3. Is the owners' plan comprehensive? _____

    _____

4. Is the owners' plan complete? _____

    _____

5. Is the owners' plan consistent? Are there items that seem contrary to each other?

    _____

6. Does the owners' plan have what I need it to have to accept it? _____

    _____

7. Does the owners' plan have what I need to direct management to implement it?

    _____

BOARD PROCESSING OWNERS' REQUESTS

When owners express concerns, raise issues, request an action, or otherwise provide information to the board they need to clearly present information and clearly state what they want from the board. The board then needs to evaluate the requests in its role as the balance point. The board chair, working with the owners, fills out the informative items. Each director considers the evaluation section before the meeting.

Board Meeting Date: _____

Action Requested by Board:
Acceptance _____ *Advice* _____ *Information* _____

What the owners are presenting to the board: _____

_____

_____

What the owners are expecting from the board: _____

_____

_____

Evaluation by each director:

1. What is the issue? What is at the root of the matter? Do I understand it? _____

   _____

2. Do I know what the owners are wanting from the board? _____

   _____

3. What does the owners' plan say about this matter? _____

   _____

4. What does the strategic plan or annual plan say about this matter? _____

   _____

5. Who owns the issue: the owners, managers, or both? Which of these groups has
   to propose a solution to solve the issue? _____

   _____

6. What is the board's role in the matter? _____

   _____

7. What direction should the board give to the managers regarding the matter? _____

   _____

8. What direction should the board give to the owners regarding the matter? _____

   _____

BOARD APPROVING
MANAGEMENT'S PLANS

When the managers present the strategic plan or annual plan (or any updates) to the board they need to clearly state what they want from the board. The board then needs to evaluate the strategic plan or annual plan (or updates) in its role as the balance point. The board chair, working with management, fills out the informative items. Each director considers the evaluation section before the meeting.

Board Meeting Date: _____

Action Requested by Board:
Approval _____ *Advice* _____ *Information* _____

Brief description of the plan presented: _____

_____

_____

What managers expect from the board regarding the plan: _____

_____

_____

Evaluation by each director:

1. Does the plan satisfy the owners' plan? Does it have what I need to explain to the owners that it meets their plan? _____

_____

2. Is the plan comprehensive and complete? For example (depending on the type of plan it is, strategic or annual), does it include

    a. Goals, strategies, tactics? Its purpose? What it wants to achieve? _____

    _____

    b. Sections dealing with the company's market, people, culture, management succession, associate development, budgets and financial projections (such as revenues, profit, cash flows, balance sheet, tax costs, etc.)? _____

    _____

    c. Investment-return analysis? _____

    _____

    d. Timelines and milestones to achievement? _____

    _____

    e. Contingency analysis? A plan B if plan A doesn't work out? _____

    _____

    f. Who has responsibility for implementing key sections of the plan? _____

    _____

3. Is the plan clear? Do I understand it? Does something seem confusing or out of place? _____

_____

4. Is the plan consistent? Are there items that seem contrary to each other? _____

_____

5. Does the plan have what I need it to have to approve it? _____

_____

6. Does the plan have what I need to hold management accountable for it?

_____

BOARD PROCESSING MANAGEMENT'S REQUESTS

When managers seek approval or advice, express concerns or raise issues, or otherwise provide information to the board, they need to clearly state what they want from the board. The board needs to evaluate any requests in its role as the balance point. The board chair, working with management, fills out the informative items. Each director considers the evaluation section before the meeting.

Board Meeting Date: _____

Action Requested by Board:
Approval _____ *Advice* _____ *Information* _____

What the managers will present to the board: _____

_____

_____

What the managers expect from the board: _____ _____

_____

_____

Evaluation by a director:

1. What is the issue? What is at the root of the matter? Do I understand it? _____

    _____

2. Do I know what the managers want from the board? _____

    _____

3. What does the owners' plan say about this matter? _____

    _____

4. What does the strategic plan or annual plan say about this matter? _____

    _____

5. Who owns the issue: the managers, owners, or both? Which of these groups has to propose a solution to solve the issue? _____

    _____

6. What is the board's role in the matter? _____

    _____

7. What direction should the board give to the managers regarding the matter? _____

    _____

8. What direction should the board give to the owners regarding the matter? _____

    _____

IDENTIFYING WHO HAS THE PROBLEM

Directors can use this form to help them identify whether the owners or the managers (or both groups) have the primary responsibility to develop a solution that aligns the interests of both groups. Owners may need to change their owners' plan. Managers may need to change the strategic or annual plans. The board may need to refocus on the process, rather than the results.

Explanation of the problem: _____

_____

	Owners	Management	Board
What is each group's responsibilities regarding the problem?			
What is each group's known position regarding its part of the problem?			
What information is needed from each group regarding its part of the problem?			

QUESTIONS FOR PROSPECTIVE DIRECTORS

1. What experience do you have with boards of directors generally? _____

   _____

2. What are your perceptions about boards? _____

   _____

3. What are your expectations about being on the board for [company name]? _____

   _____

4. What concerns do you have about being on this board? _____

   _____

5. As a director, what do you expect from management? From the owners? _____

   _____

6. Of the expectations described to you, which do you think would be the easiest for
   you to fulfill and which would be hardest? _____

   _____

7. Describe what each of the qualifications listed means to you. _____

   _____

8. Why you want to serve on a board? _____

   _____

9. Explain your philosophy of what makes a good board. _____

   _____

10. Describe your business experience. _____

   _____

11. Describe your board experience. _____

   _____

12. Describe your special skills or talents as a director. _____

   _____

13. In what company or family or business situations could you be most helpful as a
    director? _____

   _____

BOARD EVALUATION BY AN OWNER

This is an evaluation by __[name of owner]__ completed as of __[insert date]__. This evaluation is confidential; your name will not be used in any feedback the board receives. This evaluation will be given to the owners and may be given to the board chair. If shared with the board, the results will be anonymous and reported on a cumulative basis.

1. Does the board understand the owners' plan? If so, how do you know this? If not, what do you think needs to happen for the board to understand the owners' plan?

    _____

2. Does the board understand the current strategic and annual plans? If so, how do you know this? If not, what do you think needs to happen for the board to understand these plans? _____

    _____

3. Does the board act independently? Why or why not? Give specific examples.

    _____

4. Are you getting the information and support you need from the board? If not, explain what information or support you would like to receive. _____

    _____

5. Which directors do you think are doing an outstanding job? An inadequate job? List the names and reasons why. _____

    _____

6. Has the board challenged the owners? Why or why not? What was the result?

_____

7. Has the board challenged management? Why or why not? What was the result?

_____

BOARD EVALUATION BY A MANAGER

This is an evaluation of __[name of manager]__ completed as of __[insert date]__. This evaluation is confidential; your name will not be used in any feedback the board receives. This evaluation will be given to the owners and may be given to the board chair. If shared with the board, the results will be anonymous and reported on a cumulative basis.

1. Does the board understand the current strategic and annual plans? If so, how do you know this? If not, what do you think needs to happen for the board to understand these plans? _____

    _____

2. Does the board act independently? Why or why not? Give specific examples. _____

    _____

3. Are you getting the information and support you need from the board? If not, explain what information or support you would like to receive. _____

    _____

4. Which directors do you think are doing an outstanding job? An inadequate job? List the names and reasons why. _____

    _____

5. Has the board challenged management? Why or why not? What was the result?

    _____

DIRECTOR EVALUATION BY A DIRECTOR

This is an evaluation of __[name of the director]__ completed as of _[insert date]__. This evaluation is confidential; your name will not be used in any feedback this director receives. This evaluation will be given to the owners and may be given to the board chair. If shared with the board, the results will be anonymous and reported on a cumulative basis.

1.   Does the director attend board meetings? _____

_____

2.   Is the director prepared for board meetings? If so, how? If not, does this distract from the board's effectiveness? How? _____

_____

3.   Does the director understand the difference between directing, advising, and managing? Which of these actions does the director tend to do more of and how does this affect what the board does? Give specific examples. _____

_____

4.   How does the director usually contribute at board meetings? _____

_____

5.   Does the director understand the owners' plan and management's plans? Please give examples to support your answer. _____

_____

6. Does the director work toward resolution when significant differences occur?

   _____

7. Does the director support the policies, procedures, and structures that are in place? Please give examples. _____

   _____

8. Does the director act independently? Please give examples._____

   _____

CHAIR EVALUATION BY A DIRECTOR

This is an evaluation of ___[name of the director]___ completed as of ___[insert date]___ . This evaluation is confidential; your name will not be used in any feedback the chair receives. This evaluation will be given to the owners and may be given to the board chair. If shared with the chair, the results will be anonymous and reported on a cumulative basis.

1. Does the chair keep the board on task and follow procedures when running a meeting? _____

    _____

2. Does the chair encourage minority viewpoints? Please give examples. _____

    _____

3. Has the chair ever stopped the board meeting (if it got out of control or significantly off track) to talk about what is happening? _____

    _____

4. Are the agendas complete and designed for the board to direct and fulfill its responsibilities? _____ _____

    _____ _____

5. Are the agendas and other meeting information sent out in a timely manner?

    _____

6. Does the chair act independently when running the meeting? _____

_____

7. Is the chair an effective liaison to the owners and managers? If so, what makes the chair effective in this regard? If not, what improvements do you suggest?

_____

INDEX

A

ABS (alternative board structure)
  characteristics, 180
  overview, 179
ABS (alternative board structure) 1
  entrepreneur role, 184
  majority of insiders, 190
  majority of outsiders, 191
  outsiders' role, 189
  overview, 179
  role of others, 186
ABS (alternative board structure) 2
  entrepreneur role, 184
  majority of insiders, 190
  majority of outsiders, 191
  outsiders' role, 189
  overview, 180
  role of others, 186
ABS (alternative board structure) 3
  entrepreneur role, 184
  majority of insiders, 190
  majority of outsiders, 191
  outsiders' role, 189
  overview, 180
  role of others, 186
ABS (alternative board structure) 4
  majority of insiders, 190
  overview, 181
  role of others, 186
  term limits, 208
ABS (alternative board structure) 5
  board size, 206
  majority of insiders, 190
  outsiders' role, 189
  overview, 181
  role of others, 186
  situations, 191

ABS (alternative board structure) 6
  board size, 206
  majority of outsiders, 191
  outsiders' role, 189
  overview, 179, 181
  role of others, 186
  situations, 192
ABS (alternative board structure) 7
  all outsiders, 194–196
  outsiders' role, 189
  overview, 182
  role of others, 186
  situations, 196
accepting owners' plans, 122–124, 331–332
accountability
  board, 92, 134–138
  board of directors, 183
  defined, 76
  owners, directors, and managers, 138
acting independently, 153–160, 306
advising
  board actions, 229
  directors, 161–163
  examples, 164
  overadvising, 162
advisory group
  board of directors versus, 183
  defined, 7, 267
agendas
  components, 226
  explanation, 301–302
  preparing, 226–232
  sample board meeting, 298–300
  typical topics, 226–227
agreement, buy-sell, 268
allocating entrepreneur's functions, 26
alternative board structure. *See* ABS
                  (alternative board structure)
amending
  ground rules, 73
  owners' manuals, 73–74
  owners' plans, 88

350

T

beliefs, 20–25
defined, 9
entrepreneurs, 16–30, 118
examples, 18–20, 23–25
high-level, 16–17
identifying, 17–20
role changes, 16–30
within management, 18
without change, 28

trusts
defined, 272
owners' manual, 59–60

Tutelman, Cary J.
beliefs, 4–5, 266
bio, 365
Board School, The, 367

Board Evaluation by a Manager, 345
Board Evaluation by an Owner, 343–344
Board Processing Management's Requests, 338–339
Board Processing Owners' Requests, 333–334
Chair Evaluation by a Director, 348–349
Director Evaluation by a Director, 346–347
Identifying Who Has the Problem, 340
Individual Owner's Values, Needs, and Goals, 318–325
Outline for an Annual Plan, 330
Outline for a Strategic Plan, 326–329
Questions for Owners' Manual, 309–313
Questions for Prospective Directors, 341–342
Selecting a Facilitator, 314–317

U

updating
owners' manual, 121
owners' plan, 121

V

value statement examples, 76
values
owner, 291, 318–325
owners' plan, 75–76
venture capital, 41–42
voting power, board of directors, 183

W

work environment, 75
worksheets
Board Accepting Owners' Plan, 331–332
Board Approving Management's Plans, 335–337

362

CARY J. TUTELMAN, PhD,
is a business consultant and owner of CJT
Company. Cary helps closely held and
family businesses grow and move through
the complicated web of ownership,
management, board, and family issues
that transition brings. He has been
actively helping businesses since 1981.

LARRY D. HAUSE, JD,
is a business consultant and attorney with
the leading firm of Fredrikson & Byron.
He grew up in a family business, and as an
attorney, he has worked with closely held
and family businesses since 1984.
He guides entrepreneurs and other owners,
as well as directors and managers, through
the myriad challenges they face when their
businesses are in transition.

THE Board School

After years of helping closely held and family owned businesses address the issues of succession and transition, Tutelman and Hause developed THE BOARD SCHOOL.

THE BOARD SCHOOL is America's first school on boards that is specifically designed for owners of closely held and family owned businesses, their top executives, and their directors. It is a school, not a workshop. Classes are held once a week for seven weeks. It is a hands on, in depth, interactive approach that helps business owners understand how they can improve the running and transitioning of their business. Students leave The Board School with a plan to move the transition process forward.

"I found participation in the school to be a very eye-opening experience. Not only was I presented with some wonderful information, but I found myself in a setting with my counterparts at other businesses where we could freely discuss the governance issues facing our companies."
— RON MASSIE, President & CEO, Image Express

"My cousins and I are partners in our business. The school helped me to understand when I need to put on which hat—owner, manager, or brother. It gave me a structure on how to think through these roles. We had a board in the past but it really didn't work. The Board School gave me an entirely new perspective on not only the role of the board, but also the role of the owners and managers. Now we're taking a completely different approach."
— JEFFREY BERTELSON, Bertelson Brothers, Inc.

FOR MORE INFORMATION ABOUT THE SCHOOL AND REGISTRATION, VISIT
WWW.THEBOARDSCHOOL.COM

ORDERING ADDITIONAL BOOKS

Additional copies of THE BALANCE POINT
may be obtained by visiting the Famille Press web site at
www.famillepress.com.

Discounted prices are available for volume orders.

APPENDIXES & WORKSHEETS FILES

Electronic copies of the appendixes and worksheets
found in THE BALANCE POINT are also available through
the Famille Press web site. The appendixes and worksheets
may be revised and supplemented periodically.

For more information, go to www.famillepress.com.